"*Between Sundays* reflects the vintage wi[...]
pastor—and a fine preacher. Its reflecti[...]
in response to the weekday readings ar[...]
Engaging and inspiring, both down-to-ea[...]
who wants to preach or pray with the daily readings will find an
invaluable resource here."

Thomas H. Groome
Professor of Theology and Religious Education, Boston College
Author, *Educating Life*

"For those of us whose work does not allow us to attend daily Mass, Paul
Boudreau has provided us with a wonderful little 'peek' at the gospel
passages we miss when we only go on Sundays. *Between Sundays* is indeed
good news for the other six days. If we can find just five minutes a day—
over breakfast or lunch, on our commute to or from work, just before we
nod off to sleep—we can reflect on the daily Scripture, say a short prayer,
even do a quick action. Then we can go back to our busy lives and try to
put the good news into practice."

Gregory F.A. Pierce
Author, *Spirituality@Work: 10 Ways to Balance Your Life On the Job*

"Nobody preaches and nobody prays like Father Paul Boudreau. You'll
never hear the gospel the same way again! His images startle us awake
and inspire fresh insights on every page. The stories of faith he shares
here warm the heart and make us laugh despite our grim determination
to be 'serious' about God. I know we all say that God loves us: Paul really
believes it, and makes it ring true. And when I read his comfortable
conversational stories of grace, I dearly want to believe it too."

Alice Camille
Author, *Exploring the Sunday Readings* and *God's Word Is Alive*

"Years of being a professor of Scripture and preaching have convinced me
that one of the great hazards in becoming a biblical people is presuming
that we have grasped the meaning of God's word. The more familiar we
are with it, the more prone we are to missing the richness of its myriad
meanings. Blessed are those who help us to hear the word from a new
perspective. Paul Boudreau is among their number.

"The reader will finish a page, based on the daily lectionary reading
and say: 'I never saw it that way before.' And since God's word is always
an invitation with an RSVP attached, it will elicit a new response,
deepening one's own spirituality."

Fr. Stephen C. Doyle, OFM, SSL
Author, *Gospel in Word and Power*

Dedication

I dedicate this book to my bishop, Dan Hart, who gave
me the long leash I needed to write, and to the people of
the Diocese of Norwich, who received me as a pastor and
fellow disciple.

Contents

Introduction

Mary Bavier is one of the sweetest people I know. Elsa McKusick is another. They are two of the thousands and thousands of faith-filled people who attend daily mass at your church and mine on a regular basis. One morning after a weekday mass, Mary said to me, "Fr. Paul, I think your weekday homilies are better than your Sunday homilies." "I do too," Elsa chimed in. "They're so special."

Maybe I need to work on my Sunday homilies! But the "specialness" that Mary and Elsa experience on the weekdays has to do, more than anything else, with them; and with Austin and Clara, Marty, Bob, Chick, Barb, Jim and Evie, Laurie, Denise, Gail, and all the others who make up the community who attend daily Mass. Unlike the Sunday congregation, which is diverse and spread out all over the church, filling its corners, the daily gathering is small, compact, known each to the other as intimately as family—and we all sit together! When I preach among them, I am totally with them, free of all the little concerns that attend the Sunday liturgy. The homily is often a dialogue; this little community knows its freedom to jump right in and they exercise it often. As we preach together, we learn. And because we know each other's story, the happiness and heartache that attend each other's lives, we enjoy a shared wisdom and a common recognition when the light shines and gives kingdom meaning to our mundane experiences.

So it is that the weekday liturgy is my daily bread—not only because the Eucharist nourishes my body and my soul, but also because the daily good news sustains me between Sundays. Blessed, broken, and shared, the word of God fills me and gives me life. And just as the Holy Spirit day by day changes ordinary bread and wine into the living body and blood of Christ, it also transforms hundreds of ordinary ideas into the daily gospel reflections you'll find on these pages and in your own heart.

Whether you are part of this daily gathering in your parish, preacher or parishioner, or looking for a little good news to carry you through your day, I hope you will find this book useful. It is best used in tandem with a liturgical calendar, which is easy to come by in parish offices or Catholic bookstores, and a Bible or lectionary. Determine the day—with the exception of some feast days, they'll usually follow the sequence of the season—and look up the full text of the readings for the day. I have provided a few lines of the gospel, sometimes in paraphrase, but it's important to read the entire passage. Then sit back, close your eyes, and relax. Take a few deep breaths, feeling the air go in and out of your body. Desire wisdom; be an open vessel for God's inspiration.

Articulate your expectation in a prayer: "Fill me with your word, O God; enlighten me with your truth." Allow your thoughts to explore possibilities. Be alert for the subtle stirring of your heart at the prospect of fulfillment, the answer to your prayer. Read my little reflection; perhaps it will mesh with your inspiration. I have also provided a prayer and an activity for each day to help you make God's word your own flesh and blood.

I have another hope: that, as you move through your week, this book will take you deeper into the experience of God's kingdom. It is at hand, present to you, alive within you. It is a realm where life is eternal and sins are forgiven. You need but turn to enter into it, and there live and move and discover your being. And in that discovery, be fulfilled.

Advent

Monday of the First Week of Advent

Regaining Focus

MATTHEW 8:5–11

When Jesus said that he would come and heal the centurion's servant, the soldier said, "Lord, I am not worthy to have you come under my roof; just say the word and my servant will be healed."

▶ Reflection

When they came to that part of the Mass where the priest shows the host to the people and says, "This is the Lamb of God," and the people all kneel down and respond, "Lord, I am not worthy," Roland would cringe a little inside. Ever since he took that liturgy course in ministry formation and learned that this part of the Mass was a throwback to the time when folks didn't go to communion because they were taught that they were "unworthy," he had disliked this moment. "Of course we're not worthy," he thought to himself. "But Jesus taught us to eat and drink this meal in his memory. It's not a matter of 'just say the word'; we're all called to participate. They should drop this part in the next revision." Maybe they will, whoever "they" are. But in the meantime, Roland needed to regain his focus and concentrate on what he was doing: getting ready to receive the Lord in communion. Sometimes a little knowledge can be a distracting thing.

▶ Prayer

O Lord, I know there are things in our religion that need to be worked on, but in the meantime may I always worship you with an open heart.

▶ Action

The next time you recite "Lord, I am not worthy" at Mass, remember that the Lord's healing word is spoken from within you.

Tuesday of the First Week of Advent

Babies Know

LUKE 10:21–24

Jesus rejoiced in the Holy Spirit and said, "I thank you, Father, Lord of heaven and earth, because you have hidden these things from the wise and the intelligent and have revealed them to infants; yes, Father, for such was your gracious will."

▶ Reflection

It sometimes gave Annie the creeps that babies picked her out, even on a crowded bus, and just gazed at her. There was nothing unusual about her appearance; in fact, she was rather plain by any standard. She had common brown hair, starting to gray a little, and hazel eyes. She wasn't by any means a flashy dresser, either. She just wore what she termed "quiet" colors. Nevertheless, the babies stared as if they were seeing things that other people couldn't see. What Annie didn't realize was that she was a holy woman of God. She carried in her heart a profound love for people and treated the lowly in her life with dignity and respect. She listened to everyone and prayed for those in need, paying particular attention to poor people and, of course, the children. And the babies paid particular attention to her because they could see her holiness; they knew who she was.

▶ Prayer

Can babies really see things the rest of us can't, O my God? What comes over us as we grow up? Do we really lose so much to the world? By your gracious will, make me like a baby again, Lord.

▶ Action

Whether on a bus, at the mall, in church, or wherever, engage the next baby you see. Open your soul to the infant and see what happens.

Wednesday of the First Week of Advent

Eat Now

MATTHEW 15:29–37

Jesus said to his disciples, "I have compassion for the crowd, because they have nothing to eat; and I do not want to send them away hungry." So he took the loaves and the fishes, and after giving thanks, he gave them to the crowds and all of them ate their fill.

▶ Reflection

The music was playing and the procession was forming in the vestibule when the man walked up to Fr. Jim and asked him if he would hear his confession. "Gee, I can't right now," Jim replied with a smile. He had learned to be nice to such people. "As you can see, Mass is beginning and I'm the only priest. But please, join us in communion and I will hear your confession after Mass." After preaching the gospel for twenty years, it had occurred to Jim that Jesus fed people because they were hungry, not because they were "prepared." And he did not agree that people should keep themselves from communion if they had not gone to confession. "If you need to confess your sins, then by all means go to confession," he would say. "But if you're starving and you need the nourishment of the Eucharist, then come to the table of the Lord."

▶ Prayer

You are the Bread of Life, dear Lord, and you offer to me the cup of your blood to take away my sins and the sins of all the world. May I always confess my heart and be fed at the banquet of your body.

▶ Action

If you are able, fast today to the point of hunger. Compose a prayer to Jesus expressing your desire in terms of the hunger you feel.

Thursday of the First Week of Advent

Forgetting God

MATTHEW 7:21–27

Jesus said, "Not everyone who says to me, 'Lord, Lord,' will enter the kingdom of heaven. Many will say to me, 'But we prophesied, and cast out demons, and did many powerful deeds in your name.' And I will say, 'Yes, but I never knew you. Go away, you evildoers!'"

▶ Reflection

For twenty-five years Helen and Dan dedicated themselves to bringing up their four kids. Dan always had a good job and was able to provide enough income so that Helen could be a successful homemaker. It wasn't until Nicole, their youngest, went off to school that Helen and Dan noticed they hadn't really paid much attention to their own relationship over the years. They both had changed. Now that it was just the two of them, they sometimes discovered that they hardly knew each other. They needed to put aside everything else and take the time to share their hearts with each other. It can be that way with God, too. We can be devout, active in our church, attentive to our lives, but neglect our relationship with God. And sometimes the opposite is true. There are many people who haven't been to church in years, yet enjoy a rich, vibrant love affair with the Lord.

▶ Prayer

Each day I pray to you, God of my life, but I really need to open my heart more to you. You give yourself to me like a spouse; you share your body and blood with me. Help me to offer myself in return.

▶ Action

Bring God with you today. As you move through your life, talk with God. Speak your heart to the Lord moment by moment.

Friday of the First Week of Advent

Kingdom Prep

MATTHEW 9:27–31

Two blind men cried out to Jesus, "Have mercy on us, Son of David!" Jesus said to them, "Do you believe that I am able to do this?" They said to him, "Yes, Lord." Then he touched their eyes and said, "According to your faith let it be done to you." And their eyes were opened.

▶ Reflection

The paradox of the kingdom of God is so simple: The last shall be first and the first shall be last. The blind see, the lame walk, the deaf hear, the hungry are fed, the dead are raised. Sinners are forgiven. Grown-ups are to be like children and children will possess the kingdom. The virgin? Why, she's going to be the mother! Advent is the season of waiting, looking forward and preparing with joyful hope for the coming of the kingdom. When that day comes, says Isaiah, "the lowly will ever find joy," and "the poor will rejoice." The questions I need to ask are, "Where do we fit into this scene? Where is my blindness? Where am I in pain and where do I suffer? How do I utilize my money, my power, my skills, and my time—all my resources to best position myself for the coming of the kingdom?"

▶ Prayer

O Lord, look upon me and see my hurt. Heal me and heal the pain I have inflicted on others. Help me see, in the many gifts you give, a way of helping the poor know your kingdom and your love.

▶ Action

Make a true estimate of your wealth today and do something to make yourself poorer for the sake of the coming kingdom.

Saturday of the First Week of Advent

Got Ministry?

MATTHEW 9:35—10:1, 6–8

When Jesus saw the crowds, he felt compassion for them, because they were harassed and helpless, like sheep without a shepherd. He said to his disciples, "The harvest is bountiful, but the laborers are few; ask the Lord of the harvest to send out laborers into his harvest."

▶ Reflection

Is there really a shortage of priests? I don't know. Maybe. It used to be that the priests did everything because there were plenty of them to go around, and they got a *lot* of help from the nuns. Now that there are far fewer of both, laypeople are taking their rightful place in the work of ministry. We're seeing how it's not just the priests who visit the sick or teach the Bible or run the business of the parish. You don't have to be ordained to do those kinds of things. Often there are laypeople in a given community who are far more qualified and gifted for such ministries. There will always be a real need for priests and I believe we'll have priests to meet that need. But for now, the good Lord may be answering our prayers to send laborers to the harvest by inspiring men and women from all walks of life to fulfill their baptismal call to ministry.

▶ Prayer

Almighty God, your word goes out to all people. You inspire men and women to offer their lives in service to your church. May we all be good examples of the people who receive your word and act on it.

▶ Action

What are you called to do for your church? Make a list of all the things you're good at, the talents you could share with others.

Monday of the Second Week of Advent

Forgiveness Is Us

LUKE 5:17–26

Jesus said to a paralyzed man, "Friend, your sins are forgiven." The scribes and the Pharisees began to ask, "Who does he think he is? Only God can forgive sins." Jesus answered, "The Son of Man has power on earth to forgive sins."

▶ Reflection

Why does Jesus call himself the "Son of Man"? Jesus uses the term seventy-eight times in the four gospels. What does it mean? There's a reference in my Catholic Bible that points to the book of Daniel in which "son of man" is used to describe "the glorified people of God that will form his kingdom on earth" *(New American Bible* footnote, Dan 7:13). In other words, the term not only refers to Jesus as an individual, but also to the people who will continue the ministry of Jesus on earth. St. Paul writes that God gave us the ministry of reconciliation and, since God doesn't count our sins against us, we must not count the sins of others against them, either (see 2 Corinthians 5:19–20). So, that leaves forgiveness as our only option. And where God gives the responsibility, God also gives the authority. The power to forgive sins is in our hands and we're called to exercise that power liberally.

▶ Prayer

Merciful God, your forgiveness is infinite and you extend your kindness and grace to all people. Yet you rely on me to be the visible sign of your invisible love. Help me to do a good job.

▶ Action

At the end of this day, score yourself on the times you exercised forgiveness and the times you didn't. How did you do?

Waiting for the Child

MATTHEW 18:12–14

Jesus said to them, "If a shepherd has a hundred sheep, and one of them has gone astray, does he not leave the ninety-nine on the mountains and go in search of the one that went astray? Even so, it is not the will of your Father in heaven that any one of these little ones should be lost."

▶ Reflection

Who are the "little ones" of Jesus' parable? Some interpreters point to the child introduced in the previous verses, suggesting that the "little ones" are the innocent. But the whole teaching is in response to the question, "Who is the greatest in the kingdom of heaven?" (18:1). The response is that "whoever humbles himself like this child is the greatest in the kingdom of heaven" (18:4). So the child, who in the time of Jesus had virtually no social status whatsoever, becomes the symbol of true humility. The value of such a little one is expressed in the lost sheep parable. The flock was the ancient symbol of a person's wealth, power, and prosperity. But the shepherd in the story is willing to leave his flock unattended; in other words, to risk everything in order to recover the lost little one.

▶ Prayer

Dear God, your love for me is beyond my imagining. You gave up your only son to save me. Teach me to know my true value in this world so that I might come to experience that value in your kingdom.

▶ Action

Look carefully at every child you encounter today. Observe his or her behavior and reactions. Recall that they symbolize the virtues, particularly humility, that we are to practice.

Easy and Light

MATTHEW 11:28–30

"Come to me, all you that are weary and carry heavy burdens, and I will give you rest. Take my yoke upon your shoulders and learn from me, for I am gentle and humble in heart. And your souls will find rest, for my yoke is easy, and my burden is light."

▶ Reflection

As soon as Arthur walked into the conference room, the chitchat quieted down and the directors gave him their complete attention. As president and CEO of the company, he commanded a certain respect. But it was more than that. Arthur possessed a quiet confidence and peacefulness that was rare among men of his caliber. That, more than anything else, gained their awe and admiration. He worked out and kept himself trim; smoked an occasional cigar and drank only in moderation. But if you asked him what his secret was, he'd tell you that he always says a little prayer before every meeting, every important phone call, every decision. "I used to be tired all the time and often stressed out," he'd say. "Then one day at church I realized that if I wanted to survive in this business, I had to look to God. Now I cast my troubles on the Lord and my soul is at peace."

▶ Prayer

O God, thank you for your faithful presence in my life. I sometimes forget to turn to you in my need, but when I do, you are always there to comfort me, support me, and give me rest for my soul.

▶ Action

What makes you weary? What burden do you carry? Compose a prayer laying your load at the feet of Jesus and say it every day.

Thursday of the Second Week of Advent

Heaven the Hard Way

MATTHEW 11:11–15

"No one has arisen greater than John the Baptist; yet the least in the kingdom of heaven is greater than he. From the days of John the Baptist until now the kingdom of heaven has suffered violence, and the violent take it by force. For all the prophets and the law prophesied until John came."

▶ Reflection

When Janice got pregnant she had to drop out of high school to have the baby. Then her parents told her she couldn't live at home any more unless she gave up her son for adoption, so she moved in with her boyfriend for a while. But they fought all the time, which wasn't good for her or the baby, so she moved out. She lived in shelters for a while, but then she got arrested for prostitution and they found drugs on her, so they took her baby away and sent her to jail. While in prison she started reading the Bible and going to prayer meetings and came to know Christ. She repented of her sins and was baptized. Now she lives her life born again and Jesus is her Lord. Is she greater than John the Baptist? Jesus says she is. Janice is among the least born into the kingdom of God.

▶ Prayer

I look around me, Lord, and I can sometimes see that the last are first in your kingdom. When I'm tempted to be first in this world, remind me that, in your kingdom, the meek and lowly are esteemed.

▶ Action

Consider three people whom you know who are good candidates for greatness in the kingdom of God. Give them encouragement soon.

Friday of the Second Week of Advent

Jesus the Drunk?

MATTHEW 11:16–19

"This generation is like children sitting in the marketplace, calling back and forth, 'We played and you did not dance! We wailed and you did not mourn!' What I mean is John came neither eating nor drinking, and they say, 'He's crazy'; I came eating and drinking and they say, 'He's a glutton and a drunkard!'"

▶ Reflection

It's not too hard to imagine that when our Lord Jesus came to town, it wasn't long before the word got around that he liked to go to parties and eat and drink. It seems that on any Sunday we can hear a gospel story about Jesus at a dinner or telling a parable about a banquet or changing water into more wine for the feast! Yet people complained; complained about him and about John the Baptist, who wouldn't be caught dead at a party. It's too bad they both weren't seen as God's messengers of blessing and acceptance; John, who was a blessing to those who practiced their religion faithfully, and Jesus, who gathered up the lowly, broken, and discarded of the world. Jesus said he didn't come to call the righteous but sinners (Matthew 9:13), and to save what was lost (Matthew 15:24), and he knew where to find both the sinners and the lost.

▶ Prayer

My loving Jesus, you are neither a drunkard nor a glutton, but you came to save me, a sinner. And even though I don't deserve your mercy and kindness, you give it to me anyway. What a gift of love!

▶ Action

Think of the most sinful time of your life. Imagine what people would have said about Jesus if he showed up to be with you at that time.

Forgot to Die!

MATTHEW 17:10–13

The disciples asked Jesus, "Why do the scribes say that Elijah must come first?"
He replied, "Elijah has already come, and they did not recognize him." Then the
disciples understood that he was speaking to them about John the Baptist.

▶ Reflection

By the time of Jesus, there had developed an expectation among the
people that, before the messiah would come, the great prophet of the
ninth century BC, Elijah, would return as a kind of forerunner to the
event. It wouldn't be the first time in the Bible that somebody popped
up from the dead. The witch of Endor conjured up the deceased
prophet Samuel at the request of King Saul (1 Samuel 28:1–25). But
in the case of Elijah, he never died! He's one of only two characters of
the Old Testament who didn't croak at the end. (Can you name the
other?) Anyway, Elijah was "taken up" in a whirlwind (2 Kings 2:11)
and sooner or later, like anything caught up in a tornado, was
expected to come down again. Jesus said that John the Baptist was the
fulfillment of the expectation of Elijah, which says more about Jesus
than John. (The other guy who didn't die was Enoch, Genesis 5:24.)

▶ Prayer

There are some mighty strange stories in the Bible, God. That's why
I'm glad there's more to you than the Bible can contain. You're in me
and that's what really counts. Thank you for your presence and love.

▶ Action

Look up and read the references in today's gospel, Malachi 3:23 NAB
or 4:5 NRSV and 2 Kings 2:11. Reflect on the strangeness of the stories.

Marking the days of the last two weeks of Advent

There are always four Sundays in Advent. But because Advent begins on a specific *day*, Sunday, and ends on a specific *date*, December 25, the length of the season varies from twenty-eight days when Christmas falls on a Sunday, to twenty-two days when Christmas falls on a Monday. To accommodate this variation, the season switches from days to dates beginning on December 17 (with the exception of the Fourth Sunday of Advent). So, when Advent lasts for twenty-eight days, Saturday of the third week of Advent falls on December 17; when it lasts for twenty-two days, December 17 falls on the Third Sunday of Advent. (All possible days of Advent are included in the lectionary and in this book.)

How does this work for you, the reader? Simply use the daily readings for the third week of Advent during the days until December 17. Then follow the dated readings, which begin on page 21, until Christmas.

During December 17–23, special prayers called the O antiphons (named for the way each prayer begins) are proclaimed as the gospel acclamations at daily liturgy. The O antiphons prepare for the coming of Christ with titles derived from Old Testament prophecies:

O Wisdom, holy Word of God!

O Adonai, sacred Lord of ancient Israel!

O Flower of Jesse's stem!

O Key of David, royal power of Israel!

O radiant dawn, sun of justice!

O King of all the nations, keystone of the mighty arch of humankind!

O Emmanuel, desire of the nations, savior of all people!

A simple way to pray the O antiphons is by singing the verses of the hymn *O Come, O Come Emmanuel* during December 17–23.

Monday of the Third Week of Advent

What Will People Think?!

MATTHEW 21:23–27

Jesus said to the elders of the people, "Did the baptism of John come from heaven, or was it of human origin?" They reasoned, "We can't say, 'From heaven,' because he will say, 'Why didn't you believe him?' We can't say, 'Of human origin,' because the crowd regards John as a prophet." So they answered, "We don't know." Jesus replied, "Neither will I tell you by what authority I do these things."

▶ Reflection

The "elders of the people" in the gospel passage suffer from the "what will people think" syndrome. (It's the reason why a whole generation of Americans puts on clean underwear every day!) They were far more concerned with what people would think of them than they were with an honest answer to the Lord's question. Jesus, on the other hand, was unconcerned about what people would think when he drove the retailers out of the temple area, an act that prompted the question of the elders in the first place (see Mt 21:12–13). The Spirit we have received from God is a Spirit of truth (see John 14:17, John 15:26, John 16:13). When we live by that Spirit, the life of God grows within us. When we deny the truth out of fear, we kill the Spirit.

▶ Prayer

Make your Spirit steadfast within me, O God. Help me to make your presence known in the world. Give me the courage to always testify to your truth, for you live in me and we are one in Christ.

▶ Action

Claim the worst truth about yourself you can think of. Hold that truth in your heart and proclaim it to yourself throughout the day.

Tuesday of the Third Week of Advent

Calling All Sinners

MATTHEW 21:28–32

Jesus said to chief priests and elders, "Truly I tell you, the tax collectors and the prostitutes are going into the kingdom of God ahead of you. For John came to you in the way of righteousness and you did not believe him, but the tax collectors and the prostitutes believed him; and even after you saw it, you did not change your minds and believe him."

▶ Reflection

Why should the "chief priests and elders" repent? As Jesus pointed out in Mt 9:12, "Those who are healthy do not need a physician." It was understood that the clergy and the devout of the Lord's time were blessed by God because of their righteousness. They obeyed all the commandments, at least externally—which is the only way one *can* obey all the commandments. So why did they need to repent? Repent from what? Jesus knew the answer: they needed to repent from the attitude that a person can guarantee salvation through being good by sheer force of the will. A sinner, especially a known sinner like a prostitute, can harbor no such attitude. This message needs to be heard by the clergy and devout of today, just as much as it did then.

▶ Prayer

God of heaven and earth, you have poured out blessings in abundance on me and have shown me your mercy and your kindness. Keep me safe from the arrogance that would harden my heart.

▶ Action

Write down three things about yourself that would disqualify you from heaven. Carry them in your pocket and praise the mercy of God all day long.

New Covenant?

LUKE 7:18–23

John sent two of his disciples to the Lord to ask, "Are you the one who is to come, or are we to wait for another?" for Jesus had cured many people of diseases, plagues, and evil spirits, and had given sight to many who were blind. So Jesus answered them, "Go and tell John what you have seen and heard: the blind see, the lame walk, the deaf hear, the dead are raised. And blessed are those who take no offense at me."

▶ Reflection

Even John the Baptizer wasn't too sure about Jesus. John's understanding of salvation sprang from the vision of justice we find in the first reading (Is 45:6–8, 18, 21–25). God rewards the good and punishes evildoers. But Jesus seemed to be messing up the system. He was forgiving people and healing their ills. Now, how can people be punished if Jesus keeps letting them off the hook? Jesus invites John to consider something new: that the things happening around Jesus, the blind see and the lame walk and the deaf hear, are manifestations of the kingdom of God. "I did not come to condemn the world," Jesus says in John 12:47, "but to save the world."

▶ Prayer

My Lord Jesus, you came into my life to forgive me. You rescued me from the consequences of my own willful turning from what is right and good. Keep me ever mindful that you save me each day.

▶ Action

Notice the opportunities you have today to forgive sinners, lift up the lowly, and help people to see something wonderful in their lives.

Thursday of the Third Week of Advent

Least is Greater

LUKE 7:24–30

Jesus spoke to the crowds about John: "Among those born of women no one is greater than John; yet the least in the kingdom of God is greater than he." All the people who heard this, including the tax collectors, acknowledged the justice of God, because they had been baptized with John's baptism. But by refusing to be baptized by him, the Pharisees and the lawyers rejected God's purpose for themselves.

▶ Reflection

John the Baptizer was immensely popular. He took a position of poverty and powerlessness over and against the clergy of his day who were, for the most part, rich and powerful. This brought about a certain credence to his preaching of righteousness and repentance. In today's passage, Jesus makes the radical pronouncement that John is the fulfillment of the very last prophecy of the Old Testament: "See, I am sending my messenger to prepare the way before me" (Malachi 3:1). And for the second time in Advent (see Thursday of the Second Week), Jesus makes it clear that while the good and righteous John was great, the worst sinner, born again, like the tax collector, to the new and eternal life of forgiveness, is greater than he. How does our Lord's evaluation of John's life measure up against our own values?

▶ Prayer

O my God, your love reaches out to all people. You forgive all, and those who accept your forgiveness receive the greatest gift: new life. May your love and mercy always be my guiding light.

▶ Action

Make a list of your virtues and a list of your faults. Spend some time considering the value of God's forgiveness in your life.

Friday of the Third Week of Advent

Jesus, Not John

JOHN 5:33–36

Jesus said, "John testified to the truth. He was a burning and shining lamp, and you were willing to rejoice for a while in his light. But I have a testimony greater than John's. The works that the Father has given me to complete, the very works that I am doing, testify on my behalf that the Father has sent me."

▶ Reflection

The first part of John's gospel spends a considerable amount of time comparing Jesus and John the Baptist. This was made necessary by the prevailing belief at the time that Jesus actually *was* John the Baptist. (Consider the consistent answer to the Lord's question, "Who do people say that I am?"; see Matthew 16:13–14, Mark 8:27–28.) So the fourth gospel, probably composed late in the century, is careful to make the distinction. John came preaching repentance and righteousness. Jesus came proclaiming the good news of God's mercy manifested in a kingdom co-existing in time with the world. The miracles Jesus performed attested to the presence of that kingdom and the power of God's mercy. We can never achieve John's righteousness but we can receive God's mercy.

▶ Prayer

Loving God, my heart desires to be good for you. I want to be worthy of your love. All you ask is that I repent of my sins and receive your kindness. But this is the miracle of your love! Praise you, Jesus!

▶ Action

Ask a lowly person for help today, such as a child or an elderly neighbor or a low-level coworker. Receive the grace of another's compassion.

December 17

The Family Tree

MATTHEW 1:1–17

The genealogy of Jesus the Messiah, the son of David, the son of Abraham: Judah was the father of Perez and Zerah by Tamar. Salmon was the father of Boaz by Rahab, and Boaz the father of Obed by Ruth. David was the father of Solomon by the wife of Uriah. And Joseph was the husband of Mary, of whom Jesus was born, who is called the Messiah.

▶ Reflection

We now shift gears, so to speak, moving into the final days of preparation for the great celebration of Christmas, the Incarnation of God in Jesus Christ. The focus moves from John the Baptizer to Mary. The elaborate genealogy of Matthew satisfies the primitive cultural and religious need to establish the lineage of his story's heroes. (Turning to the Old Testament and looking up all the characters in the genealogy is a wonderful way to pass the day when you're snowed in!) Notice there are five women listed: Tamar, Rahab, Ruth, the wife of Uriah (Bathsheba), and of course Mary. Each held a unique place in the history of God's people, well apart from ordinary human expectations. It is in this tradition that Christ enters the human story.

▶ Prayer

I bring shame down on people, O Lord, and lay heavy guilt upon them for what I see are violations of the rules of morality. But you, O God, light up my darkness with your justice and your salvation. Let me be generous in my own understanding of the actions of others.

▶ Action

Imagine that Jesus chose to come again today. Among the people you know, who would he choose to be the instrument of his coming?

December 18

Bones of Jesus

<u>MATTHEW 1:18–24</u>

Before Mary and her husband Joseph lived together, she was found to be with child from the Holy Spirit. Joseph was going to divorce her, but an angel of the Lord appeared to him in a dream and said, "Do not be afraid! The child conceived in her is from the Holy Spirit."

▶ Reflection

"What if one day they found a hidden tomb containing what proved to be the bones of Jesus, or discovered irrefutable evidence that Mary and Joseph lived together before Jesus was conceived?" These hypothetical questions were posed in a seminary to a group of men who were about to be ordained. Some of the answers were surprising. Some of men said they would bail out. "Heck," answered one, "I'd get a law degree and become a lawyer or something and make a decent living." Others said they would have to seriously reconsider what they believed and what they were doing. But one man said it wouldn't make any difference to him at all. "Nothing can change our history. You can't go back and erase two thousand years of encounters with the risen Savior. Neither can you change the experiences of my own life. I know Jesus and you can't change that."

▶ Prayer

You sing a song in my heart, dear God, and it echoes in my soul. My body dances to the music of your presence in my life. No matter what happens, keep my faith strong and alive.

▶ Action

Consider the question that opens the above reflection. How would you answer it? Is there anything that would knock you off the track of faith? Why?

December 19

Freebie for Mary

LUKE 1:5–25

The angel said to Zechariah, "Your wife Elizabeth will bear you a son, and you will name him John. You will have joy and gladness, and many will rejoice at his birth." Zechariah replied, "How will I know that this is so? I am an old man...."

▶ Reflection

Zechariah got into big trouble for questioning the angel. He couldn't understand how he and his wife could have a baby since all their lives they had been unsuccessful and were now 'way too old. The angel reacted to Zechariah's question by striking him mute and the poor guy was unable to speak for nine months! Mary, on the other hand, had the same reaction when the angel spoke to her. Luke links the two responses with similar words: Zechariah states, "How will I know this? I am an old man." while Mary asks, "How can this be? I do not know a man." Yet Mary didn't get into any trouble at all. Why? Maybe because Zechariah was a priest under the Law and therefore received punitive recompense, while Mary was under the dispensation of grace and the mother of salvation and therefore any trespass simply was not counted against her. Who knows the mind of God?

▶ Prayer

O God, your grace and your mercy extend to all people for all time. You ask great things of each and every one of us, in our own ways. Thank you for all you've done for me.

▶ Action

Think of all the mistakes you've made for which you paid a price. Then think of all the goofs you got away with. Praise God for mercy!

December 20

God's Nuptial

LUKE 1:26–38

The angel said to Mary, "The Holy Spirit will come upon you, and the power of the Most High will overshadow you; hence the child to be born will be holy; he will be called Son of God." Then Mary said, "I am the servant of the Lord; let it be with me according to your word."

▶ Reflection

"Heaven is wedded to earth and Man is reconciled with God!" Today's announcement of the nuptials of God and Mary are echoed in the Easter Proclamation *(Exsultet)* sung at the Easter Vigil, forging a liturgical link between Easter and Christmas, the two great celebrations of the church. Then there's Pentecost. Early on in my walk with Christ I once argued with a friend over the divinity of Jesus. "What's the point?" I said. "If he were only human his message would be no less true. I could accept him as Lord even if he wasn't God." My friend replied, "I'm afraid I haven't spent much time thinking about Jesus being the Son of God. What really excites me is that we are *all* children of God." The beauty of the incarnation of God in the Son of Mary is that now God is revealed in *all* humanity. The Holy Spirit is the giver of life in all who have life.

▶ Prayer

Lord, thank you for the gift of life. In Christ you have made me your own beloved child. The life within me is no longer just me; now it is you. Your life is in me and you are in me.

▶ Action

Close you eyes and feel the life in you. Realize that the life you sense is the presence of God. You and God are one.

December 21

Labor Pains

LUKE 1:39-45

When Elizabeth heard Mary's greeting, the child leaped in her womb. And Elizabeth was filled with the Holy Spirit and cried, "Blessed are you among women, and blessed is the fruit of your womb!"

▶ Reflection

As the pain subsided, Tonya glanced nervously at the lighted clock on the dresser. She wished she could have a cigarette. The hardest thing about her pregnancy so far was giving up smoking, but she wanted to do it for the baby. Besides, it wouldn't be too much longer now. The ultrasound showed it was a girl so she and Rick named her Nykesha. She could feel Nykesha now, moving inside her, maybe getting ready to be born tonight. When Nykesha moved like that, Tonya would sing her an old African song her grandmother taught her when she was small. So she sang softly and wondered if this was how Mary felt the night baby Jesus was born. A baby stirring in a mother's womb always seems to give rise to thoughts of Christmas. She heard Rick fumble for his glasses. "What time is it, honey?" he asked, groggy. Tonya smiled and touched her husband's handsome face. "It's time for us to get up. I think this is going to be Nykesha's birthday."

▶ Prayer

O Mary, mother of Jesus and mother of the church, you were so fully and completely a woman the night you felt God was ready to be born from your body. Pray that I, too, may bring forth the Christ for others.

▶ Action

Think of a time when you really brought the grace of Christ into the life of another person. Remember what it was like and how you felt.

December 22

Embezzling Grace

LUKE 1:46–56

This was Mary's song: "God has shown strength with his arm; he has scattered the proud in their conceit. He has cast down the mighty from their thrones, and has lifted up the lowly. He has filled the hungry with good things, and the rich he has sent away empty."

▶ Reflection

As Ray knelt in his pew after communion, he reflected on his blessings. He had been, essentially, a cheater. He had spent his whole life cheating. He remembered being a kid in school and the many ways he tried to beat the system: copying homework, plagiarizing, buying reports, cribbing on tests. He cheated on his bar exam, cheated on his clients, cheated on his wife. And then he got caught and it all came apart. He went too far on a real estate deal and one day the phone rang and that was the beginning of the end. He was convicted of embezzling, served time in jail, was disbarred, lost his practice, lost his wife and family, lost everything. He turned back to God, and the Lord was there for him. God forgave him and restored him, healing his guilt and giving him a new start. Ray wept in thanksgiving when he thought of everything God had done for him.

▶ Prayer

You have healed me in many ways, Lord, and I give you thanks. I thank you, too, for the guidance that always leads me back to the right path when I go astray. Keep me always in the way that leads to you.

▶ Action

Look up and read the parables of the lost sheep and the lost coin, Luke 15:1–10. Think about how God delights in saving you.

December 23

Stand By Your Woman

LUKE 1:57–66

On the eighth day they came to circumcise the child, and they were going to name him Zechariah after his father. But his mother said, "No, he is to be called John." They said to her, "None of your relatives has this name." Then his father wrote on a tablet, "His name is John." And all of them were amazed.

▶ Reflection

When opposites attract, as is often the case, relationships are established with tremendous potential for conflict. When such relationships result in marriage, as they often do, it is especially important for the spouses to make a constant effort to support and affirm each another. A husband once told me that he discovered himself contradicting his wife just for the sake of maintaining his own autonomy over and against hers! But that's not the call of relationship, certainly not the call of marriage. It's probably a safe bet that Zechariah had spent his whole adult life wanting to have a little Zechariah Junior running around his house, carrying his name. But when the time came, his wife Elizabeth made the call, remembering the word the angel spoke to her husband some nine months before. And ol' Zech, a "good man" as the Bible tells us, stood by his woman.

▶ Prayer

Lord, I'm so grateful for the people you send into my life to be in relationship with me. Through them you teach me all about love.

▶ Action

Keep alert today for someone with whom you often find yourself in conflict. Resolve to choose compassion over competition this time.

December 24

Light in Darkness

LUKE 1:67–79

John's father Zechariah was filled with the Holy Spirit and spoke this prophecy: "Blessed be the Lord God of Israel, for he has looked favorably on his people and redeemed them. He has raised up a mighty savior for us in the house of his servant David, as he spoke through the mouth of his holy prophets."

▶ Reflection

And now Zechariah sings a song. Notice how Luke has given the lead to Zechariah in the birth of John, but Mary calls the shots in the birth of Jesus. Luke seems to be interested in drawing the distinction between the old and the new as this mysterious paradox unfolds. John, the last prophet of the law, is born to a barren woman and an elderly father in keeping with Old Testament tradition. Therefore, it is the father, Zechariah, who sings. Jesus, however, the embodiment of the New Covenant, is born of a virgin mother and a divine Father, bringing to the table something entirely new. This new light of God's love shines "on those who sit in darkness," bringing God's peace to all, and the new covenant will not be like the old one. "The days are surely coming, says the Lord, when I will make a new covenant with the house of Israel and the house of Judah. It will not be like the covenant that I made with their ancestors" (see Jeremiah 31:31–32).

▶ Prayer

Come, Lord Jesus! You bring me something new and wonderful. I am unable to rise to the goodness of God, so you come and lift me up. Be born in me now, Lord. Give me new life!

▶ Action

Just as you count up your Christmas gifts, so count up the gifts God gives you in Jesus Christ, born in you this day.

Christmas
Season

Christmas Day

Born

LUKE 2:1–14

Joseph went from Nazareth to Bethlehem to be registered with Mary, his wife, who was expecting a child. While they were there, she gave birth to her firstborn son, wrapped him in swaddling clothes, and laid him in a manger, because there was no place for them in the inn.

▶ Reflection

How many times have the circumstances of our lives drawn us into situations we didn't want to be in, yet God brought about good things for us from even the worst of events of life? Time and time again the stories of faith tell of God snatching victory from the jaws of defeat. Take for example the story of Mary and Joseph, called to travel to Bethlehem at the worst possible time, right when Mary is due to have her baby. Not only that, but of course there is no room at the inn. Yet it all works out; the worst becomes the best. This is the story of Christmas. God has thrown in the divine lot with us and he's in it for the duration. Nothing will separate us from the love of God we have in Christ (see Romans 8:35–39). No matter what happens from now on, God is with us, blessing us and making all things work together for good for us in love (see Romans 8:28).

▶ Prayer

Merry Christmas, God! Bless all the families on earth. Bless people who visit relatives and loved ones today. Keep everybody safe. When things go wrong, show your power to save and to raise up.

▶ Action

Look at your day today and decide what the worst part will be. Ask God to bless that part of the day and make it the best.

December 26

Betrayed by a Father

MATTHEW 10:17–22

Brother will betray brother to death, and a father his child. Children will rise against parents and have them put to death. You will be hated by all because of my name. But the one who endures to the end will be saved.

▶ Reflection

Mariah was sad because her father didn't show up for Christmas again. He didn't show up for her birthday this year, either, even though she turned thirteen and it would have been so special to her if he had come to her party. But he didn't, just like he didn't come for Christmas. Now it was time for her to make a decision. She came into the kitchen where her mom was preparing supper. "Mom," she said, "I don't want to see Dad any more." Theresa looked up, concerned. "But honey, he's your father. You should see him." Mariah slouched into a chair. "Yeah, but he's a lousy father. He never calls, never shows up, never does anything for us. I just don't care if I see him again." Theresa knew that this was a big step for Mariah. The girl had been deeply hurt when her father left them; she felt really betrayed. But now perhaps the healing had begun.

▶ Prayer

Father in heaven, people do betray one another, even fathers their children. But you are always faithful to me. Even if everybody abandoned me, you would still be there. Thank you for your faithfulness.

▶ Action

Think of a betrayal by a loved one that may have left you wounded in some way. Ask God to bless that person and heal your own hurt.

December 27

The Pastor's "Secret"

JOHN 20:2–8

Mary Magdalene ran to the disciples and said, "They have taken the Lord out of the tomb!" Simon Peter came and went into the tomb. He saw the linen wrappings lying there, and the cloth that had been on Jesus' head, not lying with the linen wrappings but rolled up in a place by itself. Then the other disciple went in; he saw and believed.

▶ Reflection

Everybody sees different things in different ways. Once I was staying as a guest of my friends John and Ellen at their summer house near a popular vacation spot on the water. One day I accompanied Ellen on a shopping trip to buy John a present for his birthday. While in town, we bumped into a couple of my parishioners who happened to be vacationing nearby. We exchanged greetings, introductions, and pleasantries, and continued on our way. A week later, the parishioners who had seen me with Ellen confided in me after Mass on Sunday that my "secret" was safe with them; they would tell no one of the encounter. People believe what they want to believe. The "other disciple" in the story saw the same thing Mary Magdalene saw; yet he believed something very different.

▶ Prayer

O God, when I look at the events of my day, I know you are blessing me. But sometimes it seems as if you are doing bad things to me. Heal my blindness, Lord. Help me to see the truth of your love for me.

▶ Action

Write down three reasons why you believe that Christ is risen from the dead. What do you "see" that makes you believe?

December 28

Johnny Joke

MATTHEW 2:13–18

An angel of the Lord appeared to Joseph in a dream and said, "Take the child and his mother and flee to Egypt, for Herod is trying to destroy him." So Joseph took them and fled to Egypt.

▶ Reflection

One of the great joys of having a first grader in the family is seeing what he brings home from school each day. So when little Johnny burst in the door, home from first grade at St. Michael's, drawing of the day clutched in his mittened hand, his mother was curious to see his work of art. "It's about Christmas!" he exclaimed, pulling his mittens off and dropping his coat on the floor. They worked together to get him out of his boots and finally he was able to display his work, a detailed rendering of...an airplane! "What's an airplane got to do with Christmas, Johnny?" his mom asked. "Mom!" Johnny was incredulous. "It's the flight into Egypt!" "Oh," said Mom. "And the people in the plane are...?" "Jesus, Mary and Joseph! See?" He pointed out the three faces in the windows. "And who's this up front?" she asked. Johnny couldn't believe his mother's ignorance. "Mom! That's Punt-chus, the pilot!"

▶ Prayer

Oh no! That's a terrible joke, God. You don't think I should blame you for a joke like that? Wasn't a sense of humor your idea? What? You're saying I should seek forgiveness, instead? Praise the Lord!

▶ Action

Do you think you can do better? Tell God a joke in your prayer today. The Lord could always use a good laugh. God likes to hear from you.

December 29

Consider Death

LUKE 2:22–35

Simeon took the child Jesus in his arms and praised God, saying, "Master, now you may dismiss your servant in peace, for my eyes have seen your salvation, which you have prepared in the presence of all peoples, a light for revelation to the Gentiles and for glory to your people Israel."

▶ Reflection

Browsing through the books in the children's section, Holly came across a nicely illustrated book of prayers that would be perfect for her niece, Allison. She paged through it and liked what she saw until she found a little prayer she learned as a kid: "Now I lay me down to sleep. I pray the Lord my soul to keep. Stay close to me throughout the night, And wake me with the morning light." She thought, "Whatever happened to 'If I should die before I wake'?" Holly just discovered that in a culture that sells youth and vitality, death has become a well-kept secret. Thank God that the church "encourages us to prepare ourselves for the hour of our death" (*Catechism of the Catholic Church* #1014). We still pray today's gospel, called *Simeon's Canticle*, at Night Prayer and ask for Mary's prayerful help "at the hour of our death."

▶ Prayer

Oh master of my life, if I were to die this day I would not be disappointed; nor would I feel as though I missed anything. For you have shown me love and salvation. Guide me to death and beyond.

▶ Action

Consider how you would feel if you died today. Think about what you would be angry about and what you would be grateful for.

December 30

Growing With God

LUKE 2:36–40

When they had finished everything required by the law of the Lord, they returned to Galilee, to their own town of Nazareth. The child grew and became strong, filled with wisdom; and the favor of God was upon him.

▶ Reflection

When the soda bottle broke in the freezer, Carlos had reacted badly. He had punished little Carlos and sent him to his room. Now, repentant, Carlos quietly entered his son's room and sat down next to the little guy on his bed. "I'm sorry, buddy. I shouldn't have yelled at you like that." He put his hand gently on little Carlos' head. "Sometimes I think you're supposed to know things that you can't know unless I teach you. So I guess it's my fault. Come downstairs and I'll show you what happens when you put an egg in the microwave." Little Carlos forgot his misery and happily accompanied his dad on their next adventure. We sometimes do the same to Jesus, thinking he came pre-programmed with all knowledge and wisdom. But the Bible says he grew. He learned about things the same way we do. He grew to discover who he was.

▶ Prayer

Lord Jesus, you grew up in a human family, went to school, and developed an understanding about life and about yourself. Help me to grow in wisdom and grace as you did.

▶ Action

Spend some time reflecting on your life. Consider this: as you have grown, so God has grown in you. You and God are one.

December 31

God in Human Flesh

JOHN 1:1–18

In the beginning was the Word, and the Word was with God, and the Word was God. He was in the world, and the world came into being through him; yet the world did not know him. And the Word became flesh and lived among us. From his fullness we have all received, grace upon grace. The law indeed was given through Moses; grace and truth came through Jesus Christ.

▶ **Reflection**

As a builder carefully lays a strong foundation that will support the mass of the complete building, so the author of John's gospel artfully develops a powerful and poetic prologue that will support the weight of his theological structure. For John, everything hinges on the astounding premise that "the Word became flesh"; God has become a human being! This changes everything. The understanding that follows is that God has offered a new covenant. He makes clear (and preachers need to make clear) that this is not the covenant of the law, the one with Moses. This is not the Ten Commandments. This is the gospel of God's grace shown to us in Jesus Christ. Mortal flesh will no longer be condemned by sin. Grace will win the victory!

▶ **Prayer**

With great joy I welcome you into my world, Lord Jesus. You are with me in my own body. You share my flesh and blood. In you I find hope, for in you my sins are forgiven and I become a child of God.

▶ **Action**

Close your eyes. Put all things out of your mind and listen to your breathing. Feel the life in you. That is God dwelling with you.

January 2

Not the Messiah

JOHN 1:19–28

When they sent priests and Levites from Jerusalem to ask John, "Who are you?" he confessed and said, "I am not the Messiah." "Who are you, then?" they asked. He said, "I am the voice of one crying out in the wilderness, 'Make straight the way of the Lord.'"

▶ Reflection

What was Mary and Pete's secret to their thirty years of marriage? "At some point along the way, we figured out that neither of us was the other's savior," said Pete at the anniversary celebration. "There's only one of those," agreed Mary. Early on in their marriage, Mary thought that Pete was supposed to make her happy. "But I realized that nobody or no thing could make me happy," Mary continued. "I could be happy, but Pete couldn't make me happy." Pete added, "And the same is true for me. We both believe that God created us to be fulfilled in love with God; that in God we will find our happiness. In our marriage we've learned to help each other move toward that goal." Maybe it was John the Baptist who was the first to confess that he was not the messiah. Many have since found great peace and fulfillment by realizing the same thing.

▶ Prayer

Dear Lord, your gift of grace satisfies my heart and fulfills my soul. Yet I seek after so many things. Teach me the value of your presence in my life. Show me how to be content with what I have.

▶ Action

Write down the things you feel would make you happy. Now tear up the list and throw it away. You already have everything you need.

January 3

Lamb Revealed

JOHN 1:29–34

John saw Jesus and declared, "Here is the Lamb of God who takes away the sin of the world! I myself did not know him; but I came baptizing with water for this reason, that he might be revealed to Israel."

▶ Reflection

I have to admit that I didn't know him either. Oh, sure, I was baptized. But I was about a week old at the time and the sacramental celebration didn't have a particularly rapturous effect on me. In fact, as I understand it, it marked the first time I met with disapproval in a church. (Evidently, Msgr. Kelley didn't like crying babies.) But in time, in about thirty years time, it dawned on me what I had: eternal life and the forgiveness of sins! That was a monumental revelation to me. Suddenly the Lamb of God was very real to me. He takes away the sins of the world! Here I'd been living my entire life as a victim of the sins of my parents, the sins of others, and of course my own sins. Then it suddenly occurred to me that I didn't have to. I could accept forgiveness for my sins and the sins of all the world. In an instant my life was transformed. Death had given way to new life.

▶ Prayer

When you assumed my human life, O my Jesus, it included the price you would pay for my sins. But you made the sacrifice and now I am free. You gave me life and now I live only for you.

▶ Action

Think of a sin, yours or another's, that remains unforgiven because you have not yet accepted that forgiveness. What are you going to do?

January 4

Where Are You Staying?

JOHN 1:35–42

Two disciples of John followed Jesus. Jesus said to them, "What are you looking for?" They said to him, "Rabbi, where are you staying?" He said to them, "Come and see." They came and saw where he was staying, and they remained with him that day.

▶ Reflection

The question seems innocent enough, yet when the disciples of John the Baptist posed it to Jesus, it may have been loaded. John seemed to have been a bit of an odd duck. He lived in the desert and ate locusts (yuck!) and wild honey (see Matthew 3:1–4). One can imagine the difficulty he would have endured just coming up with a meal! Could we assume that his disciples lived like he did? Well, that's what disciples are supposed to do. So, when they asked Jesus where he was staying, they were undoubtedly intending to impose on his hospitality. And Jesus graciously granted their imposition. Every time we turn to God in prayer, we are beggars looking for a handout. And though we often exploit God's graciousness, the Lord welcomes us lavishly. Yet, in the paradox of the kingdom, it is God who comes begging to us, seeking a place in our flesh and blood to stay and make a home.

▶ Prayer

Precious Lord, where do you stay? Is it truly within me that you make your home? Is my humble flesh and blood a fitting place for you? Yet you choose to be with me out of love for me. I am not worthy.

▶ Action

As you encounter the lowly today—the poor, the needy, the sick, the criminal—consider where they stay and who it is who stays with them.

January 5

Good From Williburg?

JOHN 1:43–51

Philip found Nathanael and said to him, "We have found him about whom Moses in the law and also the prophets wrote, Jesus son of Joseph from Nazareth." Nathanael said to him, "Can anything good come out of Nazareth?" Philip said to him, "Come and see."

▶ Reflection

For several years I was pastor of a wealthy parish. In order to bring across the sense of today's gospel passage, I would sometimes use the name of a rather poor, shabby town on the other side of the diocese, which I'll call Williburg. I would tell people, "It's like us saying, 'What good can come out of Williburg!'" and the folks would laugh because they got the idea. Then I became pastor of a town right next to Williburg and I couldn't use that image any more. But I found out about the wonderful things can come from the poverty and humility of lowliness. Williburg was a tremendous outlet for our Catholic Charities program and offered me and the people I served a far greater opportunity to gain kingdom wealth than I ever had in the rich town. Every instance of poverty and lowliness offers the invitation to "come and see" what good can come from what God blesses.

▶ Prayer

Sometimes I ask, O God, "What good can I do? What good can come from me?" You know, Lord, because you created the good in me. Show me. Let me see the good I can accomplish in this world.

▶ Action

Seek to discover the good above all else today. When your perception says there is no good, repent and ask God to show you where it is.

January 6

Torn Apart

MARK 1:7–11

In those days Jesus came from Nazareth of Galilee and was baptized by John in the Jordan. And just as he was coming up out of the water, he saw the heavens torn apart and the Spirit descending like a dove on him. And a voice came from heaven said, "You are my Son, the Beloved; with you I am well pleased."

▶ Reflection

I wonder what it looked like to see the "heavens torn apart." Scholars are uncertain whether this vision belonged to Jesus or to John; the pronoun is ambiguous. Either way, the image carries on the theme of Christmas: the union of God and humanity in Christ. "The heavens," in the pre-scientific understanding of the first century, was a kind of dome-like structure that housed the sun, moon, stars, and clouds. Beyond the dome was where God, the old guy with the gray beard, evidently lived. That this dome was "torn apart" meant that the division between heaven and earth was opened. God was no longer separated from humanity by an impenetrable mystery. Mark's baptism liturgy was the outward sign of a new inward reality. God was now in the human race.

▶ Prayer

O Lord, I give you thanks that you have so wonderfully revealed yourself as one who shares my human life. I'm so used to looking for you beyond me, yet you are right here within me. Glory!

▶ Action

Try to remember at least five times today that God is the life you sense right now in your body.

January 7

Lots of Wine

JOHN 2:1–12

On the third day there was a wedding in Cana of Galilee, and the mother of Jesus was there. Jesus and his disciples had also been invited to the wedding. When the wine gave out, the mother of Jesus said to him, "They have no wine."

▶ Reflection

In contemporary culture where alcoholism is a too tragic reality that has touched every life in some way, the theme of this popular story from John's gospel seems somewhat embarrassing and out of place. Yet "there's good wine a-plenty and let's drink a lot of it" was what the story meant to convey. Wine is the ancient symbol of gladness and (let's say responsible) celebration; the presence of Jesus, who is the embodiment of salvation, brings both. Like old wine, the power of the old covenant has run out. The new covenant in Jesus Christ is the abundant new wine. The surprising source of this fine vintage is the common water of the world, the human experience which washes and purifies. Like bookends, the last use of water in John's gospel is at the last supper (John 13:1–15) where it becomes the sign of the mission of Christ's followers: to forgive as they have been forgiven.

▶ Prayer

Lord Jesus, you come into my life bringing joy and gladness. I am a sinner and my sins bring sadness. But you have lifted up my heart with the wine of your forgiveness. Help me to always forgive others.

▶ Action

Remember the last really good celebration you attended. Today, create a celebration of love within your life right now.

Monday after Epiphany

Switching

MATTHEW 4:12–17, 23–25

Jesus left Nazareth and made his home in Capernaum by the sea. From that time he began to proclaim, "Repent, for the kingdom of heaven is at hand." He went throughout Galilee, teaching in their synagogues and proclaiming the good news of the kingdom and curing every disease and every sickness among the people.

▶ Reflection

In a world where it was understood that God's kingdom would come after the worldly kingdom, Jesus introduced a radical new concept: the kingdom of God was already present. One wishing to enter God's kingdom had to simply leave the world behind, which is the meaning of that word "repent." It means to turn around, to make what we would call a U-turn. It's like watching a TV with two channels: although both channels are available, you can only watch one at a time. If you want to go to one world, you have to leave the other. And since the kingdom and the world are paradoxically opposed, the effect of the switch is dramatic, like night and day: the blind see, the lame walk, the deaf hear, the sick are healed, sinners are forgiven, the dead rise, and the virgin becomes the mother. What a deal!

▶ Prayer

O loving God, you are really present to me here and now. Your heaven exists within me, even as I live in the world. Help me make the right choices today so that I may experience your kingdom in joy.

▶ Action

Be thoughtful of the kingdom today. Try to make at least three choices that will help you to leave the world behind and enter God's realm.

Tuesday after Epiphany

Never Enough

MARK 6:34–44

Taking the five loaves and the two fish, he looked up to heaven, and blessed and broke the loaves, and gave them to his disciples to set before the people; and he divided the two fish among them all. And all ate and were filled; and they took up twelve baskets full of broken pieces and of the fish.

▶ Reflection

When Jason worked for the big industrial contractor in the city, he made a lot of money. With perks and everything, he should have considered himself well off. But he didn't. As it was, there never seemed to be enough. The big house, the new cars, the fancy vacations, the nice clothes—it all seemed to gobble up his income. In time, he made radical changes to his life. He quit his job, sold his house and moved into a smaller one, stopped buying new cars, and began to spend vacations home enjoying his family. He took a part-time job teaching at a local tech school and began to enjoy life more. He got back to church and started to take his religion seriously. As he grew stronger in the practice of his faith, he began to notice that what little he had always seemed to be enough, even with some left over.

▶ Prayer

I am rich in your love, O God of all creation. I am fulfilled in your love for me and I want for nothing. The false god of money tempts me day by day, but you've shown me the truth of real wealth.

▶ Action

If you dare, ask God today and every day to show you how you can live with less so you can enjoy life more.

Fearful Chickadee

MARK 6:45–52

When evening came, their boat was out on the sea, and Jesus was alone on the land. When he saw that they were straining at the oars against the wind, he came towards them early in the morning, walking on the water. When they saw him they were terrified. He said, "It is I; do not be afraid." They were utterly astounded, for they did not understand about the loaves, but their hearts were hardened.

▶ Reflection

"Keep still and be patient. He'll come," my neighbor Bob coached. I stood like a statue, my hand outstretched and open, cradling the little cache of sunflower seeds. *"Bree bree bree bree!"* the chickadee scolded from its perch on the branch. It sounded to me like bird talk for, "Put the seeds down and back away!" I really wanted the bird to come to me, but it looked like there was no way the little guy was going to land in my hand and take the seeds. A million years of fear would not let him do it. I think the same is true for us. It seems like a million years of fear won't let us land in God's hand and receive what he has to offer, even though God has never done anything to hurt us. Repent is what we must do; that is, change our thinking about God.

▶ Prayer

For so long now, my God, you have been celebrated as the one who punishes sinners. I am a sinner so you can understand why I'm sometimes afraid of you. Help me to be not afraid.

▶ Action

Imagine if you were called to judgment right this moment. Is there any reason for you to be afraid? Why? Do something about it.

Thursday after Epiphany

What's So Special?

LUKE 4:14–22

Jesus stood up in the synagogue and read from the prophet Isaiah: "The Spirit of the Lord is upon me, and has anointed me to bring good news to the poor. He has sent me to proclaim release to the captives and recovery of sight to the blind, to let the oppressed go free, to proclaim the year of the Lord's favor." Then he said to them, "Today this scripture is fulfilled in your hearing."

▶ Reflection

Every morning when I walked to the office I would see pieces of paper and debris and cigarette butts littering the sidewalk. "Why doesn't somebody pick all this stuff up?" I asked myself maybe a hundred times before I realized that maybe God is calling *me* to pick it up! This may not sound like rocket science, but lots of times that's how we think. The people of our Lord's day were waiting for a savior. They had spent so long waiting that they'd forgotten how to do anything but wait. When Jesus announced to them that today was the day, they responded, "Isn't this Joseph's son?" In other words, what's so special about him? Yet it was in the power of all the people present to bring glad tidings, set the captives free, and announce a year of favor. Getting it done rested in their decision to act.

▶ Prayer

O God, you have placed the power to forgive and to set people free in my hands. Show me those to whom I am to announce the good news.

▶ Action

Today people will need you to forgive them and set them free. Pray for the good will to put into practice the power you've been given.

Friday after Epiphany

Giving Away Wellness

LUKE 5:12–16

A man with leprosy begged Jesus, "Lord, if you choose, you can make me clean."
Jesus touched him, and said, "I do choose. Be made clean." Immediately the
leprosy left him. The word about Jesus spread and many gathered to hear him
and to be cured. But he would withdraw to deserted places and pray.

▶ Reflection

It is curious that Jesus seemed to be trying to minimize his ministry of
healing. He often instructed those he had healed not to tell anyone of
the cure, as he did in this story. Here also, and in other stories, he fled
the crowds who came to him seeking him and his healing touch.
Some interpreters claim this suggests a kind of reluctance on his part
to advance his reputation. Clearly he wanted to heal, he could heal,
and he did. But perhaps the experience was overwhelming. In the
story of the raising of Lazarus (John 11:1–43) it says the experience
caused Jesus profound emotional disturbance. Perhaps these were like
"mini-passions" in which Jesus took on himself the ills of the people
around him, exchanging his own wellness. God's self-giving for our
benefit defies human understanding. We can only be amazed.

▶ Prayer

O God, you join me in my humanity, descend into my own flesh and
blood. You make my body your body, accepting all my human
weaknesses. Thank you, my Lord, for loving me so much.

▶ Action

Consider all the times you were sick or injured and recovered.
Embrace and celebrate your wellness today as a gift from God.

Saturday after Epiphany

Receiving Lordship

JOHN 3:22–30

They said to John, "Rabbi, the one to whom you testified is now baptizing and everybody is going to him." He answered, "I have already told you I am not the Messiah. For this reason my joy has been fulfilled. He must increase, but I must decrease."

▶ Reflection

It must have been a challenge to John to know that if he did his job right, he'd essentially be working himself out of a job. After all, he was "the Baptizer." Nobody else would ever claim that title. But baptism is a rebirth, and if one is to be born into the kingdom, one must die to the world. If Jesus is to increase in the lives of John's followers, John himself had to decrease. This challenge continues today in the hearts and minds of believers: God must increase and I must decrease. Or as Jesus would say: "Not my will, but thy will be done." In my life I receive Jesus into my body. But there ensues a struggle for lordship. To be fulfilled, I have to be like John, surrendering to Jesus because the Lord will never inflict lordship. I must give it to him. Just as Mary accepted that it be done to her, and John accepted his decreasement, so must I accept the Lord, and find my fulfillment in his increase.

▶ Prayer

Come into my heart, O Lord. Fill me with your presence. Show me the beauty of your gift of life in me. Teach me your way and deliver me from all my afflictions. May I always surrender to your love.

▶ Action

Ten times today God will point you in the right direction. Count how many times you give up your own agenda and surrender to God's.

Baptism of the Lord

Jesus the Thresher

LUKE 3:15–16, 21–22

John said, "I baptize you with water; but one more powerful than I is coming.
He will baptize you with the Holy Spirit and fire. His winnowing fork is in his
hand, to clear his threshing floor and to gather the wheat into his granary; but
the chaff he will burn with unquenchable fire."

▶ Reflection

Brought up by the priest Zechariah in the ancient traditions of Law,
John came to see the world in terms of black and white. You were
either a good guy or a bad guy. And in his mind, the messiah would
come to separate the wheat from the chaff. The righteous would be
rewarded and the wicked would burn. And that made sense to most
people; which is why when asked who Jesus was, they first said, "John
the Baptist!" Many Christians still see the law as the criterion for
salvation; saints go to heaven, sinners go to hell. But Jesus took the
refining process a step beyond John's vision. The chaff he would
remove was the sins of the world. The wheat he would keep was the
goodness God had created in every soul. That made Jesus the savior of
all, the sinner as well as the saint.

▶ Prayer

My dear Lord, there is so much chaff in my soul and so little wheat.
So much of the goodness God put there at the beginning has been
lost. Yet you came to save what was lost. Save me, Lord.

▶ Action

Clean out your sock drawer or your underwear drawer. Getting rid of
the worn out items will be like God getting rid of all your sins.

Lent

Ash Wednesday

Dirty Face

MATTHEW 6:1–6, 16–18

"Beware of practicing piety in order to be seen by others. Whenever you fast, do not look dismal like the hypocrites. They disfigure their faces so as to show that they are fasting. When you fast, put oil on your head and wash your face so that your fasting may be seen not by others but by God."

▶ Reflection

The celebration of Ash Wednesday reveals one of the great ironies of our religion. On a day when Jesus commands us to wash our faces so that no one knows we are fasting, we put ashes on our faces so that everyone will know we are fasting. Go figure. The important thing to remember is that "You are ambassadors for Christ" (2 Cor 5:20). We are the witnesses of God's kingdom present here on earth. One way I can show my kingdom citizenship is to give up something that is worldly and be deliriously happy about the fact that I am making room in my life for something lasting. Today can be the day when I proclaim my freedom from the passing things that ensnare me with their empty promises of temporary joy. Today I can give up something in this world and gain something better in the kingdom.

▶ Prayer

O Lord, you give me all I need; yet I continue to gather the things of the world to myself. Help me to fast and pray this Lent. Open my heart to give my money to the poor so that I might fulfill my mission.

▶ Action

After you receive ashes today, go home and look in the mirror. See the mark and spend five minutes pondering its meaning for you.

Cosmic Mother

LUKE 9:22–25

Jesus said to them all, "If any of you want to be my follower, you must deny yourself, take up your cross daily and follow me. If you want to save your life, you will lose will lose it. But lose your life for my sake and you will save it. What would it profit you to gain the whole world, but lose your own self in the process?"

▶ Reflection

The Christian covenant is not only a new covenant; it's a completely different one. The old one, the one made through Moses and the law, offered a worldly reward. "Long life," it promises ten times in Deuteronomy alone, and blessings upon the land. If you examine the law of Moses carefully, you can see that it's the code of the Cosmic Mother hovering over her brood, ensuring the health, well-being, and prosperity of her family. The new covenant of Jesus turns it all around. "Give it up," he says. "There is something better." So what if you live long and prosper? After you gain the whole world, then what? You die and it all passes away! That's no fun. Jesus invited his followers to believe in something beyond this passing world; a life that brings real and lasting fulfillment. But in order to get there, this world must be left behind. Welcome to Lent.

▶ Prayer

Thank you, Jesus, for teaching me about the kingdom of God. It really doesn't make any sense to pursue this passing world when all that I desire—peace, joy, love—is in the kingdom and lasts eternally.

▶ Action

Today you will have a chance to deny yourself in some way. Rate your response to the opportunity and pray to do better next time.

Friday after Ash Wednesday

Reason to Fast

MATTHEW 9:14–15

The disciples of John asked, "How come your disciples do not fast?" Jesus said to them, "The wedding guests cannot mourn as long as the bridegroom is with them, can they? The days will come when the bridegroom is taken away from them, and then they will fast."

▶ Reflection

Ever wonder why the only two days of fasting left on the Catholic liturgical calendar are a Wednesday and a Friday? The New American Bible footnotes this gospel passage and refers to that venerable second century résumé of apostolic teaching, the *Didache*: "Your fasts must not be identical with those of the hypocrites. They fast on Mondays and Thursdays; but you should fast on Wednesdays and Fridays." Well, there you go: we do Wednesdays and Fridays because the other guys did Mondays and Thursdays! But Jesus calls us to look within for the reasons to fast. While fasting expresses sorrow, feasting is appropriate for joy. Maybe that's why there are only a couple of days of fasting a year. We've got a lot to be happy about, but perhaps it's healthy on these two days to mourn the personal neglect of our own salvation. So we fast.

▶ Prayer

My Lord, you feed me with the bread of life and offer me the cup of eternal salvation. But I often hunger and thirst for the things of this world. Help me to fast and seek after the finer nourishment you offer.

▶ Action

If you are able, eat very little today. Feel what it's like to be hungry and be reminded that your true hunger is for the Lord.

Saturday after Ash Wednesday

Calling All Sinners

LUKE 5:27–32

The Pharisees and the scribes complained to his disciples: "Why do you eat and drink with tax collectors and sinners?" Jesus answered, "Those who are well do not need a physician, but those who are sick do. I have come to call not the righteous but sinners to repentance."

▶ Reflection

"Never been a sinner, I've never sinned; I've got a friend named Jesus! So you know that when I die, It's gonna set me up with the Spirit in the sky." So goes the song, "Spirit in the Sky," a seventies pop hit recorded by Norman Greenbaum. It's got a great beat, easy to dance to, but bad theology. Much to the chagrin of self-righteous and moralistic churchgoers, Christianity is not a religion for non-sinners. The righteous, or at least those who claim righteousness, have their salvation from the law, for they have obeyed every commandment and have no sin and no need of repentance. Jesus suffered and died for sinners so that, raised up from sin and death, they might share in salvation with the righteous. But since "all have sinned" (Romans 3:23), all are in need of salvation. It's popular to think that the sinless have a friend in Jesus, but it's not true. Jesus came to call sinners.

▶ Prayer

O Lord, I was a sinner and a moral failure lost in my guilt. But you found me and healed my troubled soul. Now, still a sinner, I seek your forgiveness and peace. Thank you, Lord Jesus.

▶ Action

Read Romans 3:21–24 and think about how the model of salvation expressed in that passage compares to popular understanding.

Monday of the First Week of Lent

Beggar King

MATTHEW 25:31–46

"Then the king will say to those at his right hand, 'Come, you that are blessed by my Father, inherit the kingdom prepared for you from the foundation of the world; for I was hungry and you gave me food, I was thirsty and you gave me something to drink, I was a stranger and you welcomed me, I was naked and you gave me clothing, I was sick and you took care of me, I was in prison and you visited me.'"

▶ Reflection

Bishops really like this gospel passage because it's great for pitching the annual appeal. It covers all the diocesan offices: soup kitchens, prison ministries, hospital chaplaincies, thrift stores, family services—just write one check and you're home free. There's something really compelling about winding up the pledge talk with that line, "well done, good and faithful servant." Trouble is, the good Lord is talking not about checkbooks but human hearts. Our money will be long gone by the time the sheep and the goats are divided. The coin of the kingdom is a heart that embraces the despised felon, makes room for the filthy stranger, and offers the other half of the sandwich to the grubby panhandler. To know the lowliest is to know the king.

▶ Prayer

Heavenly king, on earth you are the lowliest beggar. You joined us in poverty, humility, suffering and death, so that we might join your in kingship and glory. Help us always turn to you and serve your need.

▶ Action

Look upon the lowly today as Jesus the Lord reaching out to you for help and comfort. Show them reverence for the one they represent.

Tuesday of the First Week of Lent

Asking Mom

MATTHEW 6:7–15

"When you are praying, do not heap up empty phrases as the Gentiles do; for they think that they will be heard because of their many words. Do not be like them, for your Father knows what you need before you ask him. Pray then in this way: 'Our Father in heaven….'"

▶ Reflection

Once a kid asked me, "How does God hear all the prayers prayed by all the people all at the same time?" I had shaped my mouth to deliver a theologically correct and pastorally sensitive response when the kid speculated an answer: "Does he have, like, 'prayer waiting'?" That sounded way better than what I was going to say, so I gave him the ol' Bing Crosby smile and a friendly hair tousle and sent him on his way with a suggestion that he consider becoming a theologian. People unsure of the love of God look for ways of distinguishing their petitions so that they'll win a hearing from the target deity—like littering a church with eighty-one copies of a prayer will somehow work better than with just nine. Jesus teaches that praying to God is like sitting at the family dinner table asking Mom or Dad to pass the bread. It is God's desire to serve you (See Mark 10:45).

▶ Prayer

O Lord, you choose my body for your heaven and your holiness dwells within me. Care for me and forgive me this day. Fill me with grace that I may be forgiving to others. Protect me from evil.

▶ Action

Compose a very short prayer of less than ten words and memorize it. Recite it whenever you need God's help.

Wednesday of the First Week of Lent

Hair Ball Prophet

LUKE 11:29–32

"This is an evil generation that asks for a sign, but no sign will be given to it except the sign of Jonah. Just as Jonah was a sign to the people of Nineveh, so the Son of Man will be to this generation. The people of Nineveh repented at the proclamation of Jonah. But see, something greater than Jonah is here!"

▶ Reflection

Was Jesus yearning for a former time when the task of the prophet seemed much simpler? In the old days, after all, a little man like Jonah from a far off land could wander into a big city, slathered in fish bile and whatever else comes from being coughed up on a beach like a hair ball by a great fish, reluctantly mumble a dire but unconvincing apocalyptic warning, and get the entire population right down to the livestock to reform in sackcloth and ashes. But the people of Jesus' time want signs from heaven before they'll budge an inch. Jesus didn't know how lucky he was, however. The twenty-first century prophet has to compete with TV, movies, Calvin Klein, Madison Avenue, Sunday morning soccer, Ricky Martin, and the World Wide Web. But the offer remains the same: there is fullness of life for anyone willing to turn around and receive it.

▶ Prayer

I'm so caught up in the things of this passing world, O Lord, that I often don't even know I'm being called to repent and experience the joys of the kingdom. Keep working on me. I'll get it eventually.

▶ Action

Turn off the radio or the TV or whatever else serves as your "distraction" and listen to the voice of God coming from within.

Thursday of the First Week of Lent

Bad Rap

MATTHEW 7:7–12

"Ask, and it will be given you; search, and you will find; knock, and the door will be opened for you. For everyone who asks receives, and everyone who searches finds, and for everyone who knocks, the door will be opened. You, who are evil, know how to give good gifts to your children. How much more will your Father in heaven give good things to those who ask him?"

▶ Reflection

What gives prayer a bad rap is that so often things just don't work out. I expect my prayers to be answered with no consideration for anything or anybody else, including God. I want what I want and I want it now. But I've got to realize that there are limitations to what God has to work with here. There's time, for instance, and the infinitely complex workings of the universe. There are the imperfections of people and their unwillingness to go along with the God's plan. There are God's own promises, like the one about not killing everybody again (see Genesis 8:21). So, while "Thy will be done" is a good prayer, it's not always a sure bet that God's will is going to happen. The good news is that God's working on it.

▶ Prayer

Dear Lord, forgive me for not always trusting you. I get a little greedy in my prayer and I think you ought to jump when I snap my fingers. But you always do what is good for me. Thank you, Lord.

▶ Action

Make a list of all the things you ask God for in prayer. Put it up on your refrigerator and check them off as each is answered.

Friday of the First Week of Lent

Trashing Life

MATTHEW 5:20–26

"You have heard that it was said, 'You shall not murder.' I say to you that if you are angry with another, you will be liable to judgment. If you insult another, you will be liable to the council; and if you say, 'You fool,' you will be liable to the fire of Gehenna."

▶ Reflection

A primitive people understood and accepted violence as a method of management because primitive tribal societies were often ruled by violence. So it was assumed by a primitive people that God operated in the same fashion. If a certain behavior led to a bad end, then it was understood that God was doling out punishment. But consider: if your mother decrees that you shalt not play in the street, and you did anyway and got run over by a cement truck, would that be your mother punishing you for breaking her rules? Or would it simply be the tragic consequence of you not realizing just how much your mother loved you and looked out for your well-being? Isn't it the same with God? Jesus used the fascinating image of "Gehenna," Jerusalem's town dump. The consequence of misusing the life God gives me is that it ends up in the trash!

▶ Prayer

What a beautiful life you give me, God, yet sometimes I misuse it and treat it poorly. If evil comes my way because I pursue evil, it isn't your fault, O Lord; it's mine. Deliver me from my own sinfulness.

▶ Action

Remember a bad choice that led to a bad end and understand how you could blame the consequence on God. Then claim responsibility.

Saturday of the First Week of Lent

Hate Hurts

MATTHEW 5:43–48

"You have heard that it was said, 'You shall love your neighbor and hate your enemy.' But I say to you, Love your enemies and pray for those who persecute you, so that you may be children of your Father in heaven; for he makes his sun rise on the evil and on the good, and sends rain on the righteous and on the unrighteous."

▶ Reflection

"I really hate my mother-in-law, and I don't know what to do about it. She's cruel to me and says bad things about me to my husband and my children. I can't stay away because she's Dave's mother and the children's grandmother—and we live in the same town! I just feel really bad about it." Kathy was really struggling with the relationship. The painful feelings were building up inside her and it was beginning to play on her mind and keep her awake at night. Her pastor, Thomas, opened to the gospel for today and they prayed together. Then Thomas said a little prayer of blessing for Kathy's mother-in-law, which made Kathy think. "You know," she said, "maybe my negative feelings have been fueling the fires. Maybe what I should do is pray for her like you did. It couldn't hurt." And it might help.

▶ Prayer

Lord Jesus, you teach me to pray for those who cause me pain, knowing that the goodness I generate with my prayer will overcome the evil caused by my persecutor. You teach me wisely, Lord.

▶ Action

Who is your enemy? Write down his or her name on a piece of paper and put it in your pocket. Try to think kindly of that person throughout the day.

Monday of the Second Week of Lent

How Life Works

LUKE 6:36–38

"Be merciful, as God is merciful. Do not judge, and you will not be judged; do not condemn, and you will not be condemned. Forgive, and you will be forgiven; give, and it will be given to you. The measure you give will be the measure you get back."

▶ Reflection

The traditional religion in place during the time of Jesus saw life as a series of rewards and punishments from God. Do good, God rewards you and you prosper. Break the rules, God punishes you and life takes a downturn. But Jesus taught that life was what you lived. In Matthew 26:52 he delivers his famous line to Peter, "He who lives by the sword, dies by the sword." Apply this concept to the history of ancient Israel, which took hold of its land by force and enslaved its people, thus making violence and slavery a way of life, and you can see that it was just a matter of time before what went around, came around. Jesus suggests we live accordingly. You want forgiveness? Then forgive. You want compassion? Then be compassionate. Whatever you want given to you—money, respect, love, time—then give it to others and it will come back to you.

▶ Prayer

Loving God, you care for my needs so wonderfully and even create life for me according to how I live. Help me always to live a life of generous goodness so that I may receive, in turn, abundant goodness.

▶ Action

Consider what you need most in your life and determine what you need to give away in order to get what you need.

Tuesday of the Second Week of Lent

Scaring Priests

MATTHEW 23:1–12

"The Pharisees lay heavy burdens on the shoulders of others, but they are unwilling to help with the load. They love the places of honor at banquets and the best seats in the synagogues, and to be greeted with respect in the marketplaces, and to have people call them rabbi. As for you, call no one on earth 'Father,' for you have only one Father."

▶ Reflection

This is a scary gospel for priests. At least it ought to be. Here Jesus is saying that people need to watch out for the guys who like to wear marks of respect in public, claim titles, sit at head tables, and enjoy the chief seats in places of worship—and we put them in charge! Don't call them "Father," he says. And have you ever noticed that the "burdens" of Catholicism—marriage, divorce, sex, birth control, abortion, being single, being a woman—are all things other people carry while priests rarely help with those loads? If you're a priest, this should scare you. I'm a priest and it scares me. When this gospel comes up at church, I like to share my fears with the people I'm called to serve. They sympathize and ask how to help me change things, which is what I need because change is the heart of Lent.

▶ Prayer

O Lord, hear my prayer. You call men to serve your people as leaders, preachers, and ministers of your grace. May they always serve humbly, remembering you example of selfless giving.

▶ Action

Do you hold a title? How do you feel when people call you by your title? Try dropping it from your name and see what happens.

Wednesday of the Second Week of Lent

Kingdom Dynamics

MATTHEW 20:17–28

Jesus told them, "The Son of Man will be flogged and crucified." Then the mother of Zebedee's sons said to him, "See that my sons will sit at your right and your left in your kingdom." Jesus said, "Whoever wishes to be first among you must be the servant. The Son of Man came not to be served but to serve."

▶ Reflection

The mother of Zebedee's sons: did Jesus have her in mind when, in Mark 3:17, he nicknamed James and John, "Sons of Thunder"? No matter. She makes a legitimate request, given that she's their mother. Any mother would do the same thing regardless of how inappropriate it might seem in the light of the Lord's prediction about being flogged and crucified. Jesus, ever considerate, makes the awkward moment into a teachable one. Every desire of life must be conditioned by knowledge of the paradoxical nature of the kingdom of God. If, as Jesus has been teaching right along, the last shall be first and the first shall be last, then the wise learner so positions himself or herself to take advantage of that dynamic. So, do you want to be great in the kingdom? Then bow to serve the needs of all here on earth.

▶ Prayer

In your kingdom, Lord, the last are first and the first are last. Help me to hold this truth in my heart as I go about my day. Keep me mindful that in my service to others, I walk with you.

▶ Action

When you feel the very natural urge to dominate a situation today, repent and become the servant of others. You have nothing to lose.

Thursday of the Second Week of Lent

Kingdom Come

LUKE 16:19–31

"There was a rich man who feasted every day, and a poor man named Lazarus who lay hungry at his gate. The poor man died and was carried to the bosom of Abraham. The rich man died and went to hell. He cried out, 'Have mercy on me!' Abraham said, 'Remember that during your lifetime you received good things, and Lazarus in like manner evil things; now he is comforted here, and you are in agony.'"

▶ Reflection

The story of the rich man and Lazarus is not a story of the just reward for good or evil. It's simply a story that illustrates what happens when the kingdom kicks in. And when you die, evidently it kicks in big time! Now understand: this comes from the one who came back from the dead, so it's got some credence to it. The bad news is that once you're dead, you're done. There's nothing you can do about it. But the good news is that while you're alive, there's plenty you can do. It's really easy. There are Lazaruses lying at every gate. Heck, I walk past several of them every day just getting my mail. With a simple offering, I can gain a friend in the afterlife and put myself on track for a cozy spot in Abraham's bosom. Lent is an invitation to do just that.

▶ Prayer

O Lord, my heart is hard and I don't want to share my money with the poor. I think up all kinds of reasons why they shouldn't have my money. But you call me to faithfulness. Open my heart to give.

▶ Action

Lent is a time when we practice giving our money to the poor. What comfort can you do without today to fulfill this practice?

Friday of the Second Week of Lent

God's Servants

MATTHEW 21:33–46

"A landowner leased his vineyard to tenants and went away. When the harvest time came, he sent his servants to collect his share. But the tenants seized and killed them. When the owner of the vineyard returns, what do you think will happen to those tenants? Remember: 'The stone that the builders rejected has become the cornerstone.'"

▶ Reflection

Blind as bats, that's what we are! Who are the servants God sends to obtain his share of the harvest? In the year 2000, just one of our fifty states intentionally killed a record forty people. They were lawfully judged and condemned criminals. They showed up in our world looking for the mercy and kindness God gave to us. They got the needle instead. A million kids died in the southern hemisphere last year, too. They came seeking only the clean water God left to our care. Instead they got the dregs. A guy came up to me today and asked for spare change. Three voices in my head raised objections based on my own lack of funds, the availability of jobs, and the likelihood my money would be used to buy booze. Everything in me wants to keep the things of this world to myself, but God only asks for a share.

▶ Prayer

O God, creator of all things, you give abundance to the earth, enough for all. Your mercy and kindness win the victory over sin and evil. Help me always to share your wealth with all who are in need.

▶ Action

Write down how much money God will give you this month. Determine how much of it you should give back as God's share.

Saturday of the Second Week of Lent

Lesson in Love

LUKE 15:11–32

"The elder son said to his father, 'All my life I have never disobeyed you, yet you gave me no feast to celebrate. But when this son of yours returns, who squandered your money, you butcher the fatted calf!' The father answered, 'Son, you are always with me, and all I have is yours. But we must celebrate and rejoice: This brother of yours was dead and has come back to life! He was lost but now is found!'"

▶ Reflection

"There are two ways to learn your lessons," my wise mother used to teach me, "the easy way and the hard way. The easy way is through obedience; the hard way is through experience." The two brothers in the parable of the prodigal son had lessons to learn. The first needed to learn that his father's love was unconditional and the best place to be was in his father's house. He learned that one the hard way. The older brother needed to learn that mercy and compassion were of greater importance than even his own righteousness. He, too, had to learn the hard way. For both brothers, failure to learn would mean misery and heartache and alienation. They both needed to turn to the father's unrelenting love.

▶ Prayer

The story of the prodigal son is my story, O God, whether I am the younger or older son. Sometimes I'm one and sometimes I'm the other. Either way, my Lord, draw me to your unconditional love.

▶ Action

Make a list of the ways you are an "elder son" and the ways you are a "younger son." Change one thing from each list during Lent.

Monday of the Third Week of Lent

Town of Prejudice

LUKE 4:24–30

Jesus told them, "There were many widows in Israel in the time of Elijah, when there was a severe famine, yet Elijah was sent to a widow of Zarephath. There were also many lepers in Israel in the time of the prophet Elisha, and none of them was cleansed except Naaman the Syrian." When they heard this, all in the synagogue were filled with rage. They got up and drove him out of the town.

▶ Reflection

I was once assigned to a parish that was widely known for its large ethnic Catholic population. After weekday Mass one morning, I was invited by some of the men at church that day to join them for a cup of coffee, which I did. During our little nosh, the men started telling jokes that disrespected other ethnic groups, as well as other races. I was astonished, not that these men were bigoted and racist, but that they entertained their prejudices and expected a Christian leader to approve them. In the gospel story, Jesus invited his own hometown people to consider that God loved people of other races and nations besides their own. They threw him out. It seems the Catholic men of my old parish had thrown him out, too.

▶ Prayer

O Lord, you love all people and you call me to be a witness of that love. Through my love of them in your name, you are known. Help me to accept and respect all human life as you accept and respect me.

▶ Action

Today you will encounter someone of a different race or ethnic origin. Note and evaluate your emotional reaction to that person.

Tuesday of the Third Week of Lent

Forgiveness Math

MATTHEW 18:21–35

"The kingdom of heaven is like a king to whom a slave owed a huge amount. He could not pay, so the king forgave the debt. The slave went to a fellow slave who owed him a mere fraction, and had him thrown into debtors' prison. The king said to him, 'Wicked slave! You should show the same mercy to your fellow slave.'"

▶ Reflection

People are worth so very much to God. The translation of today's gospel says, "a huge amount," literally "10,000 talents." My resources say one talent of gold in Judea at the time weighed about 200 pounds. Ten thousand talents would make that a thousand *tons* of gold! So, you figure gold goes for a few hundred bucks an ounce. Now do the math. That's a lot of scratch no matter how you figure it. It's what we're really worth in God's eyes. Our apparent worth to each other is "a mere fraction," again the literal translation being "a hundred denarion." A denarius was a coin of about 4 grams of silver. A hundred of them would render a little less than 14 ounces, no small amount but paltry in comparison. The numbers demand that we forgive each other.

▶ Prayer

Dear God, you forgave my huge debt. You put aside my sins so that I may live in your peace. When others offend me, remind me of my mission of witness. May I forgive as I have been forgiven.

▶ Action

Whom have you thrown into "debtors' prison"? Against whom do you hold a grudge? Begin today to forgive.

Wednesday of the Third Week of Lent

Law Fulfilled

MATTHEW 5:17–19

"I have come not to abolish the law but to fulfill it. Until heaven and earth pass away, not one letter of the law will pass away until all is accomplished. Therefore, whoever breaks the least of these commandments, and teaches others to do the same, will be called least in the kingdom of heaven; but whoever does them and teaches them will be called great in the kingdom of heaven."

▶ Reflection

There is no question that Jesus played it fast and loose with the law. He clearly had an agenda when he would use the occasions of the Sabbath to work cures. Or, as a colleague recently asked, "Didn't he ever heal anybody on a Tuesday?" Yet, here he proclaims that teaching and fulfilling the law, even the least commandment, is beneficial. What gives? Well, in the whole law, with all its judgments and penalties, the worst thing that could happen is that you die. Jesus died. In doing so he fulfilled the law conclusively. But his resurrection ushered in something new, beyond the law. Heaven and earth did pass away; every letter of the law was fulfilled. Now, in Christ, all things have been made new (see Revelation 21:5).

▶ Prayer

O Lord, you have fulfilled all things with your love, and you write your law of love in our hearts. May I love others in all things and thus bring your law to perfection within me.

▶ Action

What rule do you hold sacred in your life? What happens when somebody breaks it? Could love and mercy be a greater call?

Thursday of the Third Week of Lent

Love in Flesh

LUKE 11:14–23

Jesus was casting out a mute demon; when the demon had gone out, the one who had been mute spoke, and the crowds were amazed. But some of them said, "He casts out demons by Beelzebub, the ruler of the demons." Jesus said to them, "But if it is by the finger of God that I cast out the demons, then the kingdom of God has come to you."

▶ Reflection

Jesus was thought to be in league with the devil because it seemed as if he was letting people off the hook. It was commonly understood at the time that the illnesses and infirmities plaguing certain people were inflicted on them as punishment for their sins. Keep in mind that the dietary restrictions and taboos of the Mosaic Law were, in large part, designed to keep people healthy. Reasoning to the converse was therefore understandable. Human catastrophe appeared to be God's pillory and the Lord's healing ministry must have seemed to the law keepers as one big jailbreak. But when understood from the perspective of God's inestimable love, releasing the captives was simply the mercy and compassion of God being made manifest in human form, the love of God made flesh and blood.

▶ Prayer

O God, creator of all, I was once a captive to sin, but you set me free. You rescued me from fear and guilt; you saved me from death. Now I want to live for you, Lord. Lead me in love and mercy.

▶ Action

Wrap up a small piece of bread in a napkin and put it in your pocket. Let this remind you today that you carry God's mercy with you at all times.

Friday of the Third Week of Lent

No Cigar

MARK 12:28–34

A scribe said to him, "You are right! To love God with all our hearts and to love our neighbor as ourselves is greater than all burnt offerings and sacrifices." When Jesus saw that he answered wisely, he said to him, "You are not far from the kingdom of God." After that no one dared to ask him any more questions.

▶ **Reflection**

Imagine the surprise of the scribe when, after the flush of receiving the Lord's approval for his insight and expecting to be congratulated for hitting the nail on the head, he hears Jesus tell him that he is "not far" from God's reign. Not far? But when it comes to the kingdom, a miss is as good as a mile. It would be like saying you missed the bus by only a few seconds; or being a contestant on "Who Wants to Be a Millionaire" and having Regis tell you your answer, "B," was close to the right answer, "C." It doesn't matter. You fell short and that puts an end to it. The scribe was close, but won no cigar. No wonder no one else had the courage to ask him any more questions. Perhaps the million-dollar answer that will get you on the bus as it pulls away is the awesome knowledge that God loves you with all God's heart, soul, mind, and strength, and your neighbor too!

▶ **Prayer**

Almighty God, your love is the supreme greatness, for by your love you have made all things. From your love comes you law and by your love made flesh I am saved. Keep me always in the light of your love.

▶ **Action**

Are you in the kingdom or not far from it? What can you do today that will bring you closer?

Saturday of the Third Week of Lent

Fully Forgiven

LUKE 18:9–14

"A Pharisee and a tax collector went to pray. The Pharisee prayed this way: 'God, I fast twice a week; I give a tenth of all my income.' But the tax collector beat his breast and said, 'God, be merciful to me, a sinner!' But those who exalt themselves will be humbled, and all who humble themselves will be exalted."

▶ Reflection

People often come to the sacrament of reconciliation with a list of all the good things they do for God. It's not unusual to hear a confession of righteousness: "I don't miss Mass, I don't swear, I'm faithful to my spouse, I don't get drunk," especially during Lent when people think they "have to" go to confession. (Canon law requires only that serious sins be confessed within a year.) This is the legacy of the pre-Vatican era when the consequences of sin were presented so fearfully that some people fell into the gloom of guilt while others developed denial mechanisms rather than face the reality of their sinfulness. But when forgiveness is preached and practiced, neither obsessive guilt nor denial is necessary. Forgiven utterly and completely, people can plumb the depths of their souls and air their consciences freely, confidently confessing their sinfulness.

▶ Prayer

O God, be merciful to me, a sinner. Though you have blessed me with your love and made me your own child, still I am weak; I am a sinner. But your mercy and compassion, Lord, is all the righteousness I need.

▶ Action

Know that your sins are completely and totally forgiven. Now examine your conscience fully and discover your own sinfulness.

Monday of the Fourth Week of Lent

A Sign

JOHN 4:43–54

Jesus came to Cana where he had changed the water into wine. A man begged him to come and heal his son, for he was at the point of death. Jesus said, "Unless you people see signs and wonders you will not believe." The man said to him, "Sir, come before he dies." Jesus said, "Go; your son will live." The man believed and the boy lived.

▶ Reflection

The signs Jesus performs are extremely important in the gospel of John. Indeed, the whole section of the book from the middle of the first chapter to the end of the twelfth chapter is sometimes called the Book of Signs. Today's episode even refers to the story of the first sign, changing water into wine. Yet the point of the passage is that, while a sign can make a believer out of someone, you don't need signs if you already believe. For instance: we believe that God is always creating everything new all the time (see Revelation 21:5). Further, we believe that everything God creates is out of love for us and is ordered toward our good. That means, no matter how bad things get (and they do get bad because of sin and evil), God is working to heal us and save us. Believing that, a sign is unnecessary.

▶ Prayer

Living in this sinful world, O Lord, I am sometimes the victim of my own imperfections, sometimes the victim of others' imperfections. But in every case, my God, you are there to save me and create newness for me.

▶ Action

Recall all the diseases and injuries from which you have recovered. Doctors and medicines notwithstanding, give the glory to God.

Your Choice

JOHN 5:1–16

There was a man who had been ill a long time. Jesus said to him, "Stand up, take your mat and walk." The man took up his mat and began to walk. The religious leaders said to the man, "It is the sabbath; it is not lawful for you to carry your mat." Later Jesus said to him, "Give up your sins so that nothing worse happens to you."

▶ Reflection

The Mosaic Law presents an interesting principle, that at every moment we have before us a blessing and a curse. Moses recommends, commands even, that we choose the blessing (see Deuteronomy 30:19). In the gospel story of the pool at Bethesda, the man sees the curse: that he has no one to plunge him into the pool. Jesus sees the blessing: stand up and walk! Then the religious leaders see only that the Sabbath has been broken, even though a man sick for thirty-eight years has been cured. When Jesus tells the man to give up his sins so that something worse doesn't happen, the words in the original Greek can mean, "stop making these mistakes or worse will come into being." In other words, we will experience the path we choose to walk, so choose wisely.

▶ Prayer

O God, creator of all things, in every moment of my life you create goodness for me and invite me to enter into your kingdom. Help me always to choose wisely your precious gifts of grace and life.

▶ Action

Tie a string around your wrist today to remind you that in every moment God is giving you the gift of goodness. Accept the gift.

Wednesday of the Fourth Week of Lent

Death to Life

JOHN 5:17–30

Jesus said to them, "My Father is still working, and I also am working. Very truly, I tell you, anyone who hears my word and believes in the one who sent me has eternal life, and does not come under judgment, but has passed from death to life."

▶ Reflection

Stepping into the gospel of John can be like stepping through the looking glass. It's a world of strange images and, sometimes, stranger turns of phrase. The Greek is poetic and structured artfully to create parabolic patterns of theme, called *chiasma*, designed to spotlight for the reader the theological apexes intended by the author. But often I'm left scratching my head and wondering what the heck he meant by that. The ancients imagined God as quite separate from humanity, the human side of things being decidedly dependent on and passive to God. The Fourth Gospel suggests that the union of God and humanity in Jesus has produced a kind of co-dependency; that humanity participates in this union proactively and co-creates with God. Belief is the gateway and those who actually believe this have escaped judgment and passed from mortal life to eternal life.

▶ Prayer

Dear God, you feed me with your divine life and you are in me, alive in flesh and blood. From me you create my life according to your love for me, and I am fulfilled. Thank you, Lord, for your marvelous gift.

▶ Action

Close your eyes for a moment and listen to your own breathing. Concentrate on the experience of life within. That is God within you.

Thursday of the Fourth Week of Lent

Living Law

JOHN 5:31–47

Jesus said, "I have a testimony greater than John's: The works that the Father has given me to complete. But you do not have his word abiding in you, because you do not believe him whom he has sent. If you believed Moses, you would believe me, for he wrote about me."

▶ Reflection

Jesus is the living revelation of God. He is the perfect union of God and humanity. As the Father speaks, so speaks the Son. And as the Son lives, so lives God. When we look upon Jesus and hear his words, we see God and hear the voice of God. This oneness of God and humanity is passed on to all who believe (see John 1:12). Consequently, those who choose not to believe choose not to possess the God who lives within them. And without God there is no life, only death. Those who see God only in the Law of Moses, or the structure of any religion, are limited by the law to a static god, a god who has no life. But those who see God in Jesus experience a living God; dynamic and multifarious, more faithful to humanity than humans can be faithful to God. The testimonies of John the Baptist and Moses were limited by the law. But Jesus lives beyond the law.

▶ Prayer

Your law is good and perfect, O Lord, but you call me to live by your Spirit, who gives me life and leads me according to your will. Keep me faithful to your love and your life within me.

▶ Action

When you transgress the law today, as you most certainly will, judge how the experience affects the feeling of life in your body.

Friday of the Fourth Week of Lent

Bad Cut

JOHN 7:1–2, 10, 25–30

They were looking for an opportunity to kill Jesus. He cried out, "You know me, and you know where I am from. I have not come on my own. But the one who sent me is true, and you do not know him. I know him, because I am from him, and he sent me."

▶ Reflection

Did you ever cut yourself deeply with a kitchen knife, or done some other monstrous thing to yourself that requires professional attention, like knocking a finger akimbo in a fall? The first thing we do is cover it up and close our eyes, denial always being the first stage of an encounter with our fearful mortality. Jesus was for the people of his day, an encounter with the death of all they believed about God. Those on the bottom of the cultural heap, the lepers, tax collectors, and prostitutes, who were marginalized by religious beliefs, heard the message as good news and celebrated Jesus. Those on the top, the religious and political leaders, the devout and the wealthy, heard bad news because the message did violence to all they depended on for their existence. The Lord was like a bad cut or a broken finger. They denied him, tried to cover him up, and sought to kill him.

▶ Prayer

O Lord, you challenge my position in life, my comfort, and my security. You cause me to call my values into question. You are right and true. Help me to repent and to believe your good news.

▶ Action

If you can, eat a humble meal today, perhaps soup and bread. Avoid finer food. See in humility a chance to be exalted in the kingdom.

Saturday of the Fourth Week of Lent

Bible Miscue

JOHN 7:40–53

Some in the crowd said, "This is really the prophet." Others said, "This is the Messiah." But some asked, "Surely the Messiah does not come from Galilee, does he? The Messiah comes from Bethlehem."

▶ Reflection

An elderly man came to me in distress because he felt he would not be able to get himself right with God before he died. His struggle was over the lingering memory of the terrible betrayal his own father had committed against his family. "I can forgive him for what he did," the man said. "But I haven't been able to forget it. And I know we have to forgive and forget." The poor man was laboring under a mistaken belief that the old saying, "forgive and forget," was somehow rooted in religious dogma. It isn't. We forgive because we have been forgiven. But it is humanly impossible to forget. Science tells us that every event of our lives is stored in our memory, although we may be unable to recall most of it. The Bible can be misunderstood, too. "An eye for an eye," for instance, was supposed to limit retaliation, not justify it. (Jesus revisited the quote from Leviticus 24:20 to teach love of enemy.) Sometimes, a little religious knowledge can be a dangerous thing.

▶ Prayer

You have revealed yourself through the Bible, O God, so that people may know you. Yet you also come to us in history and in creation. Most perfectly, you come in Jesus. Help me to know and love Jesus.

▶ Action

Go to the library or the Internet and look up sayings, like "God helps those who help themselves" in order to discover their origins. Does this change their meaning for you?

Monday of the Fifth Week of Lent

Human Passion

JOHN 8:1–11

The scribes and the Pharisees brought a woman who had been caught in adultery to Jesus. He said to them, "Let the one among you who is without sin be the first to throw a stone at her." When they were gone, Jesus said to the woman, "Has no one condemned you? Neither do I condemn you. Go your way, and don't make this mistake again."

▶ **Reflection**

The scribes and the Pharisees were not bad guys. They weren't any different from the rest of us. They could see that the woman they caught in adultery was doing wrong only because they themselves may not have done that particular wrong. Sexual sin is always an easy target for those who may keep a good distance from anything that could engage their sexuality. But Jesus, being a man not unfamiliar with passion, understood the woman's plight and got her off the hook. And as he judged, so would he be judged. The Lord's own passion, which we'll celebrate next Sunday, caused him the loss of his life. Yet he received the same judgment as the woman. He got off the hook of death because in Christ, God knew the power of human passion over flesh and blood.

▶ **Prayer**

Lord Jesus, you know my weakness because you yourself suffered human weakness. You died on the cross so that even the wages of my sin would not keep me from you. Thank you for saving me, Jesus!

▶ **Action**

Carry a little stone in your pocket today and remember when you're tempted to judge another that you face the same judgment.

Tuesday of the Fifth Week of Lent

Unconditional Love

JOHN 8:21–30

Jesus said to them, "You are of this world, I am not of this world. You will die in your sins unless you believe that I am." They said to him, "Who are you?" Jesus said to them, "When you have lifted up the Son of Man, then you will realize that I am."

▶ Reflection

Religious leaders live in judgment. They have to. It's the coin of their realm. We look to religious leaders for moral guidance; we want them to distinguish for us right from wrong. When they do this, when they step forward and proclaim boldly what is good and what is bad, they win the mantle of the moral compass. We follow them. Trouble is, God, the great "I Am," simply is (see Exodus 3:14). In God, there is no right or wrong, good or bad. There is only God. From the very beginning, the knowledge of good and evil is not what God intended for his creation. It caused conflict, shame, and alienation. (Look up the story surrounding Genesis 3:6–7.) The people flocked to Jesus and they believed in him because he did not distinguish the good from the bad, the sinners from the saints, but rather demonstrated God's love for all people, good or bad, without condition.

▶ Prayer

My Lord Jesus, you accept me each day just as I am. You love me with an infinite love that is not diminished by my sins. Your love transforms me and makes me a new person, eager to do your will.

▶ Action

Think of how you may limit God's love. Do you think God loves you only when you are good? Consider God's unconditional love.

Wednesday of the Fifth Week of Lent

Killing Christ

JOHN 8:31–42

Jesus said to those who believed in him, "Know the truth, and the truth will make you free." They answered, "We have never been slaves. We are children of Abraham." Jesus said to them, "But now you are trying to kill me. This is not what Abraham did."

▶ Reflection

There's a big temptation here to see Our Lord's words in this gospel passage addressed only to the Jews or the scribes and Pharisees, because his words are so harsh, perhaps the strongest he uses in John's gospel. But double-check the beginning of the passage and see that he's speaking to us, those who "believe in him." Every time I embrace the world in some way, with a judgment, a condemnation, a choice of self over others, a choice of rejection over love, I kill Jesus in my heart. I put to death the one in me who is trying to save me, and others through me, by being for others what he is being for me. That essentially tears me in half; child of God though I am, I make myself a child of the world. Yet in every moment Jesus accepts that I crucify him, reaches out in forgiveness, and offers me new life and the freedom that comes from knowing the truth about myself.

▶ Prayer

The truth about me, O Lord, is that I am a sinner. I crucify you in my heart every day, but you are always rising to new life in me, freeing me from sin, and bringing me peace. Praise you, Jesus!

▶ Action

Sit down and think about your life and try to determine where you are killing Christ. Trust in God's love, know the truth, and be free.

Thursday of the Fifth Week of Lent

Killing Christ, Part II

JOHN 8:51–59

Jesus said, "Whoever keeps my word will never see death." They responded, "But Abraham died." Jesus said, "Abraham rejoiced that he would see my day; he saw it and was glad. Before Abraham was, I am." So they picked up stones to throw at him.

▶ Reflection

The kingdom of God is irrational. Because our intellect is finite—it has a beginning and an end—any direct consideration of the eternal runs into the difficulty of our human limits. As long as Jesus teaches in parables, using finite images to explain infinite realities, I can handle it. But as soon as Jesus speaks directly of the eternal realities, i.e., "I AM," I balk. To say that God simply is, makes my attachment to the things of this passing world seem rather ludicrous. Why on earth (literally) would I seek after wealth, authority, pleasure, comfort, and security, when all I would ever need, all I could ever want, is already given to me? While I can rationalize the things that I possess, I can only accept God through faith. Once I realize there's a choice between the passing world and the eternal kingdom, I have to make it. So, rather than cut loose from the world, I seek to kill the Christ.

▶ Prayer

Eternal God, the things of this world are so inviting, so enticing to me. I want everything life has to offer. But you offer me yourself. Help me to let go of passing things that I may embrace you eternally.

▶ Action

Write down the three most important things in your life. Which one of them would you not let go of in order to make room for God?

Friday of the Fifth Week of Lent

Spirit of Life

JOHN 10:31–42

They took up rocks to stone him. "For blasphemy," they said, "because you, a human being, are making yourself God." Jesus answered, "But it is written in your law, 'you are gods.' So why am I blaspheming because I said, 'I am God's Son'?"

▶ Reflection

Jesus not only treads on Jewish theology here, he comes perilously close to trampling Christian theology as well, although the church would not be producing much of that for a while. Even so, the gnostic traditions and other early attempts at sorting out the theology of Jesus would glom onto a passage such as this one and try to extract some meaning. So the Bible says "you are gods"? Yes, in Psalm 82:6. It also says, "you are all children of God" in the same verse, but it's in rebuke for not taking care of the poor and needy as the real God would do. Nevertheless, there is the divine element in all, since all are given God's spirit of life. Jesus proclaims this as more good news, though the religious leaders continue to reject the idea that God and humanity could be one. But Jesus would pass on to all generations his own body and blood, through which he would share his divine life.

▶ Prayer

O God Most High, you came down into my humanity through your Son Jesus. And now your life is in me and we are one. You give me the power to direct your creation by prayer. What a glorious God!

▶ Action

The next time you pray, form in your mind a picture of what the fulfillment of your prayer would look like. Participate in creation!

Saturday of the Fifth Week of Lent

Reverse Caiaphas

JOHN 11:45–57

The council met and one of them, Caiaphas, who was high priest that year, said to them, "It is better to have one man die for the people than to have the whole nation destroyed on account of one man."

▶ Reflection

When a pastor is doing a poor job in a given parish and things aren't going well, the bishop usually receives many letters of complaint from people who are hurt or outraged or just plain confused by what is happening to their beloved parish. And after repeated attempts to improve the situation fail, the bishop will sometimes react along the lines of what I call "the reverse Caiaphas principle." In other words, his decisions will be based on the notion that it is better that many people should suffer for the sake of one man. That's when a parish gets stuck with a pastor who tears down the faith of the people rather than builds it up. It happens. Even though Jesus taught that the role of leadership in the community was service of the people, that role, in church as in politics, sometimes gets reversed. That's why we pray for our bishops and our clergy every day. Our priests need the prayer, love, and forgiveness of all, and the new life offered by God in Christ.

▶ Prayer

O Lord, bless my pastor. Give him a heart open to love the people entrusted to his care. Turn away evil and the self-serving spirit from his mind. Fill him with grace and grant him peace.

▶ Action

Drop your pastor a note or call him on the phone and give him your honest appraisal of his ministry. Praise or criticize where it is due.

Monday of Holy Week

Plenty of Poor

JOHN 12:1–11

Mary took a pound of costly perfume, anointed Jesus' feet, and wiped them with her hair. Judas said, "Why wasn't this perfume sold and the money given to the poor?" Jesus said, "Leave her alone. She bought it so that she might keep it for the day of my burial. The poor you will always have with you, but you do not always have me."

▶ **Reflection**

A relatively inconspicuous line, but one of the most oft-quoted of the gospels: "The poor you will always have with you." What makes this humble verse so frequently repeated? Regularly distorted, it serves as a handy rationale for ignoring the poor. "What's the point in helping the poor? Didn't Jesus say that the poor we would always have with us?" Right. But understood in the proper context, it simply means that there will be endless opportunities to help the poor. If I may borrow from another of the Lord's sayings, many are called to help the poor but few do. There will always be those who lack the personal resources to manage their lives no matter how much money you give them, and there will always be those who are in need because others have failed to help. Whom will I help today? Whom will *you* help?

▶ **Prayer**

My precious God, you fill me with blessings and make me rich with the wealth of your goodness. You send the poor to me for help. Give me the grace I need to open my hand and share my wealth with them.

▶ **Action**

Figure your gross monthly household income and then figure how much of that you give to the poor. Are you satisfied with that?

Tuesday of Holy Week

Love of Judas

JOHN 13:21–33, 36–38

Jesus was troubled in spirit and said, "One of you will betray me."
He said to Judas, "Do quickly what you are going to do." Then he said to the
disciples, "I am with you only a little longer. But where I am going, you cannot
follow."

▶ Reflection

In the ever twisting, undulating *chiasma* of John's gospel, Jesus is
pulled apart emotionally by the realization that he is going where his
friends Peter and the others cannot follow, and, at the same time, his
friend Judas is going where Jesus cannot follow: into the darkness of
treachery and betrayal. It is curious that Jesus does not try to prevent
Judas from doing what he is about to do. Instead he encourages him
and hastens him along. Even in this dire strait, Jesus refuses to judge
or condemn. Rather, he continues in friendship with Judas till the end.
In Matthew's parallel, Jesus even exchanges a kiss with Judas and calls
him, "friend" (Matthew 26:49–50). Jesus is not naive; he is simply
doing his job, revealing God's love at every turn, even the bad turns.
Not even suffering and death will keep Jesus from his mission of
showing God's love to all; to Judas, to me, and to you.

▶ Prayer

You love me, Lord. But I am a sinner and your love causes you
suffering. You died for my sins, yet you continue to love me, even
though I continue to be a sinner. I am not worthy of such great love.

▶ Action

Think about how the love you have given to others has sometimes
caused you pain. Now consider how God's love for you is the same.

Wednesday of Holy Week

Betrayed by Money

MATTHEW 26:14–25

Jesus told the disciples, "One of you will betray me; the one who has dipped his hand into the dish with me. The Son of Man goes as it is written, but woe to that one by whom the Son of Man is betrayed! It would have been better for that one not to have been born."

▸ Reflection

In a classic sense, we hear Jesus predicting the punishment Judas will receive for his betrayal. But does that punishment come from God? Or is Judas making a bed that he will eventually have to lie in himself? Jesus welcomes Judas to the intimacy of table fellowship, even dipping into the same dish as he. The Lord also accepts his own destiny. But Judas has chosen the path of treachery and betrayal, and this will lead to great pain for both his master and himself. God does not have to inflict any punishment on Judas; his actions have their own painful consequences. If you put your hand in the fire it will get burned. Jesus accepts his own part in the suffering. He will pour out the cup of his blood for the sins of the world, including those of Judas. But the betrayer didn't bargain on the pain, only the silver. Thus by money is the betrayer himself betrayed.

▸ Prayer

O Lord, how often do I betray you for the things of the world? Yet your kingdom brings me more joy and fulfillment than anything the world has to offer. Protect me and forgive me. Hold me in your love.

▸ Action

Put $7.50 worth of quarters in your pocket and carry them around all day today as a reminder that God loves you even in your sins.

Easter
Season

Holy Thursday

Washing Trespasses

JOHN 13:1–15

Jesus got up from the table, poured water into a basin and began to wash the disciples' feet. When he had finished, he said to them, "I have set you an example; you should do as I have done to you."

▶ Reflection

The parish where I go to celebrate Mass on Sunday says in its mission statement that they seek a "full, conscious and active participation in the life of the Church and the mission of Jesus Christ." The outward sign of this participation is the Sunday Eucharist where we celebrate the word of God proclaimed and the body and blood of Christ shared. The liturgy of this celebration was born at the Last Supper, which we celebrate on Holy Thursday. While all four gospels recount the meal, John's account is different: there is no bread and wine! Instead John narrates the washing of the feet. This is because the community to whom he writes, perhaps second generation and already familiar with the form, needs encouragement to participate fully, actively, and consciously in Christ's mission. Forgiveness is not simply received, but must be both received and given. Our trespass can only be forgiven if we forgive those who trespass against us.

▶ Prayer

My God, you have washed away all my sins in baptism. Now I, in turn, am called on to wash away the sins of others. Help me to forgive as I have been forgiven. Teach me the ways of your mercy.

▶ Action

Three annoying little things will happen to you today and three people will need your forgiveness. Forgive them their trespasses.

Good Friday

Cross of Flesh

JOHN 18:1—19:42

When they saw him, they shouted, "Crucify him! Crucify him!" Pilate said to them, "Shall I crucify your King?" They answered, "We have no king but Caesar." So he handed him over to them to be crucified.

▶ Reflection

What a hard thing the cross is to bear. For Jesus as well as us, the cross is the burden of being truly human. Jesus bound himself in love to his friends; coarse, difficult people, northerners with accents and crude ways. He sought out unruly people who were thickheaded and hard to handle: the inept fisherman, the political terrorist, the traitor taxman and the treacherous thief. But he bore them. He stuck with them. He wore them like flesh and he let them inside him like blood. And it hurt. The heaviest, hardest burden he carried was his mortal humanity, just like the one I carry is mine, and the one you carry is yours. In the end it is that which betrays us, judges us, condemns us, abandons us, and crucifies us. But there is more. There is always more. The love of God is always with us, defending us, saving us, forgiving us, and raising us up. When all else fails, God continues. We came from God and we will return to God.

▶ Prayer

You suffered and died for me, O Lord. It was my sinfulness you willingly carried to your death so I could know that nothing can ever separate you from me. Thank you for your faithfulness.

▶ Action

Sit with a crucifix; take it off your wall, if you have to. Look at Jesus suffering and dying and see the love God has for you.

Easter Vigil

Fear and Joy

MATTHEW 28:1–10

The women ran from the tomb filled with great fear and great joy. Suddenly Jesus met them and said, "Greetings!" They took hold of his feet, and worshiped him. He said to them, "Don't be afraid; go and tell my brothers to go to Galilee; there they will see me, too."

▶ Reflection

"Oh, I'm so nervous," Brenda said to Fr. Ortega as the church began to darken for the Vigil. The assembly had gathered, the candles were passed out, and the great, new baptismal pool was warm and ready. "Me, too," replied Fr. Ortega. He'd never done a full immersion baptism before. On the advice of his friend, a veteran pastor, he had sewn lead washers into the hem of his alb so that it wouldn't float up around him and make him look dorky. "But this is the moment I've been waiting for," Brenda went on. "I'm so glad I'm being baptized." Brenda had spent two years in RCIA preparing for this night. Now, like the women who ran from the tomb, she was half-anxious, half-joyful. An encounter with the risen Christ will always produce these emotions, blended like water and wine: fear of death, joy in resurrection. One will pass; the other will endure forever.

▶ Prayer

In baptism you raise me to a new life, O my God. You wash me clean of all my sins and make me your own child in Christ. Protect me from all fear and give me the joy of knowing you are always with me.

▶ Action

Find a small jar or container, put water in it, and carry it around in your pocket or purse during the Easter season. Remember your baptism!

Easter

Fulfillment

JOHN 20:1–9

Mary stood weeping outside the tomb. Jesus said to her, "Mary!" She turned and said to him in Hebrew, "Rabbouni!"

▶ Reflection

There was one who kept vigil for him in her heart. Even in death Jesus was for her the fulfillment of that desire for love which God placed in her heart, and places in every human heart. So, when the sabbath was over and there was just enough light for her to see, she went looking for him at the tomb. And she found him. "Mary," he said. "My Lord!" she cried, and wrapped herself around him so ardently that he had to hold her back. There would be more, he assured her. He would rise still higher, "for love is stronger than death, passion more fierce than the grave. Like fire it rages, it blazes like a flame" (Song of Songs 8:6). "God is love, and when you live in love, you live in God." God finally succeeded in winning the beloved. Now, for all time, God is with the one he loves. As a body is immersed in water, so is the beloved immersed in the lover God. As air that is breathed, so does God enter into the beloved and beget new life. As bread and wine are consumed, so is God one now with the beloved; the two become one body. It is finished.

▶ Prayer

O precious Lord, you give yourself to me so fully that now we are one, a union never to be broken. Thank you for your gift, O God.

▶ Action

Take a piece of bread and eat it. Where does it go? What becomes of it? Remember today that the bread you eat becomes *you*.

Monday of the Octave of Easter

Women Witness

MATTHEW 28:8–15

Jesus appeared to the women and they worshiped him. He said, "Do not be afraid; go and tell my brothers to go to Galilee; there they will see me." The priests, meanwhile, told the guards, "You must say that his disciples came by night and stole him away while you were asleep." And this became the story told among them.

▶ Reflection

The religious leaders, all men, set their considerable intellectual powers to the task of rationalizing the disappearance of the Lord's body. The women, filled to the brim with emotion, are sent on the mission of carrying the news of the resurrection of Jesus to the apostles. This story suggests that the female heart is a more suitable vessel for good news than the male brain. Jesus could have chosen anyone to receive this revelation: the apostles, his family, the guards. But all four gospels record the same scene, so it's unanimous. Only women were chosen by Jesus to proclaim the good news of Christ's resurrection from the dead to the apostles. Perhaps it would be a fitting custom today for woman to proclaim the Easter message to the successors of the apostles.

▶ Prayer

O Lord, just as you revealed the birth of your Son first to a woman, so his resurrection from the dead was revealed first to a woman. May your church always hear this good news proclaimed by women.

▶ Action

Consider how the good news of Christ's resurrection from the dead might seem different if it were proclaimed by a woman today.

Tuesday of the Octave of Easter

Mission Completed

JOHN 20:11–18

Mary stood weeping outside the tomb. Jesus said to her, "Mary!" She turned and said to him in Hebrew "Rabbouni!" Jesus said to her, "Go to my brothers and say to them, 'I am ascending to my Father and your Father, to my God and your God.'" And she went and announced to the disciples, "I have seen the Lord!"

▶ Reflection

In their dramatic encounter in the garden Jesus indicates to his friend Mary, that the work of unifying God and humanity is complete. In his ascension, which John's gospel sees as continuous with the resurrection and occurring on the same day, Jesus comes full circle. He comes from heaven, takes on human flesh and is born; he lives, suffers and dies; he descends, rises, and returns to heaven. He traces the path of all humanity. No human being who ever was, is, or shall be, will ever walk a path Jesus hasn't already walked. From the experience of the greatest sinner to the greatest saint, Jesus has been there and done that. Henceforth, all have a share in salvation. As Mary learns from her risen master, the God of Jesus is our God; the Lord's Father is our Father.

▶ Prayer

In your dying, Lord, you completed your humanity. In your rising you revealed the enduring power of God's love. May Easter dawn in my heart each day and may I always embrace your eternal love.

▶ Action

Today, carry a pebble in your pocket to remind you that God is with you and in you, loving you with every breath you take.

Wednesday of the Octave of Easter

The Encounter

LUKE 24:13–35

Two of them were going to Emmaus, and they met Jesus, but they didn't recognize him. They told him about the crucifixion. "Some women told us about a vision of angels who said that he was alive," they said. Then, at the table with them, Jesus took bread, blessed and broke it, and gave it to them. Then their eyes were opened, and they recognized him; and he vanished from their sight.

▶ Reflection

Jesus did not fulfill the expectation of the two disciples on the road home to Emmaus. They knew all about him; they knew his life, his message, and his mighty works. They had heard the proclamation of his resurrection. But their words were laced with doubt. Their hope of Israel's freedom fell short; the story of his appearance was too good to be true. What saved them in the end was that they had taken to heart the imperative of Christ's teaching: they had offered the hospitality of their own home to someone in need. The words of Jesus, "As often as you do this for one of the least, you do it for me" (Matthew 25:40), had been fulfilled in their presence and they returned to the fold, convinced by their encounter with the risen Lord.

▶ Prayer

O Lord, you call me to be simply a welcoming person; welcoming in my heart, my home, and my pocketbook. May I always see your presence in the lowly and the needy you send into my life.

▶ Action

Someone will come to you in need today. Welcome that person. Give to that person from what you have received from the Lord.

Thursday of the Octave of Easter

Another Encounter

LUKE 24:35–48

Jesus stood among them and said to them, "Why are you frightened, and why do doubts arise in your hearts? Look at my hands and my feet; touch me and see that it is I." Then he opened their minds to understand the scriptures, and said, "You are witnesses of these things."

▶ Reflection

Jesus, ever the teacher, stresses the need for knowledge of the Scripture. But the real experience that puts the disciples over the top is a personal encounter with the risen Savior. Down through the ages, the church's record of those who have come to believe in Jesus is starred with the names of people who have come to know the transforming power of his living presence in their lives: Paul, Constantine, Francis, Margaret Mary, and people like our own Cardinal Joseph Bernardin. A person can know a lot about Jesus; that he is the only begotten Son of God, born of Mary, who lived, suffered, died, and rose. But one can only be created anew by the awesome experience of his real presence. It is for us to seek this encounter every day of our lives.

▶ Prayer

I learn about you in church, dear God, and read about you in the Bible. But I come to know you in my own humanity, for you are flesh and blood within me. Thank you for sharing yourself with me.

▶ Action

Keep score of how many times you encounter the risen Lord in faith today. Look for him with eyes of faith.

Friday of the Octave of Easter

Ordinary Presence

JOHN 21:1–14

Simon Peter said to the others, "I am going fishing." They went out in the boat all night but caught nothing. At daybreak, Jesus stood on the beach and said, "Cast the net to the right." They cast and caught many fish. When they had gone ashore, they saw a charcoal fire with fish on it, and bread. Jesus said to them, "Come and have breakfast." And none of the disciples dared to ask him, "Who are you?"

▶ Reflection

John's gospel is a study in symmetry. In this story the themes of light and darkness, of denial and recognition, of alienation and reconciliation are balanced. The disciples toil in the darkness of unbelief, their labors spent uselessly. But at daybreak they see the Lord and their boat is filled. Where Peter denies Jesus before the charcoal fires of fear, here he recognizes him before a similar fire of invitation. Again, as in the other appearance stories, there is food to eat. Body and soul are nourished by the Lord's presence. Yet the question, "Who are you?" hovers in the minds of even the believers. The presence of Christ is so ordinary, so without fanfare or formality, that people miss it. Sometimes people only see a man on the shore.

▶ Prayer

To rise from the dead, you must first die, my Lord. And to die you must first be born of a woman, as I was. You are in my human life, O God, and there I encounter you. Open my heart to your presence.

▶ Action

Close your eyes and feel the human life within you. Get used to the realization that the life you experience is the life of God.

Saturday of the Octave of Easter

She Was First

MARK 16:9–15

After Jesus rose, he appeared first to Mary Magdalene. She told those who had been with him, but they would not believe her. Later he appeared to the eleven and upbraided them for their lack of faith and their stubbornness. Then he said to them, "Now go into all the world and proclaim the good news."

▶ Reflection

Did you ever wonder what happened to Mary Magdalene after all this? She obviously had an extremely important role to play in the life, death, and resurrection of Jesus. Catholic tradition says that the apostles continued to mistrust her. Some ancient sources say that the apostles were jealous of the attention Jesus paid to her and the support he gave her over and against them. She seemed to understand and accept Jesus far more quickly than they did, and this was said to have remained a sticking point with the men. Some biblical scholars believe the early Christian community was divided in loyalty between her and Peter. Whether this is true or not, it is evident that May Magdalene was somebody very special to Jesus. She is one of the reasons people are trying to raise women to position of leadership in the church.

▶ Prayer

Jesus, my savior, you went first to Mary Magdalene because you loved her first of all. You saw in her a heart open to believe and you drew close. Help me to open my heart in the same way. Draw close to me.

▶ Action

Imagine how different the church might be if Mary had become the first leader instead of Peter. Have fun with the image.

Monday of the Second Week of Easter

Disparage Marriage

JOHN 3:1–8

Nicodemus came to see Jesus one night and said, "I know that you are a teacher sent by God because no one could do what you do apart from God." Jesus told him, "Believe me when I tell you, you can't experience the kingdom of God unless you are born again."

▶ Reflection

Eric became cynical after the failure of his marriage. He would join his companions after work at his favorite bar and disparage wedded life over a few beers. His married friends would tend to agree with him for the sake of easy camaraderie and, for the most part, because their marriages also were given to conflict. What Eric and his friends did not realize was that they needed to make fundamental changes in their lives if they were to experience the joy of true marriage. "You cannot serve two masters," Jesus says. Eric had enjoyed the freedom of his bachelor ways before he married—and that was good. There is a freedom to marriage too, but it requires a new way of thinking, a new attitude, and a new order of priorities. Eric assumed he could just keep on living the way he did before he was married, and he was confused and hurt when it didn't work. Eric needed to be born again.

▶ Prayer

My precious savior, I have embraced the values of the world since I was young. But I long for the joys of eternal life. Help me to let go of my old ways so that I more fully delight in the way of your kingdom.

▶ Action

Write down an attitude you hold that keeps you from the kingdom. Spend the day noticing how often it comes up. Pray for a better way.

Tuesday of the Second Week of Easter

Deaf and Blind

JOHN 3:7–15

"Does it make you wonder," Jesus said to Nicodemus, "when I tell you that you must be born again? The wind blows wherever it wants. You hear it, but you don't know where it comes from or where goes. It is the same way when you're born again of the Spirit."

▶ Reflection

Nicodemus was essentially a company guy. He was part of the system of religion, government, and economy that dominated the society of ancient Jerusalem. John's gospel calls him "a Pharisee and a ruler of the Jews." Jesus simply calls him a teacher. He obviously benefited greatly from the system and would not quickly let it go. But he wanted something more, and thus he came to Jesus. "It is hard for a rich man to enter the kingdom," Jesus teaches in Matthew 19:23. The reluctance of Nicodemus is expressed in his coming to Jesus at night, a recurring theme in John's gospel, and his misunderstanding of what Jesus has to say. His attachment to the world prevents him from seeing or hearing the message of the kingdom. He is both deaf and blind. The placement of this story at the beginning of the gospel symbolizes the starting point where all of us must be born again.

▶ Prayer

O Lord, you invite me today to enter your kingdom and enjoy life to the fullest. Yet I cling to the comfort and security of the passing world. Heal me so that I may see your presence and hear your call.

▶ Action

Make a list of the ten most important things in your life. Consider what life would be like without just one of them. Would you willing to let it go for the sake of the kingdom?

Wednesday of the Second Week of Easter

Not to Condemn

JOHN 3:16–21

"God so loved the world that he gave his only Son, so that everyone who believes in him may not perish but may have eternal life. God did not send the Son into the world to condemn the world, but in order that the world might be saved through him."

▶ Reflection

The church, in its two thousand years of history, has always been in need of reform. In its very infancy, when St. Paul was spreading the message of Jesus Christ through the Roman Empire, conflicts arose between factions that had to be dealt with. A council was called, questions were resolved and the church was reformed (see Acts 15:1–32). Since then, there have been dozens of councils that resulted in reform of the church, the most recent being Vatican II. These are necessary because times change and adjustments need to be made. Also, the church, like any human institution, is imperfect and can get off the track in its articulation of the faith. Whether adjusting or correcting, the church's message must always turn back to the truth expressed in today's gospel: God wills to save, not condemn. When the church's message becomes condemnation, it must be corrected.

▶ Prayer

O Lord, I grew up in a time when it seemed like all I heard about was condemnation. But in time the church gathered in council and restored the message of salvation. Thank you, Lord, for being with us.

▶ Action

Think about the person you love most in the world. Consider sacrificing that person for the sake of others. That's what God did.

Thursday of the Second Week of Easter

In God's Hands

JOHN 3:31–36

"The Father loves the Son and has placed all things in his hands. Whoever believes in the Son has eternal life."

▶ Reflection

Evie was worried about losing her job. She and her husband Chris had just closed a deal on a new house, but now it looked like their dreams were in jeopardy. If she stopped bringing home a paycheck, how would they ever afford the mortgage? When she got home, Chris listened attentively to all her fears. Then he put his arms around her and held her close. "Honey," he said, "if they let you go, it will be because God has something much better for you. How would you be able to go out and find that new job God has for you if you spend all your time stuck in that crummy old one? Let's drive over and take another look at our new house." Chris knew that everything was in God's hands and he gently shared his faith with Evie. This is what it means to be a witness and to proclaim one's faith in God.

▶ Prayer

Dear Jesus, I believe in you, but I guess I don't always believe in you. Sometimes your ways are so far above my ways that it's hard for me to realize just how much you love me. I am so worldly that I just assume you're worldly, too. But you are not worldly; you are heavenly and your love for me is infinite. Help me always to believe in you and trust that you are creating good things for me.

▶ Action

Look at some of the things you fear might happen in your life. See them as ways God will change your life for the better.

Friday of the Second Week of Easter

To the Rescue

JOHN 6:1–15

When Jesus saw a large crowd coming, he said to Philip, "Where are we going to buy bread for them to eat?" He said this to test him, for he already knew what he was going to do. Philip answered, "Six months' wages wouldn't buy enough for each to get a little."

▶ Reflection

Mr. and Mrs. Benson ran the little country mission for their church. They cared for the rural poor and their resources were meager. Each day Mr. Benson would go into the little prayer chapel they built in a spare room with a list of all the things they needed for their mission. In his prayer he'd read from the list, holding it up to God so the Lord could "see" it. "We'd need stuff like baby clothes and wouldn't have enough money to buy it, so we figured God would have to get it for us," Mr. Benson would say. Kindly people would come to the door to drop off the things they'd need, and the needy folks would come for they things they had to have. "If we had the money," Mrs. Benson would say, "we'd never get to see the miracles God performs for us. But because we're poor, why, we can see the Lord coming to our rescue every day."

▶ Prayer

Great is your compassion, O Lord, and you are there always to fill our needs. Give me a vision to see beyond the limitations of this world to your miraculous creative power, which flows from your love.

▶ Action

Today you will come up short in some way: not enough time, not enough patience, not enough of what you need. See what God does.

Saturday of the Second Week of Easter

Making It Easy

JOHN 6:16–21

The disciples got into a boat and started across. It was rough because a strong wind was blowing. Then they saw Jesus walking toward them on the water and they were terrified. He said to them, "It is I; do not be afraid." And immediately the boat made it safely to shore.

▶ Reflection

It was a long drive across the state and Judy could feel herself getting cranky. Not only did the summer heat make her irritable, but the broken air conditioner annoyed her even more. She knew Fred had meant to get it fixed, but the need to make the trip arose suddenly and caught him off guard. In the past, before she started getting really serious about her faith in Christ, she would make Fred pay for her discomfort and make the trip miserable for them both. But now she put her faith in Jesus and decided to forgive Fred. She reached over and slipped her hand behind his neck. "How you doing, honey?" she asked, rubbing his neck and the back of his head the way she knew he liked. "Can I get you some water?" It was great with Jesus in her life. He always came to her when she needed him the most. The long trip passed quickly and before she knew it, they were there.

▶ Prayer

Dear Lord, sometimes the way is hard. But then you come to me, and everything changes. Help me to always welcome your presence in my life as the beginning of a new way.

▶ Action

Think of an area in your life where you strive for your own way and are often frustrated. Invite Jesus to show you the way of peace.

Monday of the Third Week of Easter

The Greater Gift

JOHN 6:22–29

Jesus said to the crowd, "Do not work for the food that perishes, but for the food that endures for eternal life, which the Son of Man will give you. For it is on him that God the Father has set his seal."

▶ Reflection

The crowd was hungry and Jesus had fed them. It was understandable that they were interested in how they could always be fed in such a way. But Jesus had a greater gift in mind for them. In the same way, God has a greater gift in mind for us. God gives us many gifts, which we use to supply ourselves with the things of this world that sustain our lives. But when we invest all our time, talent, and money to build our worldly estate, we misuse God's gifts. We anguish over the plight of the hungry, sometimes even blaming God for "allowing" the tragedy to go on. Yet God says to us: "Feed them; feed my sheep." There are abundant resources on this planet to care for all, even the poorest. How much is used to build the weapons of war? How much is used for private jets and yachts? How much is used to remodel your kitchen? These things aren't bad, but they are limited to this passing world and when they're gone, what do you have?

▶ Prayer

O God, day by day you give me such marvelous gifts. I have all that I need. Show me how to live simply that I may work for the lasting bread that is Jesus in me, who feeds the hungry through me.

▶ Action

Write a big check for your local soup kitchen. Talk to your pastor about giving money to Catholic Relief Services or another charity.

Tuesday of the Third Week of Easter

God a Sandwich?

JOHN 6:30–35

Jesus said to them, "I am the bread of life. Whoever comes to me will never be hungry, and whoever believes in me will never be thirsty."

▶ Reflection

Jim once again found himself in front of the refrigerator, staring through the open door, his mind empty of thought. He wanted something, but he didn't know what it was. He couldn't need food; he had just eaten dinner an hour before. Besides, he was twenty pounds overweight and he needed to cut back. Regardless, he grabbed some cold cuts, made a sandwich, and headed back to the TV. Jim doesn't know it, but the great desire in his heart, which he can feel as a kind of hunger, is the call to experience the joys of God's kingdom. He was made to know God. It's in him to do, but he has only believed in the ways of the world, so he doesn't really understand. All who hunger are called to the feast of the body of Christ, but we go to the fridge instead. We thirst and are invited to the water, but we drink the beverages of the world to excess. We are called to love, but we seek romantic gratification. We need to believe that Jesus is in us, calling to us.

▶ Prayer

O God of beauty and goodness, everywhere I look there are things to delight my eye and cause my heart to swell. But these things are passing and are meant to reveal your hand at work in our world. Help me to understand my desires and look within for their fulfillment.

▶ Action

The next time you get an urge to stick your head in the fridge, try sticking your nose in the Bible instead. See if it makes a difference.

112

Wednesday of the Third Week of Easter

Soul Soup

JOHN 6:35–40

Jesus said to them, "Everyone the Father gives me will come to me, and no one who comes to me will I ever reject. I haven't come to do my own will, but to do the will of the one who sent me."

▶ **Reflection**

Recently I was caring for a friend who had the flu. Unwrapping a bullion cube to make chicken soup, I couldn't help thinking that it wasn't too long ago when it was taught that such an innocuous little food product could send a person straight to hell if it was hidden in, say, vegetable soup and ingested, even unknowingly, on a Friday. The legacy of our pre-reform abuses caused anxiety in some Catholics, that Jesus actually would reject them for some reason, even one out of their own control. The words of today's gospel obviously contradict this fear. But even though we see it, it's sometimes hard to believe because our upbringing was so influenced by that dreadful nonsense. It's important to remember: God will not reject us. Only we can reject God.

▶ **Prayer**

In me your heart beats alive, O God, aflame with love for me. You know me. Your breath is the spirit of life within me; your body and mine are one. Know that my sins make me afraid, so often am I blind to your tender mercy and compassion. Yet your love for me is greater than all evil. Quiet my fear and make me confident of your love.

▶ **Action**

Offer someone you know a little "chicken soup" today. Revive his or her spirit with your concern and compassion.

I Could Die Now

JOHN 6:44–51

"Whoever believes in me has eternal life. I am the bread of life. Whoever eats this bread will live forever."

▶ Reflection

I know a man who is dying of cancer. Recently we journeyed to a distant monastery to fulfill a last request: to visit the priest who fostered his faith and inspired him to become a Catholic. We arrived at the abbey in time for afternoon prayer, and then my friend had a long talk with the old priest whom he hadn't seen in years. Afterward, on the way home, my friend exclaimed, "That's it! I've done everything I wanted to do. It doesn't matter what happens to me now. I could die right now and it would be okay." As we drove on in silence, it occurred to me that when he does die, he probably won't even notice it. He's caught up in God right now and dying won't change that. Dying for him will be like both falling asleep and waking up at the same time.

▶ Prayer

Do I fear death, my God? Or is it dying, the painful pathway that leads me to death's door, that makes me afraid? Either way, Lord, you yourself have suffered and died, so I know you will be with me in my suffering and dying. In you, death is no death. Rather, death's door leads to life. Jesus, may I always bear in mind the memory of your death and resurrection. Your promise of eternal life sustains me.

▶ Action

Recall a time when you were caught up in God. What were the circumstances? What has changed for you between then and now?

Friday of the Third Week of Easter

Within You

JOHN 6:52–59

"Very truly, I tell you, unless you eat the flesh of the Son of Man and drink his blood, you have no life in you. For my flesh is real food and my blood is real drink. Those who eat my flesh and drink my blood abide in me, and I in them."

▸ Reflection

A man was asked why he became an atheist. He replied that one day while he was praying, he realized he was talking to himself. Another was asked why he became a believer and replied that one day while he was praying, he realized it was all in him. The difference is subtle but significant. There's a point in life when a person perceives that he or she is all there is. Then there is the awakening to the realization that all there is exists within a person. Throughout his ministry, Jesus would wonder how best to communicate the kingdom of God (see Mark 4:30). To eat and drink Jesus is to know in a very real way that all there is exists within you. As St. Paul says in 1 Corinthians 3:21–23, "For all things are yours,…and you belong to Christ, and Christ belongs to God."

▸ Prayer

When I pray, O Lord, I sometimes wonder what it's all about. Are you really there? Then I feel your life in me, your breath moving into me, your heart pounding in my breast. Have I really died, like St. Paul said, and you now live in me? I thank you for your life and your love.

▸ Action

Stop for a moment and close your eyes. Listen to your breath and your heartbeat. Know that it is God living in you.

Saturday of the Third Week of Easter

Mouths of Babes

JOHN 6:60–69

Jesus said to his followers, "The words that I have spoken to you are spirit and life. But some among you still don't believe in me."

▶ Reflection

In a parish where I once served there was a boy who was severely retarded. His mother faithfully took him to church every Sunday, but he didn't receive communion. It came to my attention that a priest once told the mother that it would be impossible for the boy to receive Holy Communion because he did not have sufficient use of reason. So I worked with the mother to catechize the boy and the day came when he dined with us at the table of the Lord's body and blood. After Mass that day he ran up to me and hugged me wildly. Then he backed up a step, slapped his hand on his stomach and cried, "I've got Jesus in me!" Didn't have sufficient use of reason, eh? Sounded to me like he understood better than most of us do. The spirit and life of Jesus within him instantly gave him a belief he was able to express in such a beautiful and simple way.

▶ Prayer

Within me, Lord Jesus, you dwell in mystery. Forgiven and freed, I am being transformed, day by day, into your likeness, revealing your presence in the world. Lord, by your grace, keep me on the path that leads to eternal life. Let me come to you each day with arms and heart open wide.

▶ Action

Say to yourself at least five times today: "I've got Jesus in me!" Write the phrase on a piece of paper and put it in your pocket.

Monday of the Fourth Week of Easter

Gate of Love

JOHN 10:1–10
_____

"Very truly, I tell you, I am the gate for the sheep. Whoever enters by me will be saved, and will come in and go out and find pasture."

▶ Reflection

When I saw Derek, I knew right away that he was going through a hard time. He tried to avoid me, but I stopped him and asked what was wrong. He didn't want to talk about it, but I knew he needed help, so I got him to sit down with me and talk it out. "But Derek," I said, "the Lord is guiding you through this." All I got in return was a blank stare. So I tried a different twist. "Derek, God loves you." Nothing, again. No wonder he didn't want to talk with me. All I had to offer was the standard religious line. So then I said, "Gee, this must be really difficult for you." He lifted his eyes a little and said, "Yeah, it is." I asked him, "What are you going to do?" He turned to me and said, "I don't know." I said, "Wanna go to lunch and talk about it?" He said, "Sure." The gate to Derek's troubled heart was love, not answers.

▶ Prayer

Dear Jesus, you always guide me to love. It was your love for me that first opened my heart to your presence in my life. Your love sustains me and heals me every day. You call me to love others as you love me. Teach me the ways of your love. Help me always to lead others to you through love.

▶ Action

Find somebody in your life today who needs a good dose of love. Love that person the best way you know how.

Tuesday of the Fourth Week of Easter

River of Humanity

JOHN 10:22–30

*Barnabas rejoiced when he saw the evidence of God's favor. (Acts 11:23)
Some said to Jesus, "How long will you keep us in suspense? If you are the
Messiah, tell us plainly." Jesus answered, "I have told you, but you do not
believe." (John)*

▶ Reflection

The throngs of people flowed past me like a river. I was on my way to
the library across the campus near where I live and class was letting
out. Even though there were as many people walking my way as
coming the other way, I felt like I was a fish trying to swim upstream.
Sometimes big crowds like that annoy me, and today was one of those
days. "This would be a great campus," a colleague once remarked, "if
it wasn't for all the students!" But this time I was reminded from
within that God was enormously present to me in all the faces and
bodies moving past me; that each jostle and bump was the touch of
God, each voice a song sung by God into the world. God tells me
these things plainly all the time, but sometimes I don't believe. Today
I rejoiced to see the evidence of God's favor.

▶ Prayer

O God, you have created all people in your own image and likeness.
Each face is beautiful because it is your own face, each voice delightful
because it is your voice. When I forget this and am not as accepting of
others as I should be, help me to see your image in them.

▶ Action

Keep track of how many different kinds of faces and voices you
encounter today. Ask God's special blessing for each one.

Wednesday of the Fourth Week of Easter

Shining Light

JOHN 12:44–50

"I have come as light into the world, so that everyone who believes in me should not remain in the darkness. I do not judge anyone who hears my words and does not keep them, for I came not to judge the world, but to save the world."

▶ Reflection

Little Jenny was afraid of the dark, so her mom kept a night light burning in her room. One night, the light burned out and left Jenny to face the darkness. The next morning at breakfast, Jenny told her mom about the experience. "It was scary at first. I almost called you. But then I remembered what you told me; that I was a light myself." The night before, Jenny's mom had read to her the gospel verse from Matthew 5:14–16, "You are the light of the world." So Jenny went on to tell her mom that at first it was too dark to see anything. But then, gradually, as her eyes adjusted, she could see details of her room, familiar things that comforted her and gave her a feeling of security. "I wasn't afraid any more," she said. "My light was really shining!"

▶ Prayer

Sometimes I'm afraid of the world around me, Lord. There is so much darkness and evil. But you, Jesus, are the light who came into the world. You showed us that there is nothing to fear from the darkness, not even the darkness in me. Please be my light shining through me so that I may always see the good things of life.

▶ Action

Tonight, turn off all the lights and sit in the darkness. What do you see? Jesus is the light that shines in the darkness.

Thursday of the Fourth Week of Easter

Me?

JOHN 13:16–20

"I tell you truly, servants are not greater than their master. I know whom I have chosen. But it is to fulfill the scripture, 'The one who ate my bread has lifted his heel against me.' I tell you this now... so that when it does occur, you may believe that I am he."

▶ Reflection

A friend of mine who is a bishop confides in me that he's a little uncomfortable with the idea that God called him to such a position. "I would consider God's selection criteria highly questionable," he says. Yet Jesus says he knows the ones he chooses. If that's the case, I wonder why he chose Judas? And why did he also give him charge of the money? He knew Judas was a thief (look it up in John 12:6). Maybe it was because Jesus liked Judas. Maybe he wanted to give him every chance to redeem himself. Perhaps he saw in Judas some special quality, some light that shone in the darkness. Even in the end, when Judas committed his ultimate act of treachery, Jesus called him "friend" (it's in Matthew 26:50).

▶ Prayer

Why do you choose and call us, dear God? Why is it that one is a mother, another is a doctor, and another is a plumber? Why is it that some people seem so perfectly suited and others just seem out of place? Is it because your love is so great that we just don't understand it? I hope so, because sometimes I wonder.

▶ Action

Think of somebody whom you feel is really out of place. Imagine how God could be working in the world through that person.

Friday of the Fourth Week of Easter

Suitcase in Hand

JOHN 14:1–6

"In my Father's house there are many dwelling places. I will go there and prepare a place for you. Then I will return to take you with me, so that you may also be where I am."

▶ Reflection

The funeral was the next day and Paul had driven a hundred miles to attend his cousin Teddy's wake and, hopefully, to find a place to stay the night. That hope moved him to bring his suitcase to the funeral home. Perhaps one of the family would take him home and give him lodging. But as the wake moved on toward the last hour, no one offered, and Paul was left to consider driving two hours to his home and returning the next day. Then Teddy's sister Alice noticed. She was staying with another sister in a small place that was already crowded with out-of-town guests. But she said to Paul, "Come home with us. We'll give you a place to stay." Grateful, Paul went with them. The next day at the funeral, today's gospel passage was proclaimed. Paul was deeply touched, knowing he'd had a taste of the kingdom the night before.

▶ Prayer

We come to life, dear Jesus, with our suitcase in hand, not knowing where we are going. But you have promised to come for us in the end and take us home to be with you. Comfort us with this hope when we are lonely and fear the night.

▶ Action

Look through the House and Home section of your Sunday newspaper. Imagine the kind of dwelling you'd like in heaven.

Saturday of the Fourth Week of Easter

Fearing Frumentius

JOHN 14:7–14

*"If you know me, you will know my Father also. From now on you do know him
and have seen him."*

▶ Reflection

I didn't learn much about God growing up Catholic in the fifties. I
spent most of my catechetical youth learning how to dodge the grip of
Sister Frumentius. That woman had hands big enough to palm a
basketball. Most often, however, she would simply palm my face. I
used to come home with her fingerprints on my cheeks. She'd squeeze
my mouth into fish lips while she screamed at me. The secret to
surviving catechism with Sister Frumentius was getting the answers to
the questions right. So I did learn that we were created to know God,
love God, and serve God. It must be important, then, for us to get to
know Jesus, because if we know him, we know God. So I try to spend
some of my time and money studying the gospel, serving the poor,
comforting the sick, feeding the hungry, visiting the prisoners, and so
on. For as often as we do that for them, we do it for him. That's how
we get to know Jesus and, through him, God.

▶ Prayer

Jesus, you reveal God to us through your own self. You show us
through your words and your actions. O Lord, may we become like
you and reach out in compassion to the needy so that we may join
you in your union with God.

▶ Action

Look for God today in someone you might consider to be poor and
lowly. Get to know that person better. Think about what you learned.

Monday of the Fifth Week of Easter

Look-alikes

JOHN 14:21–26

"Those who hear my words and keep them are the ones who love me; and the ones who love me will be in my Father's love and my love, too. I will reveal myself to them."

▶ Reflection

My friend Bob won a look-alike contest with his dog, Tyler. Bob is kind of a bushy guy and Tyler, being a dog, is kind of a bushy guy, too. Well, they were both bushy enough to sort of look like each other, and Bob's girlfriend took a picture of them cheek to cheek and entered it in the contest and they won. I think Bob looks like Tyler because he loves Tyler and Tyler loves Bob and that's probably why he looks like Bob. They spend a lot of time together playing, going places in the car, and taking walks. Anyway, I think that they both look like each other because they love each other. If we're going to be like Jesus, which is a good idea because Jesus is in glory, then we really need to develop a liking for him. He already loves us. Loving Jesus is a matter of keeping his words, which means putting his teachings into practice. Try it.

▶ Prayer

My loving Jesus, you came into the world and you were just like me in every way but sin. You loved me so much that you suffered and died for me; then you rose and ascended so that your Spirit could be in me. Teach me to love you with all my heart and soul.

▶ Action

Next time you're in the mall, watch couples walking by and see how much the lovers look like each other.

Tuesday of the Fifth Week of Easter

Quiet in Christ

JOHN 14:27–31

"Peace I leave with you; my peace I give to you. I do not give you peace as the world gives peace. Do not let your hearts be troubled, and do not let them be afraid."

▶ Reflection

"Father Paul!" Kristina cried in horror, "You don't have a television!" My friend Denise had just dropped off her four kids at my little house and they were giving it the once over. I guess to a fourteen-year-old, the absence of a television must have been quite a shock. Her little brother Joey agreed. "Whoa," he said. "That's gotta stink." I explained to them as best I could that it wasn't as bad as it looked. I liked living without a TV. And without a stereo. No microwave. I don't even have a coffee grinder. There's a certain peace that attends my life, which I treasure. But it's a worldly peace, a passing comfort. It's simply the absence of noise. But there is an eternal peace in my life that comes from knowing that I am safe in Christ. I try to remember my salvation every day and rejoice in its comfort.

▶ Prayer

Dear Jesus, this passing world offers so many things in which to find a kind of fulfillment, but it is so limited. Help me to keep my eyes on you, my Lord. Help me to keep my life simple so that there's always room for you and a place to treasure your words.

▶ Action

Write down all the things in your life that give you peace. Now cross off all the things that will pass away. What's left?

Wednesday of the Fifth Week of Easter

Trying to Be Good

JOHN 15:1–8

"Just as a branch cannot bear fruit by itself unless it is attached to the vine, neither can you bear fruit unless you are attached to me. I am the vine, you are the branches. Abide in me and you will produce much fruit."

▶ Reflection

One of the things I learned growing up was that the fruits of the Holy Spirit are: love, joy, peace, patience, kindness, goodness, gentleness, faithfulness and self-control (look it up in Galatians 5:22–23, or the *Catechism*, #1832). Our Lord gives us the formula for a happy, happy life. The mistake I often make is that I try to be patient, or I struggle to control myself. Jesus says simply to abide in him and I will produce the fruit. What I try to do is produce the fruit myself. Can't do that, Jesus says. No more than a branch can produce fruit apart from the vine can I produce fruit apart from Jesus. My task is to abide in Jesus. If I spent as much time and effort abiding in the Lord as I do trying to be good, I think I'd be a lot further along on the way to fulfillment.

▶ Prayer

O God, in the vineyard of the soul, you are the grower who carefully tends the branches. You desire all that is good for us and you see to it that we receive all we need to live happy, fulfilling lives. May we always stay attached to Jesus so that our lives will be fruitful.

▶ Action

Sit quietly in prayer with some fruit in your lap. Think about which fruit of the Spirit you need the most and ask God for it. Then have a banana!

Thursday of the Fifth Week of Easter

Guidance for Joy

JOHN 15:9–11

"We are saved by the favor of Jesus." (Acts 15:11) "I have said these things to you so that my joy may be in you, and that your joy may be complete." (John)

▶ Reflection

"Aw, Mom! Why can't I go with Jason to the lake?" Young Brad was frustrated. He had tried everything to get his mother to let him go to the lake. But she was adamant. She wasn't going to give in, and that was that. She explained to him again that, while the boys were good swimmers, they were still too young to go to the lake alone without adults along with them. "I just want what's best for you," she added, a mantra she tagged on the end of every dispute with her son. It was true. She didn't want anything bad to happen to him. The same is true for God. God's direction in our lives comes from a profound desire that the best in life be ours. And if God is a loving, caring parent to us, then we must sometimes sound like God's whiny children. God just wants us to be happy. Why is this so hard for us to understand?

▶ Prayer

You invite us to share your joy, O Jesus. You give us all we need to be completely happy. Isn't it strange that we so often turn away to pursue passing things that will not provide us with lasting joy? Help us, dear Lord, to leave these things behind and to recognize your loving hand gently guiding us toward goodness.

▶ Action

Think of a moral law that's kept you out of trouble in your life and thank God for the loving care that kept you on the right path.

Friday of the Fifth Week of Easter

Vast Resources

JOHN 15:12–17

"You did not choose me but I chose you. And I appointed you to go and bear fruit, fruit that will last, so that the Father will give you whatever you ask him in my name."

▶ Reflection

Cindy's project was running a little behind schedule and her supervisor, June, wanted to check how things were going. "I've worked overtime almost every night this week and I still can't catch up," Cindy complained over coffee. June could see the problem right away. Cindy needed to outsource some of the work and June pointed this out to her. But Cindy was new and didn't want her employer to think she was too loose with the money. June told her, "Look, we're a big company and this project is important to us. Whatever you need, just ask. We'll back you all the way." Cindy was not used to the vast resources of the company, but she was learning. In the same way, we're not used to the power of God to give us whatever we ask for, but Jesus is working on it. He repeats today's teaching an astonishing nine times in the four gospels. The simple tradition of the church has always been that God answers our prayers. What are we waiting for?

▶ Prayer

Day in and day out, O loving God, your hand is at work in my life, creating for me everything I desire. You answer all my prayers. Thank you, Lord, for this extraordinary grace.

▶ Action

Think of what you really need in life and compose a prayer asking God to fill your need. Pray this prayer every day.

Saturday of the Fifth Week of Easter

Bus Driver Theology

JOHN 15:18–21

"If the world hates you, be aware that it hated me first. If you belonged to the world, the world would love you. But because I have chosen you out of the world, the world hates you."

▶ Reflection

As I swung into the empty seat behind the driver of the #51 bus headed home, Jimmy, the driver who I knew from church, greeted me cheerfully. "So how's it going, Padre?" he asked. "It's been a long day, Jimmy," I said as he pulled out into traffic. I'd just come from a long, difficult meeting and I was bushed. "God sure runs a crazy world," I said. "You'd think he'd lighten up on the good guys once in a while." I was just making small talk, but Jimmy wasn't. "Far be it from me to tell you anything, Padre, but I think we sometimes get the wrong idea about the Big Guy. We think because he's on our side that our lives should run like clockwork with nothing ever going wrong. Well, guess what: that ain't how it goes. We're going to live in this screwy world for a while, and then we're going to die, just like Jesus did. It's as simple as that. Why should we fare any better than God's Son?" My bus driver, the theologian!

▶ Prayer

When trouble comes my way, I turn to you, O God, and cry out for your help. "Why do you let this happen?" I complain. Then I remember that you share all my burdens. What a gift your love is!

▶ Action

Think of the biggest difficulty you have in your life right now. Could it be of your own doing? Or is it because you are a good person living in an evil world?

Monday of the Sixth Week of Easter

Computer Rejection

JOHN 15:26—16:4

"Eventually they will throw you out of the synagogues. I'm telling you this now so that when it happens, you'll remember that I told you."

▶ Reflection

Sandy heard a cry of anguish rise up from behind the partition separating her cubicle from Brian's. They were both working on the same project, so trouble on his side meant trouble on hers. She poked her head over the top to have a look. Brian had retreated to the corner of his cubicle and was on the floor curled up in a fetal position. "Whatsa matter, chum?" Sandy asked. Brian didn't even look up. "Computer crashed again?" He nodded silently. "Blue Screen of Death?" Again he nodded. "Did you save your stuff?" This time he shook his head slowly, mournfully. "Brian," Sandy shifted into her mother mode, "you know that thing is going to crash. You've got to save you work. C'mon, I'll buy you a cup of coffee." If computers are tough to deal with, life can be even tougher. Jesus warns his disciples to be ready for trouble. Living good lives in an evil world means you're going to suffer rejection and heartache. Be ready.

▶ Prayer

O Jesus, you are so good, so holy. When I think that you took on flesh to be born like me, I sigh with gratitude. You know what it's like to be human. Help me remember that you walk with me wherever I go.

▶ Action

Take a moment to think about how you experience rejection in your life. Now think of how Jesus experienced the same thing.

Tuesday of the Sixth Week of Easter

The Magic Feather

JOHN 16:5–11

"It is better for you that I go away, because if I don't go away, the Advocate will not come. But if I go, then the Spirit will come to you."

▶ Reflection

I remember as a kid going to see the animated movie, *Dumbo.* It's the story of a little circus elephant with big ears, and his friend, a mouse. In the story, the mouse discovers that Dumbo, the little elephant, can fly. But Dumbo doesn't believe it. So the mouse gives Dumbo a feather and tells him that it's magic and will make him fly. Dumbo believes this and learns how to fly (the crows teach him!), but always with the "magic feather" held securely in his little trunk. Of course, at the critical moment when he and the mouse are pushed off the top of the high wire platform in their circus act, Dumbo loses the feather. As they plummet toward the ground, the mouse screams in Dumbo's ear, "You can fly without the feather, Dumbo! The feather was just a gag! The magic is in you! You can fly!" As long as Jesus was with his disciples, they saw the Spirit in him. But once he left them, they would discover that the same Spirit was in them.

▶ Prayer

Where are you, Jesus? Sometimes when I need you the most and look for you, I can't find you. Then I remember that you are present within me. Your Spirit fills me with life and gives me power over the world around me. Thank you, Jesus, for this great grace.

▶ Action

Write the name "Jesus" at the top of a piece of paper and then list all the powers you believe are his. Then, erase his name and write yours.

Wednesday of the Sixth Week of Easter

Spirit of Truth

JOHN 16:12–15

"I have many things to say to you, but you cannot bear them now. When the Spirit of truth comes, he will guide you into all the truth. He will glorify me, and will take what is mine and declare it to you."

▶ Reflection

Truth is an incredibly heavy burden. We can no more expect to bear it than could the disciples to whom Jesus addressed his message of truth. Even the Holy Spirit can only guide us to truth; not even God can make us accept the truth. Our needs, our desires, our values and the limits of our own understanding of what is possible always condition our recognition of truth. The religious leaders who pressed for our Lord's execution believed they were operating out of truth, as did the political leaders who complied. Today our church lays claim to truths that contradict truths it claimed in the past. What is true to science today was not so a hundred years ago and will not be so a hundred years from now. That is why the Spirit is dynamic; it guides us along pathways in which we discover new and wonderful things at every turn. It is not that God is holding back from us; rather, our understanding is like the dawn. We can only gradually see the truth.

▶ Prayer

Lord, I give you thanks that you reveal all truth to me. Yet I rarely see it. I am often blind to the beauty of your presence. Heal my blindness so that I may rejoice in your truth.

▶ Action

Look up at the stars tonight. There was a time when people could not see their depth. Consider that there are trillions, just like our sun.

Unanswered Question

JOHN 16:16–20

Jesus said to his disciples, "A little while, and you will no longer see me, and again a little while, and you will see me." They said to one another, "What does he mean by this saying?" Jesus said to them, "I tell you, you will weep and mourn, but the world will rejoice; you will have pain, but your pain will turn into joy."

▶ Reflection

Sharon's divorce was a bitter one; she and her children suffered much during the process. When Linda and Tom lost their youngest daughter in a car accident, they could hardly bear the burden of grief and suffering. Jim knew it would just be a matter of time before the cancer growing in his body would begin to take his life away and leave his family without a husband and a father; his anguish was unimaginable. Sometimes, when life becomes an unbearable burden, we ask why; it is a reasonable question. But the cosmos remains silent. Even the biblical hero Job asked the question for forty-two chapters and received no satisfying answer. Maybe that's why we call Easter the "Paschal mystery." It whispers into the silence, "I am with you in suffering and death. You are with me in rising and glory."

▶ Prayer

O, Jesus, my love and my savior, you give yourself to me in body and blood so that we might be one. You share my suffering so that I might share your glory. I am *so* grateful. May I bless you all my days.

▶ Action

When you are hurt today, as you most certainly will be, remember that the suffering you feel is God's suffering as well. You are together.

Friday of the Sixth Week of Easter

Due To Arrive

JOHN 16:20–23

"When a woman is in labor, she is distressed because her hour has come and she feels the pain. But when her child is born, she no longer remembers the anguish; she is filled with the joy of having brought a new person into the world."

▶ Reflection

One night I sat up with a friend who was going to have a baby. I mean she was *really* going to have a baby, like any minute! I remember her sitting on the couch calmly reading a book while I sat bolt upright across the room in a straight-backed chair staring at her, waiting…for what? I didn't know. "Stop staring at me," she said, not looking up from her book. "I'll let you know when it's time." I have to admire the courage of Jesus. I would think twice about using the image of a woman having a baby to make a point. But I guess being the Son of God has its advantages. The kingdom of God comes like a baby being born in the night. It comes when it's ready and the time is right, and it brings joy to all who wait in expectant hope.

▶ Prayer

Loving God, I often anguish over the coming of your kingdom. The world seems so full of suffering and injustice. But the kingdom will come and it will make us glad. Thank you for your promise and its fulfillment.

▶ Action

Spend some time thinking about all the things that will happen when the kingdom comes.

Saturday of the Sixth Week of Easter

Wrestlemania

JOHN 16:23–28

"Very truly, I tell you, if you ask anything of the Father in my name, he will give it to you."

▶ Reflection

Seth, who was about ten years old and really big into wrestling, announced to me at supper, "You've got to take me to Wrestlemania tonight at the Civic Center. I've got tickets." I was caught off guard. "Your mother didn't tell me anything about taking you anywhere. I don't think...." Seth howled in protest. "But I've got tickets! Mom said I could go!" I was skeptical. "Well, there's nothing written on the instructions about...." Seth ran to his room screaming in agony. He wailed for an hour. Then, hearing nothing, I crept to his door and listened. Reverently, from within, came his desperate plea: "Dear God, please let me go to Wrestlemania. You said you'd do anything for me if I asked. Please." Well, what could I do? I took him. Randy Savage almost got the best of Hulk Hogan that night, but the Hulkster won in the end. He wasn't the only winner. Seth won, I won, and God won, too, because God always answers our prayers.

▶ Prayer

Is it true, Almighty God, that whatever we ask you in the name of Jesus, you will do for us? Your love is so great. Your mercy and kindness are beyond my understanding. Give me the grace, dear Lord, to have faith in your love. Teach me to always turn to you in my need.

▶ Action

What do you need the most in your life? Spend some time thinking how it will be when God provides it for you.

The Ascension of the Lord

Snakes Alive!

MARK 16:15–20

"Go into all the world and proclaim the good news. These signs will accompany you: using my name you will cast out demons; you will speak in tongues; you will pick up snakes in your hands, and if you drink a deadly thing, it will not harm you. And you will lay hands on the sick and they will recover."

▶ Reflection

A classmate from seminary tells the story of going to a prayer meeting in a rural part of the country where they practiced snake handling. Of course, he didn't know at the time that they were snake handlers. But as the meeting warmed up, out came the big box of snakes and they started passing them around. Talk about a crisis of faith! My friend said he ended up taking one because he was afraid that if he turned it down, they would've handed him two! While I don't think I could warm up to snake handling, I do think there is a certain faith that accompanies true believers. And that is that no matter what, the worst thing that could happen is that we die. And even if we die, we are one with Christ who is with God in heaven.

▶ Prayer

Dear Jesus, you ascended into heaven to be with God, yet you are always with us. That means that whether we live or die, you are with us, saving us and raising us up. Please, dear Lord, when I am afraid, remind me of your promise.

▶ Action

Call to mind the scariest thing you can think of. In this vision, what's the worst that could happen to you? In faith, what would happen?

Down the Drain

JOHN 16:29–33

"The hour is coming when you will scatter and leave me alone. Yet I am not alone because the Father is with me. I have said this to you so that in me you may have peace. In the world you face persecution. But take courage because I have conquered the world!"

▶ Reflection

Rosemary is an investment banker for a major insurance company. Her voice was a whisper over the phone: "I just lost sixty-four million dollars of the company's money!" "Yikes!" I whispered back. "Do you remember where you put it last?" "Don't be funny," she said. "It's down the drain. I'm glad Jesus loves me because I'm in *big* trouble with my boss right now. Say a prayer for me." I did. Rosemary is a real woman of faith. I guess you have to be when you throw around that kind of money. One thing is for sure: she's confident in the love of God. Jesus loved his friends beyond their weaknesses. The most fearful times of my life are when I think I have pushed God beyond the limits of divine love. But there are no limits to God's love. God's love is infinite, enduring the sins of the world.

▶ Prayer

You love me beyond my sins? O dear God, such love is beyond me. Yet, such love is my desire. Teach me to love as I am being loved. Allow me to join Jesus in conquering the world.

▶ Action

Think of the worst thing you ever did. God's love for you is greater than anything you can do, even the worst sin. Know that you are forgiven and that God still loves you and always will.

Tuesday of the Seventh Week of Easter

Pulling Teeth

JOHN 17:1–11

Jesus prayed, "Father, the hour has come; glorify your Son so that he may glorify you."

▶ Reflection

Have you ever tried getting people to be eucharistic ministers at church? Has anyone ever asked you to be a eucharistic minister? I tell you, it can be like pulling teeth. The standard answer I get from people is something like, "Oh, I couldn't do that. I'm not worthy." Well, I know that. And God knows that, too. There is a certain worldly value we carry around and, unfortunately, we apply it to God. We think that God is best glorified in people who are close to moral perfection. And when we fall short in some way, we think that somehow God is not glorified in us as much as in someone else who has it more together. But Jesus says that God is glorified in people who love each other and offer the same ongoing forgiveness to each other that God offers us. Jesus is glorified in his disciples because they will be at peace in him, even though they will have scattered and abandoned him. Living in the same love for each other, they will reveal the glory of God's love.

▶ Prayer

God of love, your new covenant of love is not like the old covenant of law. You give us your love, infinite, unconditional, ever present, greater than sin, greater than death. May we receive your love and give it freely to others.

▶ Action

Think of something you do for your church that you don't feel worthy to do. Imagine God wrapping it as a gift and giving it to you.

Wednesday of the Seventh Week of Easter

Chicken Heaven

JOHN 17:11–19

Jesus prayed, "And now I am no longer in the world, but my disciples are in the world as I come to you. Holy Father, protect them so that they may be one, as we are one."

"It is more blessed to give than to receive." (Acts 20:35)

▶ Reflection

The chicken died. Amanda had loved it as best she could. Even when it was no longer the cute little fuzzy yellow chick her well-meaning aunt bought her at the store for Easter, but had become a gawky, scraggly, adolescent hen, Amanda took care of it. She fed it and kept its water dish filled and cleaned its cage. She took it for walks in the back yard and even carried it about the neighborhood so her friends could pet it. But then one day it began to fail. Amanda's Dad figured there was something wrong with it, but Amanda thought it was just lonely for other chickens. On its last day, Amanda held it tenderly as it expired. "I know she's in chicken heaven now," Amanda said tearfully at its funeral. "She taught me how to love someone smaller and more helpless than I am. She was so special to me." I think caring for us is as good for God as caring for others is good for us.

▶ Prayer

O God, you care for us so. And you give us the poor and the lowly so that we, in turn, can also care. May we always find joy in doing your will and spreading your love on earth.

▶ Action

Spend some time and energy today caring for someone who needs your help. Know that you are being like God.

God In Us

JOHN 17:20–26

Jesus prayed, "My Father, the world does not know you, but I know you; and my disciples know that you sent me. I made your name known to them so that your love for me may be in them."

▶ Reflection

I went to the funeral of a friend recently. After communion, many people came forward to offer their remembrances of Dale and the contribution he made to their lives. Dale was the kind of guy who would give you the shirt off his back and was equally generous with his time and his energy. People saw a lot of God in him. St. Paul wrote in Galatians 2:19–20, "It is no longer I who live, but it is Christ who lives in me. And the life I now live is by faith in the Son of God, who loved me and gave himself for me." Our Lord Jesus Christ revealed a God who is so in love with us that he is willing to be crucified and die rather than be apart from us. This love of God is the Holy Spirit, the Lord and giver of life. When we accept this love, which forgives our sins and the sins of all the world, then the Holy Spirit lives in us.

▶ Prayer

Source of Love, from you comes the Spirit who forgives sin and raises us to eternal life. By the power of the Holy Spirit Jesus became a human being like us. He forgave sins and rescued people from death. Send your Spirit again upon the church so that we might continue.

▶ Action

Think of someone in your life who really needs forgiveness. Pray earnestly for that person and offer forgiveness from your heart.

Friday of the Seventh Week of Easter

All You Need

JOHN 21:15–19

When they had finished breakfast, Jesus said to Simon Peter, "Simon son of John, do you love me?" Peter answered, "Yes, Lord, you know that I love you." Jesus asked him three times, "Simon, do you love me?" And three times Peter responded, "Yes, Lord, I love you." Then Jesus told him, "Tend my sheep."

▶ Reflection

The apostle Peter was an ignorant fisherman from Galilee, and not a very good one. He had little to recommend him for appointment to a leadership position. His fierce loyalty to Jesus was diluted by a moral weakness, which, when the chips were down, caused him to bail out. The evidence of the gospel stories indicates that he emerged as the leader among the twelve not by any strength of character, but by force of personality. At the critical moment he faltered. But Jesus taught that the one who was forgiven much, loved much (see Luke 7:47). If the flock was to be tended, it would have to be by someone who loved much. Peter, forgiven a great deal, was the one for the job.

▶ Prayer

Dear Jesus, you showed us that the love of God is stronger than sin, stronger even than death. You offer this love to everyone. You forgive our sins and give us the power to set others free from sin. Please, Lord, may we always live in the freedom of your love and pour that love into others by our constant forgiveness.

▶ Action

Think for a moment of the greatest offense you ever committed against God. How does it feel to be completely forgiven?

Saturday of the Seventh Week of Easter

Rx Miracle

JOHN 21:20–25

Jesus did so many other things that if they were all written down, the world itself could not contain the books that would be written.

▶ **Reflection**

The doctor at the walk-in clinic quickly diagnosed my problem and wrote me a prescription. Then she asked if there was anything else I needed. "Sure," I said. "I'm a poor man and I was wondering if you could give me a break on the cost of this visit." She took back the prescription and said, "Then you don't want this. You'll faint when you see how much that costs." Then she went out into the main office and started poking around on the shelves. I closed my eyes and quickly said a little prayer. "O Jesus, help her find what she's looking for." She returned with a little box and handed it to me. "You're a Catholic priest, right?" I nodded my head. She said, "Well, you must really be connected, because this stuff is hardly ever on hand in the office. But it was there when I looked for it." I exclaimed joyfully, "I said a little prayer!" She said, "Well, it worked. Say one for me." This was just another one of the "many other things" Jesus did.

▶ **Prayer**

O God, send your Holy Spirit upon us at Pentecost. Give us the power to be the witnesses of your love throughout the world. You show us your mercy and kindness. Help us, dear Lord, to trust in you and always turn to you in our needs.

▶ **Action**

Open your journal or a notebook, or just take a piece of paper and write down all the answers to your prayers that you received this year.

Pentecost

Sin Destroyed

JOHN 20:19–23

On that first day of the week, Jesus came and said, "Peace be with you." Then he breathed on them and said to them, "Receive the Holy Spirit. Whose sins you forgive, they are forgiven; whose sins you hold bound, they are held bound."

▶ Reflection

The resurrection of Jesus won the victory over death. But how did he win the victory over sin? What mystical action broke the power of perdition forever? The answer is simple: he forgave it. Sin cannot hold up against forgiveness. It dissolves like smoke. It is the power of God's love and mercy brought to bear against evil. But we Catholics have so long associated the power of forgiveness with priests and the sacrament of reconciliation that we've forgotten that the Holy Spirit was "breathed" upon the whole church! The power to forgive sins is given to all. We inhale it with every breath we take, and in exhaling can speak words that forgive others or hold them bound. And it is in holding sins bound that we breathe life into evil. Held bound to our own sins, we experience death; holding others bound, we chain them to death as well. But sin cannot survive forgiveness; it is put to death.

▶ Prayer

Jesus, savior of the world, in dying you destroyed my death, in rising you restored my life. By your cross and resurrection, you have set me free. May I always share your gift of forgiveness with those in need.

▶ Action

Close your eyes and imagine Jesus standing before you. He breathes upon you. Breathe in. Imagine his Spirit in you, forgiving your sins.

Ordinary
Time

Monday of the First Week of the Year

The Two Kingdoms

MARK 1:14–20

After John was arrested, Jesus came to Galilee, proclaiming the good news of God, and saying, "The time is fulfilled, and the kingdom of God has come near; repent, and believe in the good news."

▶ Reflection

I like the oldies, and "Did You Ever Have to Make Up Your Mind" by the Lovin' Spoonful is one of my favorites. It speaks well of the dilemma faced by potential followers of Christ. The good news of Jesus is that the kingdom of God is at hand. The bad news, if you want to call it that, is that in order to enter the kingdom, you have to reject the world—and vice versa. You can only "Say yes to one, and leave the other behind." You can't have both. Essentially, Jesus tells people they must choose. The word "repent" simply means to: turn around, make a fundamental change. This is necessary because the kingdom is paradoxically opposed to the world. In the kingdom the last are first, the poor are blessed, the virgin is a mother, and to die is to live; the kingdom is coming but the world is passing away. One will end and the other will endure forever. So "you'd better go home, son, and make up your mind."

▶ Prayer

Thy kingdom come, Lord. Help me today to enter your kingdom in all the ways you will reveal to me. Help me to abandon this passing world and embrace the beauty and lasting joy of your kingdom.

▶ Action

How many ways will you encounter the kingdom today? Look for the doorways of poverty, humility, surrender, and reconciliation.

Tuesday of the First Week of the Year

Fix Instead of Kill

MARK 1:21–28

*A man with an unclean spirit cried, "What have you to do with us, Jesus of
Nazareth? Have you come to destroy us? I know who you are, the Holy One of
God!" Jesus rebuked him, saying, "Be silent, and come out of him!" The
unclean spirit convulsed the man and shouting, came out of him.*

▶ Reflection

Once again Larry left church feeling angry. He supported capital
punishment in his state, but the pastor had reiterated the bishop's call
to end the death penalty. "We need to rid our population of these
animals who victimize us and our children," he grumbled to his wife
Kathy as they got into the car. Larry then commenced the elaborate
starting ritual necessary to bring his old Chevy to life. He set the
choke, pumped the gas pedal twice and held it halfway, then hit the
starter. The worn out machine responded with a puny click and
nothing more. "Needs a new solenoid," he sighed. Then Kathy said,
"Honestly, Larry. You keep this old heap alive because you love it, and
so you fix whatever goes wrong with it. Don't you think God would
rather we fix the people he loves than kill them?"

▶ Prayer

O God, maker of all things, in your own image and likeness you have
created our human family. Yet sin has degraded us, some worse than
others. By your love, help us to restore what was lost.

▶ Action

Imagine what a condemned prisoner on death row would be like after
he or she was restored to wholeness.

Wednesday of the First Week of the Year

Our First Call

MARK 1:29–39

Early in the morning Jesus got up and went out to a deserted place to pray. Simon tracked him down and said, "Everyone is looking for you." He answered, "Let's go on to the neighboring towns, so I can proclaim the message there, too. That's what I came here to do."

▶ Reflection

It was difficult for Cindy at work. She wanted so much to do a good job and compete with the men at her level. She was the second woman ever to hold the position of assistant director in her company and she knew it would be a major accomplishment for her to break through the "glass ceiling" that kept her gender from entering the upper echelons of the industry. At home with her husband Frank, she expressed her frustration. Frank supported her one hundred percent, but cautioned her: "Remember when I got so stressed out trying to get that promotion? You reminded me why I was there in the first place: to be a light for others, like Jesus taught. That's your job too, babe. Let's both keep focused on our first call to be living witnesses of God's goodness." Cindy agreed, adding that being a woman in a man's world added another challenge: to show how a woman does things.

▶ Prayer

Dear God, you made me to know, love, and serve you in this world, to be a living sign of your saving grace. Help me today to always remember the purpose of my life.

▶ Action

Write down three ways you could be a witness to God today. Check each one off as you accomplish it.

Tanya's Broken Leg

MARK 1:40–45

A leper came to Jesus and begged him, "If you want to do so, you can make me clean." Moved with pity, Jesus reached out and touched the man, and said to him, "I want to heal you! Be made clean!"

▶ Reflection

"It's not that you need to be important in the eyes of the world," Tanya's dad told her as she lay in the hospital bed, her shattered leg held painfully in place by a contraption that could have passed for a medieval torture device. "God will definitely hear your prayers." "But does God even know who I am?" she whimpered pitifully. "Oh, God made you, baby. You're very special to God," Dad replied. She thought about that for a while and then said, "Dad?" He took her hand softly. "Yes, baby?" he replied. She said, "If God thinks I'm so special, why did he let me break my leg?" Dad paused thoughtfully. "I think God wanted you to score that goal, baby. The big girl wasn't supposed to tackle you from behind. That's against the rules. People break the rules, Tanya, and sometimes God's will isn't done. But God will heal your leg in time and make you an even better player. You'll see." And Tanya *did* see.

▶ Prayer

Merciful Lord, you fill me with healing goodness. Even when things go wrong, you are there to help me and heal me and restore me so I can take up life again. Keep me always faithful to your love.

▶ Action

Ask yourself, "Would it be God's will that I be run over by a train?" Yet, what would happen if you jumped in front of one?

Friday of the First Week of the Year

Forgiveness Is Possible

MARK 2:1–12

Some of the scribes were saying, "Only God can forgive sins." Jesus said to them, "Why do you question this? You must know that the Son of Man has authority on earth to forgive sins." Then he said to the paralytic, "Stand up and walk!" And he stood up and walked, and they were all amazed.

▶ Reflection

You can forgive sins. You have been given complete authority to forgive. That "Son of Man" title Jesus uses in the gospel stories refers to himself as a representative of all people, and any person as a member of the human race. Just as Jesus forgave in the name of God and demonstrated that forgiveness by healing the afflicted, so do we forgive in the name of the human race and demonstrate that forgiveness by our actions. But forgiveness rarely comes easy. Jesus agonized over his ultimate and eternal act of forgiveness and suffered through the process. So do we. Sometimes our forgiving comes through years of trying. But without the trying, it is not accomplished. And for us to walk with Jesus, we are called to forgive as we have been forgiven.

▶ Prayer

Our Father in heaven: forgive us as we forgive one another. Give me the grace and mercy I need today to share your love with others by forgiving them as you have forgiven me.

▶ Action

At the end of this day, make a list of all the people who needed your forgiveness and check the ones who actually got it. How did you do?

Saturday of the First Week of the Year

In Love with a Sinner

MARK 2:13–17

The Pharisees asked the disciples, "Why does he eat with tax collectors and sinners?" When Jesus heard this, he said to them, "Those who are healthy don't need a doctor, but those who are sick do. I have come to call not the righteous but sinners."

▶ Reflection

It took me a long time to realize that God was calling me to close relationship. I grew up Catholic in the forties and fifties and, like a lot of people, got the idea that God likes you when you're good and doesn't when you're bad. So, being pretty much a sinner from my youth, I didn't think I had any kind of a chance with God. At the first opportunity I stopped going to church and assumed that was that. I figured I'd take my chances with the hereafter when the time came. But God's call was relentless. It wasn't until I was thirty years old that it dawned on me that the Lord was offering me friendship. I thought, "Why me? I'm a sinner." It seemed God was replying, "Yes, I know. That's why I want you. I've loved you all these years but you hardly know me." I've spent the time since then getting to know this God revealed in Jesus. What a loving God I have discovered!

▶ Prayer

God of love, your goodness and mercy are beyond me, are more than I can understand. I know only that Jesus rejected no one and offered your kindness and compassion to all. Help me always to believe.

▶ Action

Write down all the reasons why God should *not* love you, then tear them up and throw them away. In God's eyes, they don't exist.

Monday of the Second Week of the Year

New Wine

MARK 2:18–22

The Pharisees asked Jesus, "Why do John's disciples fast, but yours don't?" Jesus said, "You don't patch an old shirt with pieces from a new one. Neither do you put new wine into old bottles. You put new wine into new bottles."

▶ Reflection

"Let me get this straight:" Don was attending the RCIA inquiry so he could learn a little something about Christianity. "In the Old Testament, if you followed the commandments, God blessed you. And if you sinned and broke the commandments, God punished you. Right?" Yeah, that's about it. "Well, who punishes you in the New Testament? Jesus?" No, in the New Testament Jesus forgives you. "Oh." Don was a very thoughtful inquirer. "Well then, how do you keep people from sinning?" You don't. The Holy Spirit transforms people and makes them into new creations bent on virtue, not sin. "Oh." Again Don thought. "Really? That's different from what you usually hear." Yes it is. There's a part of "new" that some people just don't understand. To really be a Christian, you have to take on a whole new way of thinking.

▶ Prayer

Lord, you have revealed your ultimate plan of salvation through Jesus Christ. He gave up his body and poured out his blood for the sins of all the world. Help me to live his victory over sin and death.

▶ Action

Look up the blessings and curses of the law in Deuteronomy 28. Compare this with 2 Corinthians 5:17–21.

Tuesday of the Second Week of the Year

Challenged by Freedom

MARK 2:23–28

It was the Sabbath and Jesus led his disciples into the fields where they picked grain to eat. The Pharisees said to him, "What you are doing is not lawful on the sabbath." He replied, "The sabbath was made for people, and not people for the sabbath."

▶ Reflection

The sabbath law referred to in the gospel was Exodus 20:8–11, the third commandment. The interpretation of the time did indeed forbid what Jesus and his disciples were doing. But Jesus introduced a whole new way of understanding the Scripture and the religious authority. He recognized that God's purpose was always love. Love, specifically love for people, was the beginning and end of all God did. Once a person recognizes the love of God in all things and can respond from the same foundation of love, that person transcends law and religious authority. He or she becomes "lord of the sabbath." Rather than break the law, which he most certainly did in the eyes of the religious authorities, Jesus went beyond the law and invited his disciples to follow. Human authority always seeks power over others, while the authority of God's love always serves others in freedom.

▶ Prayer

Lord, by your cross and resurrection you have set us free! You have shown us the way of God's love, which brings us peace and heals our souls. Help us always to serve others in peace.

▶ Action

If you were hungry and Jesus offered you a cheeseburger on a Friday in Lent, what would you do?

Wednesday of the Second Week of the Year

WWJD?

MARK 3:1–6

Jesus said to Pharisees, "Is it lawful to do good or harm on the sabbath, to save or to kill?" But they were silent. That angered him and he was grieved at their hardness of heart. Then he healed the man with the withered hand. So the Pharisees conspired to kill him.

▶ Reflection

Father Al was at the end of his rope. Tony and Nita were desperate to return to communion, but Tony had a former marriage that the church just wouldn't annul. Al had tried every avenue, but the tribunal was unrelenting. It seemed to Tony and Nita that their thirty-six years of marriage and service to their parish counted for nothing. Now that their granddaughter was receiving first communion, they really felt it necessary to join her in the sacrament. Al agreed, but the church said no. Al asked his pastor, Msgr. Fregeau, about it. "Have you considered the 'internal forum solution'?" the wise old priest asked. "But I thought we weren't supposed to use that," Al replied. The Monsignor chuckled. "We're not," he said. "I just asked if you considered it. Sometimes, Al, you've got to use the WWJD approach; and ask yourself: what would Jesus do?"

▶ Prayer

O my God, you overwhelm me with your love. Your trust in me is greater than I deserve, yet your Spirit moves me to live in the light of your truth and to walk in your ways. What freedom you give me!

▶ Action

If you were suddenly made pope, what things about the church would you change? What do you imagine Jesus would think about that?

Thursday of the Second Week of the Year

Demons Are Like Klingons

MARK 3:7–12

All who had diseases pressed upon Jesus to touch him. Whenever the unclean spirits saw him, they fell down before him and shouted, "You are the Son of God!" But he sternly ordered them not to make him known.

▶ Reflection

Jesus didn't want the demons to make him known because he knew the demons! Evil will always try to subvert the truth. They're like the Klingons in Star Trek: you can never trust the demons, even if they're making Jesus known. We only need to look back over two thousand years of Christian history and see some of the evil that has been done in the name of Jesus. In just the past decade the pope has apologized for the way the church treated the Jews and admitted the church's error in the infamous seventeenth-century prosecution of Galileo. Are there emotionally and mentally disturbed teachers of the faith and preachers of the gospel making Jesus known today? I would answer with an unqualified yes. That's why it is important that individual Christians take responsibility for knowing the gospel of our Lord Jesus Christ and the traditions of church teaching.

▶ Prayer

You have given me a Spirit that witnesses to the truth, O God. You have placed your law in my heart and enlightened my path with your love. May I be the sheep who always knows the shepherd's voice.

▶ Action

Have you ever heard something at church that you thought was just plain wrong? Call a trusted priest and find out for sure.

Friday of the Second Week of the Year

You're Choosing These?

MARK 3:13–19

He went up the mountain and called to him those whom he wanted, and they came to him. He appointed the twelve, whom he also named apostles, to be with him, and to be sent out to proclaim the message.

▶ Reflection

Whom did Jesus want with him? And to whom did he entrust the mission of proclaiming the message of the gospel that would change the history of the world? For starters, a very unsuccessful fisherman; you may recall from the other gospel stories that when Peter caught a fish, it was a miracle! James and John, two other less than stellar fishermen, were two brothers who argued about which one was greater. There was the cynic, Nathanael; the skeptic, Thomas; the political radical, Simon the Zealot; Matthew, who sold out to the enemy and collected taxes for the Romans; Jude, who became the patron of lost causes (I wonder why!); and of course Judas, who was known to be a thief, who would steal from the group's communal funds, and who would eventually turn Jesus in. This is the foundation of our apostolic church. It is obvious from this that Jesus had a profound trust in the power of the gospel to transform human lives.

▶ Prayer

When I look at my life, Lord, I wonder how I am going to accomplish any good in this world. Then I remember that you are with me, changing the water of my life into the wine of your kingdom.

▶ Action

At the beginning of the day, consider what you are called to be as a Christian in the world. Ask God for the grace to make it so.

Not Crazy

MARK 3:20–21

At that time such a crowd came together that they could no longer even eat. When Jesus' family heard about all this, they went out to try and take charge of him because people were saying, "He has gone out of his mind."

▶ Reflection

"I'm sick of people saying I'm crazy. I'm *not* crazy!" Arnie was venting to his psychotherapist. The shrink replied, "Well, Arnie, you *are* a little neurotic." Arnie laughed. "*Everybody's* a little neurotic. But that's not the same thing as crazy. I'm just different. I see things differently; I want different things; I live differently than other people do. I'm normal, but just in a different way." Arnie may not know it, but he has a lot in common with Jesus. John the Baptist was said to be crazy, too (see Matthew 11:18). What passes as "normal" is often just what the majority settles for: safe, secure lives that fulfill expectations and provoke little controversy. To respond to passion and detect "call" and live by spirit is not what others do; it will not be seen as "normal." It will not necessarily gain approval, not even from one's own family. One must live so for God alone.

▶ Prayer

Lord, you have called me by name. I know it; I can feel it. Your Spirit is within me, giving me the life and energy to follow. People may think I'm crazy. (Sometimes *I* think I'm crazy!) But I will follow.

▶ Action

Take the opportunity to do three things today that others don't do, that mark you as a follower of Jesus. Celebrate them with gladness.

Monday of the Third Week of the Year

The Unforgivable Sin

MARK 3:22–30

The scribes said, "He casts out demons by Beelzebub." Jesus replied, "No one can plunder a strong man's house without first tying up the strong man. Truly I tell you, people will be forgiven for their sins and whatever blasphemies they utter; but whoever blasphemes against the Holy Spirit can never receive forgiveness, but is eternally guilty."

▶ Reflection

Sometimes people ask, "But if all I do is forgive people, won't I be letting them off the hook and just giving my permission for them to do wrong again?" The question presents the possibility that by doing right (forgiving) we might be doing something wrong (assenting to sin.) This is the classic Catch-22 of moral thinking. In other words, it's the sin against the Holy Spirit. Rejecting forgiveness rejects forgiveness, so how can it be forgiven? We need always remember that the kingdom of God is a paradox. In it, the last are first and the first are last. The blind see, the lame walk, the deaf hear, and the virgin is the mother. As it says in Mary's song, the Magnificat, the weak win the victory over the strong. So it looks to worldly minded people that Jesus is doing something wrong.

▶ Prayer

O Jesus, you forgive all my sins. That makes my heart so glad. It makes me cry when I think of how much you love me. Please, I want your love to transform me and make me a better person.

▶ Action

Don't let go of God's love today. No matter what happens, no matter how much your sinfulness manifests itself, trust in God's love.

Tuesday of the Third Week of the Year

New Family

MARK 3:31–35

The crowd said to Jesus, "Your mother and your brothers and sisters are outside asking for you." He replied, "Who are my mother and my brothers?" And looking at those who sat around him he said, "Here are my mother and my brothers! Whoever does the will of God is my brother and sister and mother."

▶ Reflection

Back in Mark 3:21 we heard that the family of Jesus was coming to get him because people were saying that he was out of his mind. In today's gospel, they arrive. Despite the images of family harmony we like to present at this time of year, the Bible paints a somewhat different picture of the interplay between Jesus and his relatives. Rather than affirm his relationship with his mother and siblings, Jesus takes the occasion to distance himself from them, preferring instead the company of his followers. Blood may be thicker than water, but spirit rises above blood. New life in Christ includes a new family. Those born again of water and the Holy Spirit discover a whole new world of parents, sisters and brothers, bound by a spirit of love that transcends kinship.

▶ Prayer

O Lord, you give me parents and a family to birth me and raise me and protect me while I'm a child. But when I'm grown, you offer me a new family, a heavenly father and mother. Thank you, Lord.

▶ Action

Consider your father and mother, and consider God and Mary. As good as your parents may be, maybe there's something better.

Silly Farmer

MARK 4:1–20

Jesus taught them a parable: "A sower went out to sow. Some seed fell on the path and the birds ate it up. Some fell on rocky ground where it sprang up quickly, but was scorched because it had no root. Some fell among thorns, which grew up and choked it. And some fell on good soil and yielded grain, thirty and sixty and a hundredfold."

▶ Reflection

In a primitive agrarian culture like that of first-century Palestine, the farming images Jesus used to convey the meaning of the kingdom would have been easily understood. But because Jesus taught using parables, his agricultural stories always had a few twists to them. In this case, the farmer's sowing style is a little unorthodox. He does nothing to prepare the ground, opting rather to simply spread the seed with no concern for where it lands. The farmer's confidence was not in the quality of the ground that received the seed, but in the potential of the seed to produce more than enough from good ground to make up for that which fell into unsuitable areas. In his subsequent explanation, Jesus makes it clear that we are in charge of how our "ground" receives the seed.

▶ Prayer

How you trust in the seed of your word, O loving God! Yet, within me I see how much has grown from its planting. So powerful is your word; by it I am transformed. Keep me near to your word.

▶ Action

Put some soil in a dish, dampen it with water, drop a seed in it, and place it on a window sill. Watch it every day.

Thursday of the Third Week of the Year

David's Measure

MARK 4:21–25

Jesus said to them, "Is a lamp brought in to be put under the bushel basket, or under the bed, and not on the lampstand? For there is nothing hidden, except to be disclosed; nor is anything secret, except to come to light. Pay attention to what you hear: the measure you give will be the measure you get."

▶ Reflection

King David of the Old Testament was a very imperfect person. He was an adulterer and a murderer. Yet God favored him and bestowed blessings in abundance one him. David didn't escape his sinfulness; he paid the price (see 2 Sam 12:15–19, 24:10ff). Still, the Lord put a light in David and he let it shine. He was a great leader, a military commander, a poet, and a composer. But most of all David was a man of prayer. His relationship with God was born of a humble spirit and nurtured by a truthful heart. God puts a light in everybody. It is the truth of who we are, who God created us to be. Prayer keeps us in touch with God, with the way that leads to God's blessings and the house God builds for each one of us. With such wealth in our lives, our measure of giving can be great.

▶ Prayer

Your love in me was hidden for so long, my God, but in time you brought it out and now I am a sign of your love for others. May I always be a living witness of your saving love.

▶ Action

Go beyond the normal measure of your love today and give love in abundance. Give of yourself as much as you can and see how it feels.

Friday of the Third Week of the Year

Big Tree

MARK 4:26–34

"The kingdom of God is as if someone scatters seed on the ground. Then day after day the seed sprouts and grows, but he does not know how it happens. The earth seems to produce of itself, first the stalk, then the head, then the fullness of the wheat. But when the grain is ripe, he wields the sickle because the harvest is ready."

▶ Reflection

In a 1998 interview on the PBS TV show *Frontline* called "Angel on Death Row," Sr. Helen Prejean, CSJ, author of the monumental book *Dead Man Walking*, remembered the moment she saw a spark of compassion in the brutal, remorseless murderer facing execution on death row. "And boy I latched on to that," she recalled. "I knew that was a little part of his soul." Sr. Helen looked on a barren field with eyes of faith and saw the kingdom of God. In a word or gesture no bigger than a mustard seed, she could see a spreading shade tree in which birds could make their homes. Our Lord invites us all to look upon all in our world with such faith. God knows the seed of goodness is in even the most despicable criminal or hated enemy, because God put it there.

▶ Prayer

Sometimes I am a barren field, Lord, but you have placed the seed of your love in my heart and you know that in time it will bring forth fruit. May I always love others as you have loved me.

▶ Action

Today you will need to be patient with someone because his or her seed is not yet grown. Evaluate how well you do.

God in My Boat

MARK 4:35–41

A great storm arose and the boat was being swamped. But Jesus remained asleep on a cushion. They woke him and said, "Teacher, do you not care that we are perishing?" He woke up and rebuked the wind, and said to the sea, "Peace! Be still!" The wind ceased and all was calm. Then he said, "Why were you afraid? Have you no faith?"

▶ Reflection

Sometimes in the midst of the storms of my life, my little boat begins to sink and I wonder why God doesn't seem to care. As usual, I get it wrong. God is not the problem; it's my understanding of God that needs an upgrade. God is the creator who loves me. That means God is always working to bring about what is best for me out of a profound and infinite love for me. That doesn't mean there won't be storms. After all, weather is what makes life possible, and life, because it is so manifold and complex, sometimes looks to be a little crazy. But when the craziness of life seems to be overwhelming, God is still with me, loving me and creating a future that will save me. This is true whether I believe it or not. I just need to believe it and live according to that belief.

▶ Prayer

O my God, you hold the whole world in your hands and order life in such a way that it always benefits your beloved. In your love for me, keep me safe from all harm and help me to believe in your love.

▶ Action

Think back to the worst time you ever had in your life and trace the way God led you out of it.

Monday of the Fourth Week of the Year

Whacking Swine

MARK 5:1–20

Jesus met a man with an unclean spirit. Night and day the man would howl among the tombs and bruise himself with stones. Jesus asked him, "What is your name?" He replied, "My name is Legion, for we are many." Jesus sent the spirits into a herd of swine, which ran off a cliff and drowned themselves in the sea.

▶ Reflection

As if to demonstrate his parables of the empty field and the mustard seed, Jesus encounters a truly hideous person. Mark, who writes the shortest gospel, is uncharacteristically wordy in describing the afflictions of this loathsome individual. Try to imagine someone so horrible and revolting as the man in this story. Yet Jesus looked upon him with compassion. What did Jesus see in him? A brother? Maybe he saw him as a fellow traveler in human form, weak like himself, distinguished only by degree. At any rate, he drew from him what was good and sent the rest away. The people of the village reacted negatively because what Jesus did upset their understanding of how things work—to say nothing of the loss of a valuable herd of swine. But a life had been saved!

▶ Prayer

You have created all things, my God, and have made humanity in your own image and likeness. Open my eyes to see your identity impressed on even the lowliest of my sisters and brothers.

▶ Action

Look for a truly despicable person today and try at least to image how God would be present in that person.

Tuesday of the Fourth Week of the Year

Arise! Be Free!

MARK 5:21–43

She came up behind him and touched his cloak, for she thought, "If I but touch his clothes, I will be made well." And immediately she felt in her body that she was healed. Then he went in where the child was. He took her by the hand and said to her, "Little girl, get up!" And immediately the girl got up. They were overcome with amazement.

▶ Reflection

In the anthropology of first-century Palestine, there was no one lower on the cultural scale than a little girl. She possessed no social value; she was, in fact, a bit of a liability because she would have to be married sooner or later and that would cost money. Being sick diminished her value further. Being dead…well, she was off the scale. And the woman with a hemorrhage was equally valueless. Religious superstitions and the prejudices of a male-dominated society completely marginalized her. In both cases, there was nothing that could be done. Into this hopeless situation steps Jesus. With the powerful words spoken by our Lord, "Arise!" and "Be free!" he reestablished the status of the sick, the lowly, the powerless, and the female for all time.

▶ Prayer

As much as you are Father, O God, so you are Mother as well, for male and female are the expressions of your image and likeness. Help me always to celebrate your presence in the weak and the lowly.

▶ Action

Just as we imagine God as an old man with a gray beard, spend some time today imagining God as a young woman, lovely and lively.

Wednesday of the Fourth Week of the Year

Missing the Familiar

MARK 6:1–6

Then Jesus said to them, "Prophets are not without honor, except in their hometown, and among their own kin, and in their own house." He could do no deed of power there, except that he laid his hands on a few sick people and cured them, so amazed was he at their unbelief.

▶ Reflection

"The church should do more to promote belief in the Real Presence of Christ in the Eucharist," Tom pronounced over dinner. He had a particular awareness of God dwelling within him, and he genuinely wanted to share the joy of this experience, and its power, with others. The only concrete experience of this reality he knew was the Eucharist, the outward sign of the inward mystery, and he felt more should be done to teach about it. "But, Tom," his dinner companion objected, "Listen to the Eucharistic Prayer. It says it all." Of course! How could Tom have missed something so obvious? We are so familiar with the prayer we hear every Sunday that we sometimes forget to listen to it. The words are there. So powerfully do they speak of the mystery we celebrate that they actually make the presence of Christ real for the assembly. We just need to pay attention.

▶ Prayer

You constantly reveal yourself in all creation, my Lord, and the world sings of your presence. Help me today to discover you in the ordinary and familiar of my life. May I see your face at every turn.

▶ Action

If you can, set your watch to signal you every hour of the day. When you hear the beep, look for God in whatever surrounds you.

Thursday of the Fourth Week of the Year

Making Room

MARK 6:7–13

Jesus sent out the Twelve giving them authority over unclean spirits. He told them to take nothing for the journey but a walking stick—no food, no sack, no money in their belts. So they went off and drove out many demons, and anointed the sick and cured them.

▶ Reflection

All things of this world have their finite limits, and our pockets are no exception. Filled with worldly wealth, there is no room for the gift of God. Jesus sent the disciples on a mission to bring God's kingdom to bear on the people of a passing world. They were to carry with them the wealth of God's grace and nothing more: no luggage, no hotel reservations, and no per diem. Without security of any kind, they were to rely completely on God's ability to create a world that would receive them and care for them. What if they were to hedge and bring along enough money to cover their expenses? Would it have crowded out a component of grace necessary to work many cures? Possibly. Look around today and see what wealth, comfort, and a well-stocked pantry have done for the apostolic church. When's the last time you saw a present-day apostle work a cure?

▶ Prayer

Build my faith, O precious savior, so that I may put my trust in you alone. Wealth, security, and comfort are a constant attraction to me. May the help of your grace be always sufficient for me.

▶ Action

Make a list of three things you believe you simply have to have in order to be fulfilled and happy. Could God do better for you?

Friday of the Fourth Week of the Year

Where's the Power?

MARK 6:14–29

People were saying of Jesus, "John the Baptist has been raised from the dead; that is why mighty powers are at work in him." Even when King Herod learned of it, he said, "It is John whom I beheaded. He has been raised up."

▶ Reflection

The information technology of Jesus' day was word of mouth. There was no television, no radio, no newspaper, no Internet, no FAX; there were no pictures to show. So when people heard about Jesus, they were ready to believe that it was probably John the Baptist (see Matthew 14:2, 16:14; Mark 6:14, 8:28; Luke 9:19; John 1:8, 19–20). Could it be because John just made more sense to them? John was a teacher of the covenant law given to Moses, and he was relentless in its application. He stood before King Herod, the most powerful man in Israel, declared he was living in a way that was not right, and it cost him his freedom and his life. Jesus, on the other hand, simply forgave people. It was inconceivable to the people of his day how there could be any power at all in forgiveness. So when they heard of the miracle worker, they assumed it was John. But there *was* power in forgiveness, the power to heal (see Mark 2:1–12).

▶ Prayer

Lord, you have forgiven all my sins. You have set me free from mortal fear and killing guilt. You have made me whole.

▶ Action

Today you will have at least one opportunity to forgive rather than condemn. See if you can discover the divine power in forgiveness.

Saturday of the Fourth Week of the Year

Friends and Strangers

MARK 6:30–34

The apostles returned to Jesus and he said to them, "Come away and rest a while." People saw them leaving and many hastened on foot from all the towns and arrived at the place before them. When he saw the vast crowd, his heart was moved with pity, for they were like sheep without a shepherd. So he began to teach them many things.

▶ Reflection

I think of the friends that I enjoy, their company, and the adventures we share. I remember once, after a wedding, a group of us rented a van and drove up the coast for a few days, visiting out of the way places of great natural beauty and just being together. It was a delight! I would run off with good friends at the drop of a hat. But would I do the same thing with strangers? Not likely. It is just such an amazing scene that Mark paints of Jesus in this story. With great care for his closest, most intimate friends, he goes away with them for rest and relaxation after an exhausting mission. When total strangers show up, he has the same concern for them, caring for their needs and sharing with them the same treasures of wisdom, knowledge, and understanding he shares with his closest friends. How about that?

▶ Prayer

O my God, how good you are to the least and the greatest! Those far from you enjoy the same favor as those close to you, because you are always there for those who turn to you. Thank you for your love.

▶ Action

Write down the name of the person you think is closest to God, then the name of the one who's farthest away. Consider where you fit in.

Monday of the Fifth Week of the Year

God's Got Freebies!

MARK 6:53–56

People recognized Jesus and scurried about the surrounding country bringing in the sick on mats to wherever he was. In whatever villages or towns or countryside he entered, they laid the sick in the marketplaces and begged him that they might touch only the tassel of his cloak; and as many as touched it were healed.

▶ Reflection

Hat Day, Bat Day, whenever the local sports stadium has a giveaway, people come. The same is true for our church. Celebrations like Ash Wednesday, Palm Sunday, and the feast of St. Blaise hold special appeal because there are "goodies" to be had, something anybody can get no matter what be the marriage situation or the last time one's gone to confession. We can cop an attitude here and say they just come to get something, but isn't that why God gives? As soon as people heard Jesus was in town, they didn't stop to praise and thank him. Nor were they concerned to get their lives in order so they could go out to meet him. They simply gathered their sick and brought them to him. And he received them, curing them all, no obligation, no purchase necessary. God's grace is free.

▶ Prayer

What I need most from you, my God, is absolutely free. Your grace flows like water, like abundant wine for my pleasure and well-being. Lord, may I reflect this same grace to all the people I meet today.

▶ Action

What is the one thing you would like most in your life? How much would you pay for it? Consider getting it from God for nothing.

Pius or Practical?

MARK 7:1–13

The Pharisees observed that some of the disciples ate their meals without washing their hands. So they questioned Jesus, "Why do your disciples not follow the tradition of the elders but instead eat with unclean hands?" He responded, "You hypocrites! You disregard God's commandment but cling to a mere human tradition!"

▶ Reflection

"Oh, Father," gushed the woman after Mass. "I just love it that you wear the cincture. It's so pious and it means so much to me." She was, of course, referring to that simple rope we priests sometimes wear around our middles to gather our albs or contain our stoles for Mass. In my case, I wasn't trying to be pious; as the "weekend guy" helping out on Sundays at a nearby parish, I didn't always have my own alb with me and the one I was wearing was a little long. The cincture kept it from getting under my feet so I wouldn't do a nosedive down the altar steps, a move having no liturgical grace whatsoever. But the significance of the gird was important to the woman and I thanked her, wondering if she'll consider me less pious next week when I don't wear one.

▶ Prayer

O Lord, I love the religion you have given me. But I know that sometimes I can put religion ahead of the love you pour out for all people. Help me always to recognize that my first duty is to love.

▶ Action

Someone today will violate a code of civility or offend you in some way by being rude or irreverent. See how quickly you can forgive.

Wednesday of the Fifth Week of the Year

Source of Evil

MARK 7:14–23

He said to them, "Are even you likewise without understanding? Do you not realize that everything that goes into a person from outside cannot defile, since it enters not the heart but the stomach and passes out into the latrine? All evils come from within and they defile."

▶ Reflection

The lack of scientific sophistication in the 2000-year-old text of Mark's gospel is evident in this passage. There was, of course, no knowledge of germs in the time of Jesus. That discovery was eons away. But there was a primitive awareness of the connection between what you touch with your hands and what you put in your mouth. The trouble was, good sense hygiene had evolved into religious rituals that set God up as the bad guy who made you sick if you didn't wash your hands before eating. That may appeal to my aunt Tillie, but Jesus rejected it out of hand and pointed to the real source of evil in the world. God does not inflict bad things on you; you inflict them on yourself. Now you march right back to the sink and wash those hands before you eat.

▶ Prayer

My Father, you made me to be in harmony with the world you created for me. I know I eat some pretty strange things, but you keep me safe. Help me not put evil things into your world.

▶ Action

At the end of this day, write down three evils that came out of you into the world. Ask God to help you contain them next time.

Divinity Within

MARK 7:24–30

A Syrophoenician woman begged Jesus to drive the demon out of her daughter. He said to her, "It is not right to take the food of the children and throw it to the dogs." She said to him, "Lord, even the dogs under the table eat the children's scraps." Then he said, "For saying this, you may go. The demon has gone out." The woman went home and found the child in bed and the demon gone.

▶ Reflection

In the divine act of creation, God favored the human race with qualities that distinguished it from all other animals. Along with high intellect and a capacity to reason, humans can recognize and appreciate attributes of humor, wisdom, poetry, sarcasm, and irony, among others. This constellation of capacities may have led the earliest theologians responsible for the Genesis story to conclude that humans were made in God's own image and likeness. Perhaps it was a collection of these subtle qualities in the Syrophoenician that made Jesus take notice that there was more going on here than an encounter with one of the historical chumps of Israel's story. She challenges him with wit and irony and he discovers a sister in need.

▶ Prayer

In every creature you put value, O Lord, even beyond my ability to know. Help me to see your handiwork in every person. Make me a living channel of your saving love.

▶ Action

Consider someone whose race, ethnicity, or religion makes him or her less than likable to you. Spend time praying for that person.

Friday of the Fifth Week of the Year

Strange and Bizarre

MARK 7:31–37

They brought to him a deaf man who had a speech impediment and begged him to lay his hand on him. He took the man off by himself, put his finger into his ears, and spitting, touched his tongue; then he looked up to heaven and groaned, and said "Ephphatha!" ("Be opened!") The man's ears were opened and he spoke plainly. Then Jesus ordered them not to tell anyone.

▶ Reflection

An old seminary classmate wrote his diocesan newspaper recently about the scourge of demon Pokémon. He claimed that Ash, Pikachu, and all their little friends are just dupes of the devil and parents should be protecting their children from them. That strikes me as being a little over the top. Jesus didn't seem to have a problem with strange rituals and bizarre incantations. When in Rome—or in this story's case the Decapolis—do as the Decapoleans do. The formula Jesus used, perhaps familiar to the locals, connected the man to his faith and effected a cure. But there is no evidence that it was in keeping with Jewish custom. He would probably have gotten in trouble for it then, as he most certainly would today. No wonder he didn't want them to tell anybody!

▶ Prayer

Thank you, Lord, for revealing your love to people of every race, language, and religion. Help me to accept the strangeness of others.

▶ Action

Think of the strangest religious ritual you ever saw. Make an attempt to understand how God works to love people through this ritual.

Saturday of the Fifth Week of the Year

Without Blame

MARK 8:1–10

There was a great crowd without anything to eat, so Jesus said, "My heart is moved with pity for the crowd, because they have been with me now for three days and have nothing to eat. If I send them away hungry to their homes, they will collapse on the way, and some of them have come a great distance."

▶ Reflection

This is the well-known story of the multiplication of the loaves. Because of the components of bread and the narrative of taking, blessing, breaking, and distributing, and the dismissal at the end, the story has an obvious eucharistic significance. But what can sometimes become lost in the powerful symbolism is the simple humility of Jesus, who was genuinely concerned for the welfare of the people, even though their predicament was the result of their own failure to prepare for the obvious. Sometimes I'm tempted to have less compassion for one who is the victim of his own folly. But Jesus just wanted to serve a need, regardless of whose fault it was. When I care for the needy like Jesus did, I step into the power of the kingdom, where a little can go a long way.

▶ Prayer

O Lord, your love reaches beyond blame and you care for those who should know better than to get themselves in trouble. Lead me to the purity of your love so that I may be a sign of your kingdom.

▶ Action

Help someone today just for the sake of helping. Listen to yourself judge, but step beyond the judgment.

Monday of the Sixth Week of the Year

Faith Is Great

MARK 8:11–13

The Pharisees came and began to argue with him, asking him for a sign from heaven, in order to test him. And he sighed deeply in his spirit and said, "Why does this generation ask for a sign? Truly I tell you, no sign will be given to this generation." And he left them, and getting into the boat again, he went across to the other side.

▶ Reflection

While Jesus was annoyed at the Pharisees for trying to test him, his question has an answer. We look for outward signs, things we can see, to speak to us of inward realities, things we can't see. That's why our church celebrates sacraments. They are the signs of Christ's presence among us and within us. But somewhere along the line we have to accept God at face value, even though God isn't showing a face. It would be nice if we got signs and wonders to verify every impulse and inkling; just wait for a shaft o' light to show us the way. But that would preclude faith, wouldn't it? And for the adventuresome, it would certainly take the fun out of it. No, God calls us to trust. God whips up a creation that will accommodate an infinite number of choices. Our job is to choose. Then God has something to go on in order to create a future that will accommodate our choices.

▶ Prayer

God of the universe, in this moment of time you create infinity so that I may step boldly into the next moment, confident of your presence. Help me to choose the way of my Lord, Jesus Christ.

▶ Action

Carry a pebble in your pocket today to remind you that God is always with you no matter where you go or what you do.

Tuesday of the Sixth Week of the Year

Beyond Imagining

MARK 8:14–21

The disciples had forgotten to bring any bread. When Jesus said, "Beware of the yeast of the Pharisees and the yeast of Herod," they said to one another, "It is because we have no bread." Becoming aware of it, Jesus said to them, "Why are you talking about having no bread? Do you still not perceive or understand?"

▶ **Reflection**

Jesus asks his stupefied disciples, "Do you still not understand?" You can almost hear them reply, "Understand what?" You see, Jesus made a remark about yeast and they presumed he was mad at them because they forgot to bring bread. The Lord's continued disappointment with his disciples reveals in some way God's ongoing frustration with us. We think that somehow we are supposed to do something for God and we get anxious when we don't accomplish anything because we think somehow that God is going to be mad at us. Yet God is revealed as the one who wants to do something for us; who sacrificed his only begotten Son to save us from the wrath. Doesn't that count for anything? The call here is to stop worrying about what we do for God and start trusting in what God wants to do for us.

▶ **Prayer**

Your Spirit fills me and gives me life, my God. You direct creation to serve my needs, yet my desire is to serve you. In our love for each other, protect me from anxiety and faithlessness.

▶ **Action**

At the end of the day, ask yourself, "In what way have I failed God today?" Decide if Jesus would accept the answer.

Wednesday of the Sixth Week of the Year

Big Secret

MARK 8:22–26

They brought a blind man to Jesus and begged him to touch him. So he led the man by the hand out of the village. Then he put saliva on his eyes and laid his hands on him and the man's sight was restored. After that he sent him away, saying, "Do not even go back into the village."

▶ Reflection

It's not hard to guess why the thing with the spittle never made it into the healing rituals of Christianity. Somehow putting saliva on people, even the divine spit of the Lord, is a little too much for most folks to swallow. Maybe that's why Jesus didn't want the man to even go back into the village where he would be sure to spread the news. Like the man Jesus cured with strange rituals and incantations in Mark 7:31–37, this man is instructed not to reveal what scholars have called "the messianic secret." The secret is that Jesus is the presence of God's kingdom apart from any religious rite or ritual. It is not a matter of getting the words right or showing up at the correct building. The gift of God comes where it is needed and we receive it through faith.

▶ Prayer

Dear Lord, your love makes you present in all the moments and actions of my life. You insist on no "right" way of worship, yet you are revealed in the rituals of religion. Thank you for your goodness.

▶ Action

Take an inventory of all the different ways people worship God in your life. Reflect on how God is revealed to them.

Thursday of the Sixth Week of the Year

Paradox of Power

MARK 8:27–33

Jesus asked his disciples, "Who do people say that I am?" They answered him, "John the Baptist." But Peter said, "You are the Messiah." Then Jesus told them that he had to suffer and be killed. Peter began to rebuke him, but Jesus said, "Get behind me, Satan! You are setting your mind not on divine things but on human things."

▶ Reflection

Success is always measured in worldly terms. That's why most people thought Jesus was John the Baptist. John enjoyed a large following. He preached a message that made sense to people: God rewards the good and punishes the bad. So when people heard of the miracles Jesus was performing, they figured it must be John bringing God's reward to all the good people. That's what they wanted to believe. But Jesus preached a radically different message: your sins are forgiven. Righteous people and power people would not be able to abide by that proclamation because righteousness would no longer have value and power would be in weakness, turning the whole system upside down. It would be a while before the disciples could figure that out.

▶ Prayer

I pray that your kingdom come every day, O Lord, yet I hardly know what to expect from its coming. I know I need to let go of my worldly values. Please help me with your grace every day.

▶ Action

Try to imagine a world in which the poor and weak are blessed and the rich and powerful are destitute. Where do you fit in?

Friday of the Sixth Week of the Year

Exercise in Futility

MARK 8:34—9:1

Jesus said, "If you want to become my followers, you must deny yourselves, take up your cross and then follow me. If you want to save your life, you will lose it, but giving up your life for my sake, and for the sake of the gospel, will save it. What will it profit you to gain the whole world and forfeit your life?"

▶ **Reflection**

Consider any given church congregation on a Sunday morning. Chances are a large majority of them are functional atheists. Oh, they believe in God all right. They believe that God exists. They may even concede that Jesus is the Son of God, and that he died and rose. They would probably accept heaven, hell, forgiveness, resurrection, maybe even the Real Presence. But if you were to tell them that all their striving to gain wealth and comfort in this world is an exercise in futility; that the consequence of their efforts to be successful will be a forfeit, and that everything they put into saving their way of life for future generations will simply result in destruction, they would not believe it. It's easy to believe in God. It's another thing entirely to believe in the teachings of Jesus and put them into practice.

▶ **Prayer**

I grew up in this world, O Lord, and was taught to pursue the wealth and comfort of success. Repenting of this way of life and embracing your kingdom is hard. Please give me the courage to change.

▶ **Action**

Make a big switch for the kingdom today. Be last when you could be first. Give away what you would rather receive. Live the kingdom.

Saturday of the Sixth Week of the Year

Reincarnation?

MARK 9:2–13

The disciples asked Jesus, "Why do the scribes say that Elijah must come first?" He said to them, "Elijah is indeed coming first to restore all things. How then is it written that the Son of Man is to go through many sufferings? But I tell you that Elijah has come, and they did to him whatever they pleased, as it is written about him."

▶ Reflection

Catholics don't believe in reincarnation, but this passage about the return of Elijah makes you think twice. But of course Elijah never died. He was one of those Old Testament guys who just got taken up. Enoch was the other (see Genesis 5:24 and 2 Kings 2:11). Also, one must always be cautious about taking the Bible too literally as the fundamentalists do. But since Elijah didn't die, the Jewish tradition had been maintained that he would return to usher in the messiah (see Malachi 3:23 NAB or 4:5 NRSV). That's why a place is customarily left empty at the Jewish seder meal, just in case he shows up. The real question, though, is why the messiah had to suffer and be killed. The answer is simple: the rulers of the world reject the paradox of the kingdom. You have to in order to be a worldly ruler.

▶ Prayer

My God and savior Jesus, you teach a truth that only those who leave worldly things behind can know for themselves. Help me to let go of all my wealth and comfort so that I may better experience you.

▶ Action

What teaching of Jesus do you reject? love your enemy? turn the other cheek? give away your money? Spend time with your doubts.

Monday of the Seventh Week of the Year

Everything is Possible

MARK 9:14–29

A man said to Jesus, "I asked your disciples to cast out the demon from my son, but they were unable." Jesus answered, "You faithless generation! How much longer must I put up with you?" The father said, "If you are able to do anything, have pity on us." Jesus said, "If you are able?! All things can be done for those who believe." The father said, "I do believe. Help my unbelief!"

▶ Reflection

Once again the Lord's frustration with his disciples breaks through. Their fight against evil is stymied by their unwillingness to accept God's readiness to save and to heal. It's one of those difficult situations in which it seems that nothing works. As long as the disciples think it's hopeless, that they can't do it, then it won't get done. It's like when I'm looking for my keys: I'll establish in my mind that I can't find my keys, so even though I may look right at them, I don't see them because my belief is that I can't find them. Jesus reiterates over and over that it is people's faith that saves them and makes them whole. Activities like prayer and fasting, motivated by belief and undertaken with confidence, connect faith and healing.

▶ Prayer

I fail to comprehend the mystery of your love, my God. For so long I thought you would love me only if I was good. Now I know that you always love me. Help me to get used to the miracle of your love.

▶ Action

Write down some of the ways you believe things won't go well for you because you're less than perfect. Change your way of thinking.

Tuesday of the Seventh Week of the Year

Merest Children

MARK 9:30–37

Jesus said, "The Son of Man is to be betrayed and killed. Yet three days after he will rise again." But they did not understand what he was saying and were afraid to ask him. Instead they argued with one another about who was the greatest. So he took a little child and put it among them and said, "Whoever welcomes a child welcomes me, and whoever welcomes me welcomes the one who sent me."

▶ Reflection

Mark cast the disciples in a pretty dim light. They just don't get it. They have failed utterly to understand what Jesus is trying to tell them. They're anxious, afraid, and intimidated by Jesus. Despite the Lord's constant teaching and demonstration, they have missed the point entirely. I wonder if at some point Jesus didn't have second thoughts about the criteria he used to select his followers. It looks like these ignorant Galilean fishermen just aren't cutting it. So here is where Jesus will have to practice what he preaches. Can he maintain faith that this sorry lot can be fashioned by God into the foundation upon which Christ will build the church? Prospects look bleak, but where the flesh is weak, the Spirit is still very willing.

▶ Prayer

O Lord, my God, you choose the lowly and exalt them while humbling the great. Help me to know my own humility, for you have chosen me, too. Make something wonderful out of me!

▶ Action

Write down a short list of your own faults and shortcomings and then consider what a wonderful challenge you are to God!

Wednesday of the Seventh Week of the Year

The Black Jesus

MARK 9:38–40

John said to him, "Teacher, we saw someone casting out demons in your name, and we tried to stop him, because he was not following us." But Jesus said, "Do not stop him; for no one who does a deed of power in my name will be able soon afterward to speak evil of me. Whoever is not against us is for us."

▶ Reflection

There's a church in downtown Port au Prince, Haiti, with the most extraordinary frescos depicting the life of Jesus. Native-born black artists were invited to paint them after the overthrow of dictator Jean-Claude "Baby Doc" Duvalier in 1986, giving them a wonderfully distinct style and parochial flavor. Jesus, Mary, Joseph, John the Baptist, and all the characters of the gospel stories are given the identity, garb, and settings of black Haitians. It can be a bit of a shock for American *blans* (white people) to see this, but it serves as a reminder that our church, our faith, is universal. Just because people look different, sound different, do things differently, or don't gather with us, it doesn't mean they are against us. And whoever is not against us is for us.

▶ Prayer

Precious Lord, your Spirit gives life freely to all people of every race and nation, for you have created them all in your own image and likeness. Help me see you in all the rich variety of humanity.

▶ Action

Imagine God present in every different person you meet today. How often does it surprise you?

Kingdom Checkbook

MARK 9:41–50

"If a hand or foot causes you to stumble, cut them off; it is better to enter life maimed than end up in hell with your hands and feet. And if your eye is your problem, tear it out; it is better to enter the kingdom of God half blind than have two eyes and end up in hell."

▶ Reflection

When something is expensive, we say "it costs an arm and a leg." Well, the kingdom of God is expensive: it'll cost you an eye, a hand, and a foot! While some think it boorish to talk about money at church, money is the deal. It's nice to want to include time and talent with treasure, the big three of stewardship. But most of us cash in our time and talent for a paycheck. What is clear is that those who have the money are holding back from those who don't. Recently the population of the world crossed a statistical line: the 200 richest people in the world have more than the two *billion* poorest. Most of us are far closer to the 200 than we'll ever be to the two billion. What's important to remember is that God provides for all and it is the stewards, you and me, who are responsible for managing the funds. If your checkbook is your difficulty, take it out and open it.

▶ Prayer

My God, you have blessed me with riches and called me to faithful stewardship, sharing my wealth with the poor and the needy. Help me let go of this passing treasure in the joyful hope of a lasting reward.

▶ Action

Sit down with your checkbook and write a check to the local soup kitchen. Make it a big one, for the kingdom is coming!

Friday of the Seventh Week of the Year

Divorce Trick

MARK 10:1–12

The Pharisees asked to test him, "May a man divorce his wife? Moses allowed divorce." Jesus said, "That was because of your hardness of heart. But God made them male and female. Therefore a man shall be joined to his wife, so they are no longer two, but one."

▶ Reflection

In the gospel stories, whenever the antagonists, in this case the Pharisees, ask Jesus a trick question, the Lord gives a trick answer. The question about divorce was designed to "test" Jesus. Taking a side in the issue, which was at the time controversial, would put him at odds with one group or another. So Jesus, as he often did, referred to Scripture. This left his listeners nonplussed. "Then it is better not to marry," the disciples say in Matthew's parallel story (19:10). St. Paul would agree (1 Cor 7:8). Nonetheless, most of us marry. It's a sacrament of the church… sometimes. Many marriages, even those attempted in the church, fail. Church law recognizes this reality and does not bind members to marriages that suffer from nullifying defects. Our people need to know that when an attempt at marriage fails, the church is there to help pick up the pieces.

▶ Prayer

You call your people to marriage, O God, and we respond as best we can. But it's hard and sometimes we fail. Thank you for always helping, no matter what. Teach me to always trust in your love.

▶ Action

Whether you're married, divorced, or single, think how God calls you to union with others. Seek God in your relationships.

Saturday of the Seventh Week of the Year

Becoming Children

MARK 10:13–16

People were bringing little children to Jesus so that he might touch them. When the disciples spoke sternly to them, Jesus became indignant and said, "Let the little children come to me; do not stop them. It is to such as these that the kingdom of God belongs. If you do not receive the kingdom like a little child, you will not enter it." And he took them up in his arms and blessed them.

▶ Reflection

It is obvious what God has in mind when he creates people. If you'll notice, God doesn't create grown-ups; God creates little children. I think that's the way God wants it. God did create a couple of grown-ups once, saw how it worked out, and has been creating little children ever since. The strange thing is that we take these wonderful little children God gives us and we make them into grown-ups just like ourselves. That's why Jesus warns us to think twice about how we treat the little ones. And that is why God continues to send us little children: not so that we might make them like ourselves, but so that we might change and become like them. There is a little child in you who wants to come to Jesus. Do not stop that little child.

▶ Prayer

O God, you formed me in my mother's womb to be her child and yours. You made me in your own image and likeness so that I may discover you hidden in me. Help me to be the child you created.

▶ Action

Do you remember how to skip? How about finger paint? Do something today that reconnects you to your childhood.

Monday of the Eighth Week of the Year

Joyful Stewardship

MARK 10:17–27

Jesus told a rich man, "You lack one thing: Go, sell what you own and give the money to the poor so you will have treasure in heaven. Then come and follow me." The man was shocked and went away sad, for he had many possessions. Jesus said, "How hard it is for the rich to enter the kingdom of God!"

▶ Reflection

It's not that God has anything against wealth. On the contrary, it is God who entrusts people with wealth so that they might use it for God's purposes. The difficulty, however, is getting this idea of stewardship through to our worldly way of thinking. The forces of the retail establishment hit us every way and everywhere with the gospel of consumerism. Never are our eyes and ears far from the blast of marketing hype. Why, you can't live without this, you won't be happy without that! Buy, buy, buy; have, have, have. Sometimes it's hard not to believe it. But the illusion that wealth can make us happy and secure is an ugly, ugly lie. Jesus, ever the lover, invites the rich man to do something truly beautiful. Are we willing to show the rich men and women how beautiful it is?

▶ Prayer

Lord, you give me everything I need. Yet the world tries to convince me that I should have more. And often I want what the world offers. Help me to hear the lie. Make me faithful to the call of stewardship.

▶ Action

Cross off something from that list you have in your head of things you need. You'll be better off for it.

Tuesday of the Eighth Week of the Year

Fundamental Option

MARK 10:28–31

Jesus said, "Truly I tell you, there is no one who has left house or brothers or sisters or mother or father or children or fields, for my sake and for the sake of the good news, who will not receive a hundredfold now, and in the age to come eternal life. But many who are first will be last, and the last will be first."

▶ Reflection

It isn't as if we don't have a tried and true product here; we're not offering a pig in a poke. Plenty of people in history have renounced all their wealth for the sake of the kingdom and reported, "Hey! This works!" Saints Francis and Claire of Assisi come to mind. Saints Peter Canisius, Matilda, Jane Frances de Chantal, Charles Borromeo, and a host of others bear enduring witness to the joy and fulfillment that comes with giving up worldly wealth and following in the footsteps of Jesus. But it seems the rich aren't buying it; they like the things money can buy. Only the poor and the lowly who have little to lose are willing to give it a shot. Peter didn't really leave much; by all accounts, a failing fishing business. Are there any willing to give up wealth today?

▶ Prayer

What good is my wealth, O Lord, if I cannot find eternal joy in your kingdom? But you show me the way that leads to life. Give me the courage to give it all away for the sake of the kingdom.

▶ Action

Remember when you were a kid and didn't want to share? Today, share something with the poor. Give away food, clothes, and money.

Wednesday of the Eighth Week of the Year

Worldly Ways

MARK 10:32–45

James and John said to Jesus, "We want to sit at your right hand and at your left in your glory." Jesus said to them, "You do not know what you are asking. Whoever wishes to become great among you must be your servant, and whoever wishes to be first among you must be slave of all. The Son of Man came not to be served but to serve, and to give his life a ransom for many."

▶ Reflection

Jesus is talking suffering and James and John are looking for the best seats in the house. If I were Jesus, I would've taken them to a crucifixion (understanding that it was a fairly common occurrence), pointed to the poor soul on the cross and said, "Okay, boys, that's my seat. Which one do you want?" Learning the ways of the kingdom is hard because we grow up learning the ways of the world. If you want to be first (and who doesn't want to be first?), then you have to strive to be first. It is what the first reading calls "the futile way of life your (parents) handed on to you." James and John were just doing what they were taught to do. But in the kingdom, the last are first. The seat you take here inversely determines your seat in the kingdom.

▶ Prayer

I want to sit at your right hand in glory, too, dear Lord. But I don't want the cross any more than you did. Help me to walk humbly and carry my own cross faithfully. Make me last in this world.

▶ Action

When given the opportunity today, make yourself last instead of trying to be first. See what happens.

Thursday of the Eighth Week of the Year

Seeing In Blindness

MARK 10:46–52

Bartimaeus, a blind beggar, cried out, "Jesus, Son of David, have mercy on me!" Jesus stopped and called to him. Throwing off his cloak, he sprang up and came to Jesus. "Rabbi," he said, "let me see again." Jesus said to him, "Go; your faith has made you well." Immediately he regained his sight and followed him on the way.

▶ Reflection

In order to hope for a world in which the last are first, you need to be in a hopeless situation. In order to see it, you have to be blind. In yesterday's gospel, James and John, blind to the kingdom, could only apply worldly standards to their hopes. They asked for glory. In today's gospel, set in opposition to yesterday's story, the beggar Bartimaeus "sees" the presence of the kingdom because he is blind to the world. He asks humbly for pity. James and John hold on to their worldly values. The beggar "throws aside" the cloak in which he kept all he owned. We might remind ourselves that if the apostles didn't get it, what makes us think that we do? Maybe today we ought to take a look at our values and determine if they fit the kingdom. Maybe there is something in our lives we need to throw aside.

▶ Prayer

Awaken me to your kingdom, O God. Heal me of the blindness that keeps me from seeing your presence in my life. Give me strength to fight the temptation of worldliness. May I follow only you.

▶ Action

Is there a hopeless situation in your life right now? If there is, maybe it's time to really believe that God is leading you to wholeness.

Friday of the Eighth Week of the Year

A Bad Halo Day

MARK 11:11–26

Jesus came to a fig tree and found nothing but leaves, for it was not the time for figs. He said, "May no one ever eat fruit from you again." Then he entered the temple and began to drive out those who were selling and buying in the temple. He overturned the tables of the money changers and the seats of those who sold doves. In the morning they found the fig tree withered.

▶ Reflection

If you've been looking for "the wrath of God" in the gospel stories, here it is. Jesus is really upset. It could be he's having a "bad halo" day. In any event, the merchants' market gets wrecked and an innocent fig tree gets withered. So, does that mean God's wrath is violent and capricious? No, the cursing of the fig tree was symbolic. It was to remind us that God gives life for the purpose of bearing fruit. No fruit, no life. And apart from the practicality of having a market in the temple, the thievery of commerce has no place in a house of prayer. God's wrath is real. It's a kind of tough love designed to move people back to where they need to be. So today it costs a fig tree and a little business. There's plenty more where that came from.

▶ Prayer

My loving God, I was brought up to be afraid of you, yet you are full of kindness and compassion. When I get off the track, bring me back. If you have to scare me to do it, fine. I trust in your love.

▶ Action

Imagine that Jesus showed up at the front door of your life right now. What do you suppose he would be upset about? Why?

Macho Men

MARK 11:27–33

The chief priests, the scribes, and the elders said, "Who gave you authority to do these things?" Jesus said, "I will ask you a question; Did the baptism of John come from heaven, or was it of human origin?" They answered, "We do not know." And Jesus said to them, "Neither will I tell you by what authority I am doing these things."

▶ Reflection

Authority lies at the heart of the human conflict with God. Who's in charge? Humans want to be, especially the males. It is the ultimate ego trip. Being in charge means it's your turf, your way. You get what you want. Listen to the gripes about life and you'll hear the discontent that comes when somebody else is in charge. The chief priests, scribes, and elders in the gospel story were upset with Jesus because he was acting on his own authority. Not a good idea when you're messing with a male-dominated organization, especially a religious one. The Catholic church runs into the same difficulty. Every movement toward something new can be perceived as a challenge to authority. Compassion is not the default reaction when power is at stake. "Thy will be done" is easy to say, hard to do.

▶ Prayer

Father in heaven, you are God and Jesus is Lord! Yet within me is a will that strives to take command. I want things my way but your way is so much better. Humble me so that I may follow your will always.

▶ Action

Today, if you get snatched up in a direction you would rather not go, surrender and see where it takes you. You can leave God behind.

Monday of the Ninth Week of the Year

The Rejected Stone

MARK 12:1–12

"A man leased his vineyard to tenants and sent a servant to collect his share. But they sent him away empty-handed. So he sent his son to them, but they killed him. What should the owner of the vineyard do? He will come and destroy the tenants and give the vineyard to others. Have you not read this scripture: 'The stone that the builders rejected has become the cornerstone'?"

▶ Reflection

Piety, virtue, discernment, self control, care—these are the cornerstones of a fruitful life, a life that is lived to the fullest. Yet the builders of life in this world tend to reject such qualities in favor of those that will result in worldly gain: shrewdness, competitiveness, ruthlessness, an appetite for the things money will buy, and a willingness to profit at all costs. But this is where we have to answer one of life's fundamental questions: who made us? If the world made us, then we should embrace worldly values. Then, once having gained the world, the world will pass away and we will pass away with it, and that will be that. But if God made us, then we ought to perhaps consider what will give us lasting value.

▶ Prayer

You made me, O Lord. You have revealed the truth about your creation. I know I miss the point so often. I think the money you give me is for my own comfort. Help me to know and live the truth.

▶ Action

Take a good stock of all you possess: bank accounts, house, furniture, car. Then spend some time remembering who made it all possible.

Tuesday of the Ninth Week of the Year

God's Face

MARK 12:13–17

The Herodians asked Jesus, "Is it lawful to pay taxes to the emperor, or not?"
Jesus said to them, "Whose face is on the coin?" They answered, "Caesar's."
Jesus said to them, "Give to Caesar the things that are the Caesar's, and to God
the things that are God's." And they were utterly amazed at him.

▶ Reflection

Whenever the religious leaders in the gospel stories try to fake Jesus
out, Jesus fakes them back. He never gives them a straight answer. This
story is not about paying taxes. It is about who you are and to whom
you belong. A guy asked me the other day if I had ever seen the face of
God. I gave him a speculative answer, long and drawn out, with
multiple cognitive nuances. It was a lousy answer to a simple
question. I should've said, "Yes, I see God all the time. I'm looking at
God right now." Every life bears the inscription of God; each person is
the image and likeness of God. In the end, everything gets sorted out.
What belongs to the world passes away with the world. What belongs
to God goes to be with God. So pay taxes and give yourself to God.

▶ Prayer

O God, you live within me, sharing my life and my body. You create
the world around me and unfold my day like a map before me. May I
always surrender to your loving direction and caring will.

▶ Action

If you were to take an inventory of everything in your life, what would
last and what would pass away? What do you want to keep?

Wednesday of the Ninth Week of the Year

Ask a Silly Question

MARK 12:18–27

The Sadducees, who say there is no resurrection, questioned Jesus. He said,
"Those who rise from the dead neither marry nor are given in marriage, but are
like angels in heaven. Have you not read in the book of Moses, in the story
about the bush, how God said to him, 'I am the God of Abraham, the God of
Isaac, and the God of Jacob'? He is God not of the dead, but of the living."

▶ Reflection

There's an old saying that goes, "Ask a silly question and you get a silly
answer." Jesus applies the maxim to the Sadducees' question. Again,
like in yesterday's gospel, the answer isn't meant to settle the question.
So the grieving widow who fully expects to be reunited with her
husband in heaven need not be alarmed by this teaching. But when
Jesus uses angels to illustrate his answer to the Sadducees who
specifically don't believe in angels (see Acts 23:8), you know the Lord
is tweaking somebody's nose. Nonetheless, he makes a subtle point:
he counts Abraham, Isaac, and Jacob among the living. He challenges
their denial of a functional resurrection with the suggestion that life
continues unbroken by death.

▶ Prayer

How often I am frightened by death, O God. But you have assured me
that my life goes on; that I am like you and will never die. Still, I
wonder about life after death. Keep me confident in your love.

▶ Action

Make a list of people you'd like to see when you die. Spend some time
imagining what that will be like.

Not Even Total Love

MARK 12:28–34

Jesus said, "The first commandment is, 'Hear, O Israel: the Lord our God, the Lord is one; you shall love the Lord your God with all your heart, and with all your soul, and with all your mind, and with all your strength.' The second is this, 'You shall love your neighbor as yourself.' There is no other commandment greater than these."

▶ Reflection

I keep thinking there's not enough love for God in me to make it work. I don't love God with all my everything. There are people, experiences, even things I spend more time and energy loving than I do loving God. And to tell the truth, I'm not all that crazy about my neighbor, either. I could consider myself a moral failure—and I do! But Christianity isn't about how well I measure up to the demands of God's law. If that were the case, I'd be lost with no chance of ever finding lasting joy in heaven. No, my salvation is a gift of God. I'm saved by the mercy of God shown to me in Jesus Christ. Maybe that's why the Lord's measure of the scribe's response found further on in this passage, was that he was "not far" from the kingdom. Hearing this, they were all afraid to question him further.

▶ Prayer

I am a sinner, my Lord, yet you give me all your love. You save me from evil and raise me to life. You pour your love into me and it flows out to others in spite of my weakness. You are a wonder God!

▶ Action

Make a list of the things and people you love, and honestly fit God in there somewhere. Then guess who's at the top of God's list.

Friday of the Ninth Week of the Year

Word Play

MARK 12:35–37

While Jesus was teaching in the temple, he said, "How can the scribes say that the Messiah is the son of David? David himself, by the Holy Spirit, declared, 'The Lord said to my Lord, "Sit at my right hand, until I put your enemies under your feet."' David himself calls him Lord; so how can he be his son?" And the large crowd was listening to him with delight.

▶ Reflection

The people got a kick out of Jesus playing with the Scripture because they knew he was making fun of how the scribes taught. The passage, Psalm 110:1, wasn't controversial. There was no question that the song, probably composed during the time of King David or King Solomon, was addressed to the king and that "my lord," a completely different word than "the Lord," was simply a form of polite address used frequently in the royal court (see the note on Ps 110:1 in the New American Bible). Of course you're not supposed to make fun of religious teachers, so there were some in the crowd who weren't delighted. Jesus didn't insult the intelligence of his listeners like some of the scribes of his day did or like some high-placed religious teachers do today.

▶ Prayer

O God, you guide me day by day through this wonderful world. Arrogance and pride tempt me along with lust for power and wealth. Lead me along a humble path. Keep me safe and fill me with light.

▶ Action

Today, notice the difference between people who seem "higher" than you and those who seem "lower." This is a worldly illusion.

Priest or Scribe?

MARK 12:38–44

Jesus said, "Beware of the scribes, who like to walk around in long robes, and to be greeted with respect in the marketplaces, and to have the best seats in the synagogues and places of honor at banquets! They devour widows' houses and for the sake of appearance say long prayers. They will receive the greater condemnation."

▶ Reflection

It took a child to notice. She came up to the priest after Mass and asked, "Are you a scribe?" The priest, a kindly man, asked what she meant. She said, "Jesus said to beware of the scribes who like to wear long robes and sit in the chief seats and recite long prayers, and who like marks of respect and titles of honor. So I thought maybe you were a scribe." The priest considered this for a moment and said, "No, honey. I'm a priest. But it sure sounds like I'm a scribe." Then he asked the little girl, "Would you pray for me every day so that I don't turn into a scribe?" The little girl agreed that turning into a scribe would not be a good thing and promised to pray for the priest every day. He thanked her for her insight and her promise to pray. Then he thanked God for showing him something he'd not seen before.

▶ Prayer

O Lord, in our church men wear long robes and sit in the chief seats. Bless them and keep them humble in your work. May they always use their authority to serve and not to be served.

▶ Action

Look at the authority of your own life. Consider the temptations of being a grown-up or a parent or a boss. Ask God for humility.

Monday of the Tenth Week of the Year

The Money Man

MATTHEW 5:1–12

"Blessed are the poor in spirit, for theirs is the kingdom of heaven…. Blessed are the peacemakers, they shall be called children of God."

▶ Reflection

In the comedy movie *Life of Brian*, some people on the edge of the crowd listening to Jesus preach don't quite hear him say, "Blessed are the peacemakers." One of them, a maker of cheese, insists that he said, "Blessed are the cheese makers." There is a somewhat less comedic but no less interesting difference between Matthew 5:3–12, called The Beatitudes, and Luke's account of the same teaching (6:17–49). Luke is starkly material ("Blessed are you who are poor… Blessed are you who hunger…") while Matthew clearly has a much more intangible cast ("Blessed are the poor in spirit… Blessed are those who hunger and thirst for righteousness…") I wonder if the difference had anything to do with Matthew being a person of money—he was a tax collector and, presumably, made a lot of it; and Luke being poor—he was a physician, not a very lucrative profession in the first century. What you value determines what you hear.

▶ Prayer

O Jesus, you have given me so many gifts and I love them all. I love the things of the world you give me for my use while I live. Teach me to always use your gifts wisely and not let anything possess me but you.

▶ Action

Think about what you value in this life and try to connect your values to the way you see God.

Tuesday of the Tenth Week of the Year

Got Salt?

MATTHEW 5:13–16

"You are the salt of the earth and the light of the world. Let your light shine so that people can see your goodness and give praise to the God who created you."

▶ Reflection

The cook is at the stove preparing something in a pot. Dipping a spoon and offering it, he says: "Try this and tell me what you think." She tastes it, smacks her lips thoughtfully, and says, "Needs salt." A boy is reading by a window as the day fades into evening. Mom walks in the room and flips the switch. "You need more light," she says. I used to think that we were created and placed in this world to be tested in order to determine if we were worthy of heaven. But Jesus says no, we're here because the world needs salt; it needs more light. We need to get over the idea of a worried life lived under a severe and critical God, and begin to take Jesus at his word. We're here to celebrate God and make the goodness of God known in the world.

▶ Prayer

O my God, you made me who I am for better or for worse. Help me to be the person you want me to be so that people can see your hand at work in my life.

▶ Action

Make a list of all the qualities and traits you possess. Think about how to use each one to show God's glory.

Wednesday of the Tenth Week of the Year

Love Comes First

MATTHEW 5:17–19

"Whoever breaks one of the least of these commandments will be called least in the kingdom of heaven."

▶ Reflection

"I was always too strict with my daughter," the mother complained bitterly, "and now that she's gone, she won't have anything to do with me." The woman poured out her story of regret and loneliness, recounting all the mistakes she'd made as a mother, agonizing over the broken relationship between her and her daughter. She realized, maybe too late, that she had laid the law down too hard on her daughter while she was growing up. Now she was suffering the consequences. The Jewish community, to whom Matthew's gospel was addressed, was critical of Jesus for not reaffirming the law as the way to salvation. Jesus taught that moral righteousness is of value in the kingdom, but even those who break the law have a place in the kingdom. Jesus places the relationship between God and humanity above maintaining moral righteousness.

▶ Prayer

O Lord, you invite me to walk with you day by day, and day by day I fail to live up to what is right and good and perfect. Yet you wait for me; you don't allow me to fall behind. I am *so* grateful for your love. Help me to always trust in your mercy and compassion. Amen.

▶ Action

Have you been too hard on somebody? Take a moment and think of all the times God has forgiven you.

Thursday of the Tenth Week of the Year

Upping the Ante

MATTHEW 5:20–26

"You have heard that it was said to those of ancient times, 'you shall not murder;' and 'whoever murders shall be liable to judgment.' But I say to you that if you are angry with a brother or sister, you will be liable to judgment."

▶ **Reflection**

It seems at first blush that Jesus is simply upping the ante on the law, giving us just so many more reasons to worry about the salvation of our immortal souls. And in a way he was. Understand that Jesus was teaching people who actually did measure their chances of salvation by how well they followed the law. So if a person never killed anybody, he could check off the fifth commandment. Not so fast, says the Lord. In reality, nobody measures up to the law. The law is perfect (Psalm 19:8) but we are not. In his teaching, Jesus is simply making it clear that there can never be point where we can say we don't need forgiveness. All have sinned (Romans 3:23). But the blood of Christ was shed for all so that sins might be forgiven. Therefore, salvation in Jesus Christ is a matter of accepting forgiveness, not following the law.

▶ **Prayer**

How I have worried about the salvation of my soul, dear God. I wasn't a very good witness of your mercy and forgiveness. Then I came to believe that my sins were forgiven. Oh, what joy!

▶ **Action**

Think of an example of how you break each one of the commandments. How does it feel to be forgiven?

Friday of the Tenth Week of the Year

Opt for Mercy

MATTHEW 5:27–32

"You have heard that it was said, 'You shall not commit adultery.' But I say to you that everyone who looks at another with lust has already committed adultery."

▶ Reflection

The man was very angry and upset. His son had just "come out" to him, telling him that he was gay, a homosexual. Now the man was outraged, pounding on the arm of the chair. "How will he ever be saved from the fires of hell?" he cried. I felt bad for him. He seemed to think that God had already separated the sheep and the goats! Some say that homosexuals are the goats because they commit sexual sin. But according to Jesus, we all commit sexual sin. The Bible says precious little about homosexuality, but it says plenty about adultery. We know that we sin in thought, word, and deed. So we're all committing adultery, one way or another. Now who are the goats? It seems to me that, if we're faithful to the teaching of Jesus, we ought to put the stones down because none of us is without sin. In reality, we're all under the same condemnation. But we've all been offered the same gift of salvation. So, unless we're confident that we can make it through life without sinning, we'd better opt for mercy.

▶ Prayer

O God, in your infinite mercy and love, you have forgiven all my sins. Help me to be forgiving as I have been forgiven.

▶ Action

Make a list of sins our society tends to condemn. If you can detect the same sin in your heart, cross that one off the list.

Saturday of the Tenth Week of the Year

Taking Vows

MATTHEW 5:33–37

"Again, you have heard it said, 'You shall not make a false oath, but carry out your vows to the Lord.' But I say to you, don't make any vows. Just say yes or no; anything more comes from the evil one."

▶ Reflection

Poverty, chastity, and obedience; till death do us part; so help me God. I wonder how the whole business of "vows" crept into our religion. Jesus seems pretty clear in this teaching that vows are to be avoided. Anything beyond "yes" and "no" comes from the devil, he says. That's certainly understandable. Human weakness severely impedes our ability to keep the vows we make. Once we make a vow, the devil has us over a barrel. If we break the vow, as we almost certainly will, the devil has a field day condemning us and taking away our peace. Perhaps even worse, if we actually manage to keep the vow, then the devil can set us up as self-righteous. As it is, our brothers and sisters who fail at marriage, priesthood, or religious life seem to come under a kind of condemnation from us, even though Jesus warned us not to make vows at all.

▶ Prayer

Loving God, hear the intent of our vows. We mean well; our efforts at marriage, religious life, and telling the truth celebrate your love and faithfulness. May your love keep us safe from the evil one and bring us to the fulfillment of our hopes. Amen.

▶ Action

Take a moment to consider the vows you have made in your life. Say "yes" to your call of life today.

Monday of the Eleventh Week of the Year

The Other Cheek

<u>MATTHEW 5:38–42</u>

"You have heard that it was said, 'An eye for an eye and a tooth for a tooth.' But I say, do not resist an evildoer. If anyone strikes you on the one cheek, turn and offer the other."

▶ Reflection

Jack was irate, shaking his fist at me. "The Bible says, 'an eye for an eye,'" he fumed. He was reacting to what I said in church about the American bombing of Iraq. Jack needs to upgrade his theology. That "eye for an eye" line always gets plenty of play when folks are searching for a justification for war or the spirit of retaliation that sustains war. Somehow the precept makes it okay to smash somebody in the face if he hits me first. Well, as Mahatma Gandhi once said, "An eye for an eye will make the whole world go blind." In reality, the rule, found in Leviticus 24:19–20, restricts retaliation in order to avoid escalation. Be that as it may, Jesus teaches no retaliation at all. Rather, one who believes in the power of God to save is called to surrender, to live in such a way so as to demonstrate God's ongoing care and protection. This is tough faith. In order to drive this teaching home, Jesus surrendered to the suffering and death of the cross.

▶ Prayer

Jesus, my Lord, you surrendered to evil so that you might show God's power to save. Each day I am offended in little ways and in big ways. May I always trust in the power of your grace to save me.

▶ Action

Today, let somebody get away with an offense against you. Pray for the grace you need to allow God to work it out for you.

Tuesday of the Eleventh Week of the Year

It Will Work

MATTHEW 5:43–48

"You have heard that it was said, 'You shall love your neighbor and hate your enemy.' But I say love your enemies and pray for those who persecute you."

▶ Reflection

Back in 1999, Barry was the "Y2K specialist" at the company where he worked. His job was to see to it that the computer system would survive the turning of the millennium when the computer date went from 99 to 00. On December 31, his boss was nervous. "Trust me," Barry said. "This is going to work." In the same way, Jesus says to us, "Trust me. This will work." Our society is very nervous about surrendering to our enemies. We spend most of our resources building weapons of war to defend ourselves against our enemies. If an attack comes, we will blow our enemy to kingdom come. Without a strong defense, our country would fall victim to the tyrants and the despots and the Hitlers and the Saddams. We would end up losing everything. If what we say we believe is true, however, then we would actually be gaining everything. The world for us would pass away and the kingdom would come. So whom do we trust?

▶ Prayer

O loving God, your mercy and kindness reach out to all people, regardless of whether they are good or bad. Your love is universal. Make us instruments of your peace.

▶ Action

Think of somebody who persecutes you; a neighbor, a coworker, or a relative. Ask God to bless that person.

Wednesday of the Eleventh Week of the Year

Andy Rooney Theology

MATTHEW 6:1–6, 16–18

"When you fast, do not look miserable like the hypocrites do. They put on sad faces so others can see they are fasting. When you fast, wash your face and fix your hair so nobody knows you are fasting. But your Father in heaven knows and he will reward you."

▶ **Reflection**

This sounds like something out of Andy Rooney. Isn't it strange that Jesus tells us to wash our faces when we fast so that nobody will know we are fasting, and then on Ash Wednesday, when we begin our season of fasting, we put ashes on our faces so that everybody will know we are fasting? And even though Jesus tells us to keep our charitable giving a secret, we insist on plaques with our names on them, or the names of loved ones, to indicate to all that we gave the money! And imagine giving presents on holidays and special occasions without a card indicating from whom it came. And no thank-you notes! Jesus teaches that simple acts of self-denial produce a kind of cosmic debt that is paid in the next life. Or, we can seek our reward in this life in the form of respect and admiration from others. One corrupts and passes away, the other blesses and endures for ever.

▶ **Prayer**

Lord, you give me so much, yet I seek more from the world around me. I want people to thank me and respect me and admire me. Yet, all I need is your love. Help me to value only what is from you.

▶ **Action**

In the spirit of today's gospel, send a card or a gift to someone today without indicating that it's from you. Just make it an anonymous gift.

Inhaling A Prayer

MATTHEW 6:7–15

"There is no need for you to recite many prayers in order for God to hear you. Just say: Our Father in heaven, how blessed is your name. May your kingdom come and your will be done. Give us our daily bread and forgive our debts as we forgive our debtors."

▶ Reflection

I couldn't believe what I was hearing. The man could actually recite the Act of Contrition while both exhaling and inhaling! I was impressed. I mean, he could say it twice as fast as anybody else. But by the time I could think of something to say, he was gone from the confessional. I wanted to ask him to stop and think about what he was saying. We pray the Lord's Prayer all the time. But do we think it through? Don't we want more from God than just our daily bread? And don't we want all our debts forgiven, not just as we forgive our debtors? And while we really want the kingdom to come, I'm not sure we really want the world to pass away. Our prayer to God could be so easy and so beautiful if we just gave it half a chance.

▶ Prayer

Our Father, you give me everything I need, yet always I want more. I hold people bound to their transgressions, yet I want you always to be merciful and forgiving to me. I wait for your kingdom to come, but not always in joyful hope because I love the things of this world. Help me, Lord, to repent of my ways and love you with all my heart.

▶ Action

Take your time and repeat the Lord's Prayer. Pause and reflect over each word, each phrase. Listen carefully to what you are saying.

Friday of the Eleventh Week of the Year

Shopping Cart Treasures

MATTHEW 6:19–23

"Do not store up the treasures of earth for yourselves. Moths will eat, rust will corrode, and thieves will steal. Instead, store up for yourselves treasures in heaven where it will be preserved from moths, rust, and thieves. Your heart will be wherever your treasure is."

▶ Reflection

I watched the woman pick through the rows and rows of fruit stacked on the supermarket shelf. She pinched some, squeezed others, sniffed a few, and carefully eyed each one, turning it over a few times to get the complete picture. Those that passed her inspection won the right to enter her shopping cart. Those that didn't were put back for the carts of the less discriminate. She was a wise shopper, knowing which fruits would last and satisfy and which would not. So it is with us who seek the kingdom of God and its treasures. We need to develop our senses to discern what will last and what will pass away. Love, mercy, and kindness will last. Care for your loved ones and time spent growing in love will endure. Money, power, and material things will pass away. Our hearts will last in lasting things.

▶ Prayer

You create all things so beautifully, almighty God, that my heart desires to possess them all. But you show me what will last and what will satisfy. Teach me to be careful about what I seek. Help me to see the difference between worldly things and heavenly things.

▶ Action

Make a list of five passing treasures and five eternal treasures. Ponder the list. What do you need to do in your life?

Saturday of the Eleventh Week of the Year

Choosing Creation

MATTHEW 6:24–34

Jesus said, "Do not worry about your life, what you will eat or what you will drink, or about your body, what you will wear. Is not life more than food, and the body more than clothing? And can any of you by worrying add a single hour to your span of life? But strive first for the kingdom of God and his righteousness, and all these things will be given to you as well."

▶ Reflection

"But how will I know which path to take? What if I go the wrong way?" Kathy was worrying about her life, so she was seeking guidance from her pastor. He tried to calm her fears by explaining that God didn't work like that. God didn't create just one path for her. God creates an infinite number of possibilities for her to choose from every moment of every day of her life. She needed only to choose and God would create the next moment based, of course, on her choice. Then she would choose again and the cycle would repeat itself. And in each moment of creation God would be loving her and blessing her and saving her and raising her up, because that's what God does. She just needed to concentrate on making good choices.

▶ Prayer

Lead me, Lord. Show me the way to go. When I choose well, give me peace and well-being. When I choose poorly, rescue me, heal me, and restore me, and I will thank you and praise you all the days of my life.

▶ Action

Stop and consider the next moment of your life. See in the variety of choices the variety of futures God can create for you.

Monday of the Twelfth Week of the Year

Opposites Attract

MATTHEW 7:1–5

"Do not judge and you won't be judged. The same judgment you make for others will be used to judge you. And the measure you use to give to others will be the measure used to give to you."

▶ Reflection

Lou and Missy were attracted to each other like magnets. They were opposites, and like magnets, could feel the strong attraction through the opposite poles of their genders, their personalities, and their psyches. But because they were so different, they spent a lot of time and energy trying to change each other, trying to make the one be more like the other. But each time one attempted to change the other, the other would resist and swing back to where he or she was in the beginning, like a needle on a compass, because that's the way magnetic attraction works. Opposites attract. The trick was for them to learn to change themselves; then it was amazing what happened to the other. They began to really enjoy their marriage. Just like moving one magnet will, in turn, move another, so changing ourselves often works to effect change in others around us.

▶ Prayer

God of heaven and earth, you have fearfully, wonderfully made us all and placed us together so that we might find each other and, in our communion of love, discover you. Remind me each day of my need to reform so that I may experience you in my love for others.

▶ Action

Consider a conflict in your relationship with a friend or a family member. Change yourself and see what happens.

Tuesday of the Twelfth Week of the Year

Mean in Me

MATTHEW 7:6, 12–14

"Do to others as you would have them do to you. Living this way fulfills the law and the prophets. The gate that leads to life is narrow and the road is hard, and there are few who find it."

▶ Reflection

Slam! It was the third telemarketer of the day and I had had enough. All they were going to get from me was dial tone from now on. There is a spirit of meanness in me that I tend to reserve for rude clerks, idiot motorists, and telemarketers. At all times I seek to be good and kind toward those with whom I share the planet; that is, until I encounter one of the aforementioned subgroups. Then all bets are off and I cut loose with a barrage of…well, sinfulness. I seem to give myself easy permission to be mean to them, rationalizing that after all, they deserve it. But in the final analysis, it is I who deserves better. The best thing I can do for myself is to be good and kind to all, regardless of how I am treated. It's a little harder that way, and a little narrower, but it is the way that leads to life for me. I have a choice each day to let evil or good be my guide.

▶ Prayer

Each day, O Lord, your love guides us in the way that leads to life. You give us the example of Jesus who suffered and died because of our sins. Still he continues to suffer and die in those we hurt and abuse through violence and neglect. Help us to change each day.

▶ Action

Think about the last person you treated poorly. Given the above teaching, devise a plan for your next encounter.

Wednesday of the Twelfth Week of the Year

The Good Path

MATTHEW 7:15–20

"Beware of false prophets who come to you like wolves in sheep's clothing. You will know them by their fruits. Every good tree bears good fruit, but the bad tree bears bad fruit."

▶ Reflection

"How do I know I'm on the right path?" goes the often-asked question. Anyone reading this book is seeking to follow the straight and narrow. Yet the signposts are often ambiguous and sometimes misleading. There are those who wear big religious symbols and can quote the holy books and by every measure appear devout, but their lives are filled with anger, distrust, stinginess, mean-spiritedness, and hardness of heart. Then there are those who have nothing to do with religion and treat Sunday like any other day of the week, yet live in beauty and do good and their lives are rich in kindness, mildness, peace, joy, and charity. Jesus teaches that you will know the rightness of your path by the fruit you produce. If the fruit is good, the path is good. If the fruit is bad, so is the path.

▶ Prayer

You have placed your Spirit within us, O God, giving us life and opening our eyes to the presence of good. Teach us always to examine carefully the fruits of our lives so that we may know our path and discern the path of others.

▶ Action

Think of the religious leaders you know, like priests, nuns, or bishops. Which ones would you follow based on the above?

Thursday of the Twelfth Week of the Year

Building On Rock

MATTHEW 7:21–29

"Many will say to me, 'Lord, Lord, did we not prophesy in your name?' I will declare to them, 'But I never knew you; go away from me, you evildoers.' Everyone then who hears these words of mine and acts on them will be like a wise man who built his house on rock."

▶ Reflection

This past Sunday, when I ate and drank of the body and blood of the Lord, I touched the source of my Christian life. As St. Paul writes in Galatians 2:20, "Now it is no longer I who live, but Christ who lives in me." So when I reconcile with an offender, give to a beggar, offer no resistance to an attacker, keep my deeds of mercy hidden, pray for my persecutors, renounce worldly treasure, stop passing judgment, treat others the way I want them to treat me, and generally follow the life and teachings of Our Lord Jesus Christ, I come to "know" him and gain intimate relationship with him who lives in me. ("Knowing" in the biblical sense is a very real physical union, like the union of a husband and wife.) Doing this, my life may diminish on a worldly scale. But I am joined with Christ in his dying and in his rising. I am building a lasting house.

▶ Prayer

You have married me, Lord. You have made me your spouse. In our union we enjoy fullness of life. As you share your life with others, so may I too be a channel of your grace and an instrument of your peace.

▶ Action

Today, as you face your decisions, ask yourself: "What would Jesus do?" Write "WWJD" on a business card and carry it in your pocket.

Friday of the Twelfth Week of the Year

Choosing Life

MATTHEW 8:1–4

A leper said to Jesus, "Lord, if you choose, you can make me clean." He stretched out his hand and touched him, saying, "I do choose. Be made clean!" Immediately his leprosy was cleansed. Then Jesus said to him, "See that you say nothing to anyone."

▶ Reflection

Jesus demonstrates that experiencing the kingdom of God is a matter of the choices we make. Every moment presents us with options that will in turn produce new sets of choices. What we choose now will determine what our next choices will be—and life will be, generally speaking, the consequence of our choices. (I say "generally" because you have to factor in everybody else's choices, too. That's where it can sometimes get difficult.) What if Jesus chose not to heal the leper? Then life would be diminished by that much. It would be a step backward. Instead, Jesus advances the kingdom through compassion, courage, and care. Notice, too, the Lord's attention to detail: he makes every attempt to see to it that his good deed is kept secret (see Matthew 6:1–6). Jesus built a life of goodness so that when life failed him, as it most certainly would, he would have a lasting reward.

▶ Prayer

O Lord, you give me life and you set me free to invest my life in this world for good or for bad. Keep me in the light of your love so that I might live by your light and produce lasting fruit.

▶ Action

At the end of this day review your choices. Rate them according to the gospel and decide if you built up the kingdom or tore it down.

Saturday of the Twelfth Week of the Year

According to Faith

MATTHEW 8:5–17

A centurion appealed to Jesus, "Lord, my servant is in terrible distress." Jesus said to him, "I will come and cure him." The centurion answered, "Lord, I am not worthy to have you come under my roof; but only speak the word, and my servant will be healed." Jesus said him, "Go; let it be done for you according to your faith."

▶ Reflection

God creates according to my choices and I will always experience the consequences of those choices. If I choose to jump out the window, God will create a world to accommodate my choice according to the laws of creation, in this case, the law of gravity. I will probably injure myself. But from the instant I fall, God will be creating to heal me and raise me up. God is love and God creates; that's how it works. My faith plays a huge role. I will move in the direction of my faith. If I believe God loves me, I will move in the direction of love. If I believe God is punishing me, I will move in the direction of punishment. If I believe God makes good things for me, I will look for the good. Or, I will look for the bad if I believe God is working against me. All things are done for us according to our faith.

▶ Prayer

O God Almighty, what a great creator you are! You make a world for me out of love for me. And even though I am a sinner, you always raise me up when I fall. Praise you, Lord, and bless your holy name!

▶ Action

Take stock of your faith. Write down what you believe God is doing either for you or to you today. Evaluate it according to the gospel.

Monday of the Thirteenth Week of the Year

Leaving Parents

MATTHEW 8:18–22

A scribe said to Jesus, "I will follow you wherever you go." Jesus answered, "Foxes have holes, and birds of the air have nests; but the Son of Man has nowhere to lay his head." Another said, "Lord, first let me go and bury my father." But Jesus said to him, "Follow me, and let the dead bury their own dead."

▶ Reflection

We understand almost immediately the need to surrender our connection to the material things of the world: our possessions, our comfort and security, our homes even, if that's what it takes. Things of the world pass away, while the kingdom endures forever. But then Jesus, as always, drags it one step further. Are we willing to give up what we would call "family values" for the sake of the kingdom? We have made loyalty to family a *fait accompli* of the Christian ethic. Yet Jesus recognizes that families, like people, are imperfect. The fourth commandment of the law, like the others, will impede our progress toward God's kingdom if we follow it dogmatically and unreasonably. Sometimes it's best to leave a mother and father behind when the next step toward the kingdom requires it.

▶ Prayer

My God, out of love you call me to enter your kingdom, because your kingdom is the fulfillment of my existence. Help me leave behind the passing world for your eternal realm.

▶ Action

Consider your relationship with your parents, for better or for worse. Determine how it might impede your progress in the kingdom.

Tuesday of the Thirteenth Week of the Year

Screaming

MATTHEW 8:23–27

A storm arose at sea and the boat was being swamped. They cried out, "Lord, we're doomed!" He said to them, "Why are you so afraid?" Then he spoke to the wind and the sea, and all was calm.

▶ Reflection

This week my friend Maggie expressed some anxiety over a situation in her life. We chatted back and forth over the e-mail for a while until she resolved the problem. She realized that while her fears were understandable, they were inconsistent with her trust in God. She chided herself for her lack of faith: "If I were in the sinking boat with Jesus," she wrote, "I'd be the last one to stop screaming!" I thought that was a pretty funny line, so I promised her I would get it into print. It's funny because it makes a universal point, the same one as today's gospel. Though Jesus is in the boat with us, we often fear we are perishing. "Do not fear," Jesus commands us in Mark 5:36, "only believe." In a world where we learn to live according to fear, that's easy to say—but tough to do.

▶ Prayer

Dear Jesus, when life is contrary and the way grows hard, when things go wrong and we feel that you have abandoned us, remind us that you are with us and that we have nothing to fear. Calm the storms of conflict and keep our fragile boat afloat, for the wind and the waves frighten us and cause us to sometimes lose faith.

▶ Action

Where is the boat sinking in your life? Spend some time picturing in your mind the presence of Jesus where you need him most.

The Joke is On You

MATTHEW 8:28–34

The demons begged Jesus, "If you're going to cast us out, send us into the swine." So Jesus said to them, "Go!" They entered the swine and the whole herd ran down to the cliff and plunged into the sea.

▶ Reflection

The concept of political correctness was still some two thousand years away when Matthew wrote his gospel for the Jewish community of Christian believers. At the time there was no doubt some ethnic and religious humor circulating among the Galileans about their non-Jewish neighbors, the Gadarenes, across the lake. And since the Jews didn't eat swine, probably a few swine jokes, too. We really need to suspend our standard picture of a somber congregation listening to the gospel being droned by a dour cleric, and imagine a Robin Williams rabbi telling this story to a Comedy Central audience. If ever there was a knee-slapping Jesus yarn for kosher Jews, this is it. It was written and proclaimed not only to teach faith, but also to entertain. Yes, Virginia, there are gags in the Bible.

▶ Prayer

Ha, ha! You're pretty funny, God. Well, at least I think you are. I imagine that this joke worked a lot better in first-century Judea than it does here and now. Some people don't think you're funny, but you must be. You included a funny bone when you made us, and every day we see things in your creation that make us laugh.

▶ Action

Take a minute to think of a few jokes God has pulled on you lately. Now go share a few jokes and a laugh with someone.

It's All Yours

MATTHEW 9:1–8

Jesus said to the scribes, "You need to know that the Son of Man has authority on earth to forgive sins." So he said to the paralytic, "Stand up and go your way." And he stood up and went home. The crowds marveled that God gave such authority to human beings.

▶ Reflection

Although Theresa was winning the lawsuit, she still carried bitterness in her heart against the state system that wronged her. She didn't want to forgive them because she was afraid that by doing so, she'd be letting them off the cosmic hook. She was right. Today's gospel story indicates that the divine power to forgive sins is granted to human beings. Imagine what we could do if we really believed we had the authority to free people from their sins. Theresa needed to forgive her oppressors for two reasons: so she herself could be free of the bitterness which followed the offense and get on with her life, and so she could do her part to heal the system that wronged her. Forgiveness is our right and our obligation.

▶ Prayer

God our Father, forgive us our trespasses as we forgive those who trespass against us. Help us to participate in your divine power by both forgiving and being forgiven. May the healing power of your love and forgiveness heal our hearts and make us ambassadors of reconciliation.

▶ Action

Forgive someone today from your heart. If there's no one you can think of, just wait; the person will show up shortly.

Friday of the Thirteenth Week of the Year

Kids Beat Evil

MATTHEW 9:9–13

When the Pharisees saw Jesus dining with sinners, they complained to his disciples. When he heard this, he said, "Those who are well don't need a doctor, but those who are sick do. I haven't come to call the righteous, but to call sinners."

▶ Reflection

Larry is very anxious because he sees his kids hanging out with the wrong crowd. I wonder how the Blessed Mother felt when she heard her son was eating with the sinners. I wonder if she was anxious and upset. Based on the popular characterizations of Mary, she could have been serenely confident that the goodness in her son was greater than the sinfulness of the people he was hanging out with. I wonder if it would be possible for parents like Larry today to believe that the goodness of their children would provide a positive influence on their peers instead of the other way around. If we believe in the power of goodness to eventually win the victory over evil, is it possible our children are called by God to hang around with the wrong crowd? Are we willing to trust enough in the power of goodness to let it happen?

▶ Prayer

There are times when we need greater confidence in your goodness, O Lord, and a greater faith in your Son's victory over sin and death. When the darkness of evil threatens us, may we always believe in your love.

▶ Action

Think of someone who has positively influenced you in your life. Consider what you'd be like today without that influence.

Saturday of the Thirteenth Week of the Year

New Wine Gospel

MATTHEW 9:14–17

"You don't put new wine into old wineskins. If you do, the skins will be ruined and the wine will be lost. You put new wine into fresh wineskins so that both are preserved."

▶ Reflection

I saw a wonderful bumper sticker in town the other day: "Don't make me come down there!—God." We tend to think of God in terms of that image: that God is watching over us, waiting for us to do something wrong, and then God's going to "come down" and we're going to get it. It's a very authentic Old Testament understanding of God, but it doesn't fit the image of God revealed in Jesus Christ. Jesus constantly presents the kingdom of God as a constant invitation to enter a celebration of love. All are invited. The sinner is not excluded because sins are forgiven. The dead are not prevented because Jesus has risen from the dead. So we've got a choice: the old wine or the new wine. Choose one or the other, but don't ever see the gospel and the Ten Commandments as the same thing. They're not.

▶ Prayer

O God, your law is good and right and just. But your people, the work of your hands, are weak and sinful, and cannot measure up to your goodness. In the mercy and kindness you have shown to us in Jesus Christ, keep us near to you and don't let us be lost. Help us to live in your love.

▶ Action

Think of how your life measures up to the Ten Commandments. Now consider that your sins are forgiven. Do you feel thankful?

Monday of the Fourteenth Week of the Year

The Brawl

MATTHEW 9:18–26

When they came into the house, there was a crowd making a commotion. Jesus said, "Go away; the girl is not dead but sleeping." But they ridiculed him. But when the crowd had been put outside, he went in and took her by the hand, and the girl got up.

▶ Reflection

Let's call this passage, "Jesus gets into another brawl." When the party arrives at the synagogue leader's house, a crowd has assembled, as was the custom, to mourn the death of the child and to offer comfort to the grieving parents. Jesus addresses them harshly. His "go away" is as harsh and abrupt in the original Aramaic as it sounds in English, and deeply offensive to the crowd. Their response, which was ridicule and derision, is meant to be offensive in turn. Then the story says the crowd was "put out." The Greek word carries a notion of violence. Can you imagine what it looks like to "put out" a hostile crowd that doesn't want to go? All this is in contrast to the humble plea of a brokenhearted father, the fearful touch of a broken woman, and the tender life of a little girl.

▶ Prayer

Sometimes I, like the people in the story, can't imagine that you care about the little things in my life, dear Lord. Yet you raise the little girl and you care for me. When I doubt your infinite love for me, remind me what you did for the people in the story. Thanks.

▶ Action

Think about what you might consider to be beyond saving in your life. Try to put that attitude "out" and call upon Jesus.

Tuesday of the Fourteenth Week of the Year

Forgiveness Hostility

MATTHEW 9:32–38

The Pharisees said, "He casts out demons by the prince of demons." But he had compassion for the crowds because they were harassed and helpless, like sheep without a shepherd.

▶ Reflection

The Pharisees were hostile toward Jesus because they believed a person's afflictions were the result of sin; what a person suffered was a kind of just deserts for the wrong they had done. To heal them was, in a way, letting them off the hook so that they didn't suffer the consequences of their sinful actions. Therefore they accused Jesus of being in league with the devil because he seemed to be giving people license to sin with impunity. Unfortunately, that kind of attitude puts a shepherd at odds with the sheep, especially the ones in need of the shepherd's care. Jesus saw things differently. He understood his mission as one of salvation, not of condemnation (see John 3:17). He believed that mercy was an expression of God's love and had the power to transform a person from the inside out. Forgiving sin is indeed letting people off the hook. But mercy and compassion will achieve what punishment never could.

▶ Prayer

You have given us your law to follow, O God. But even though I try and try, I fail. Yet your love and forgiveness raises me up and frees me from my sins, and for this I give you thanks.

▶ Action

Keep track of the number of times God forgives you today. At the end of the day, offer God fitting praise and thanksgiving.

Wednesday of the Fourteenth Week of the Year

Not Far

MATTHEW 10:1–7

Jesus sent out his disciples with the following instructions: "Go to the lost sheep of the house of Israel and proclaim the good news that the kingdom of heaven has come near."

▶ Reflection

When I was growing up Catholic in the fifties, all I seemed to hear was the bad news. It seemed that the possibility of heaven was just so far away. Condemnation, on the other hand, was always at the door. I remember how I grew fearful late in the week when I had sinned sufficiently to warrant hell (which wasn't hard to do in those days) but it wasn't yet Saturday night when I could go to confession and be reinstated in grace. Into this world was proclaimed the good news that heaven wasn't so far away after all. Heaven was near and I just had to turn and enter it; turn from my old idea about God, sin, and hell, and embrace the new revelation of God shown to me in Jesus Christ. The good news is that my sins were forgiven. I could always celebrate that truth in sacrament of reconciliation. But it's also true that I'm always safe in the hands of God. No more fear. No more doubt.

▶ Prayer

Dear God, you have rescued me from sin and death. Yet from time to time I am afraid because I am a sinner. Teach me to trust in your love. Tell me again and again the good news that you are near me, that heaven is at hand.

▶ Action

Remember that in your baptism God promised you eternal life and the forgiveness of your sins. Enjoy that memory.

Thursday of the Fourteenth Week of the Year

No Just Deserts

MATTHEW 10:7–15

"Cure the sick, raise the dead, cleanse the lepers, cast out demons. If people won't welcome you or listen to your words, it will go easier on the judgment day for Sodom and Gomorrah than for them."

▶ Reflection

The man in the television commercial told me I should buy a new car because I deserved it. That sounded mighty fine until I realized that getting what I deserved may not be such a good thing. Looking at my life, I judge myself a sinner. What I deserve is the just punishment given to the wicked, which is the consequence of sin. But Jesus Christ has forged a new covenant between God and humanity, rescuing me from the punishment due my sins and setting me free to serve God without fear and to be a living witness to God's saving power. Now for every consequence of sin there is an act of divine mercy. So now I don't rely on God's justice; I bank on God's mercy! If I didn't accept this new covenant, I'd be stuck with the old one and I don't think that would work out very well because I would be in big trouble!

▶ Prayer

O my Jesus, you forgive us our sins and save us from the fires of hell. You lead our souls into heaven, we who are most in need of your mercy. May we always live in the light of your love. May rejoicing and thanksgiving be the witness of our lives.

▶ Action

Think of what you deserve as punishment for your sins. Now consider that your sins are forgiven. Compose a prayer of thanksgiving to God.

Friday of the Fourteenth Week of the Year

In Her Face

MATTHEW 10:16–23

"I am sending you out like sheep in the midst of wolves. Do not worry about what you are to say. What you are to say will be given to you when you need it."

▶ Reflection

The woman next door was livid. Too many times she had been made to wait while poor Colleen struggled to get her invalid father and his wheelchair into their van just as the neighbor was trying to use the driveway Colleen was blocking. Now the neighbor was in her face. "How long will this go on?" she fumed. "Um, n-n-not for long," the gentle Colleen stammered. "The doctor said he only has a few more weeks to live." The impatient neighbor blanched and backed away. Colleen's reply had left her speechless. Dragged before the one-woman tribunal of the neighborhood, Colleen had been called to witness on account of the love she was showing her broken father. That witness completely disarmed her accuser. It may not have meant much in the cosmic order, but it gave some respite to the beleaguered woman. It's amazing how God works through gentle, humble souls, especially when fear and anxiety are not allowed in the way.

▶ Prayer

O God, when I am called to account for my love before the tribunal of the world, be with me and give me the strength I need to be your witness.

▶ Action

Think about the times you were called upon to witness to God's love in your life. How did you do?

Saturday of the Fourteenth Week of the Year

Better Than Birds

MATTHEW 10:24–33

"Do not fear death. Two sparrows are worth a penny, yet God knows when just one of them falls to the ground. So do not be afraid; you are worth more than a whole flock of sparrows."

▶ Reflection

Ken makes a modest living off the stock market and often uses the image of a roller coaster to describe the ups and downs of his day. Sometimes it gets pretty scary for him, but his confidence gets him through. He knows that the key to investing is to weather the storm, to trust in the power of the economy. It makes me think about the times I've gone to the amusement park and ridden the roller coaster. I know it's going to be scary, but I have a certain confidence in the design and construction of the machine and trust in its operation and maintenance. It is the same with life. Our fears are understandable; life can look pretty scary sometimes. But our fears should not keep us from following our hearts and being who we're called to be. Jesus tells his disciples not to be afraid and to have faith in the designer and maker of life. The life of a single sparrow is a concern to God. Imagine how concerned God is for you!

▶ Prayer

When life is scary, my creator, remind me who makes life. Keep me confident that you will see me through, even if I die. As you value me above all other creatures, may I value you more than anything else.

▶ Action

Think about the most scared you've ever been. How did it work out? Remember how God delivered you and preserved you.

Monday of the Fifteenth Week of the Year

Constant Hassles

MATTHEW 10:34—11:1

"Don't think that I have come to bring peace, for I have come to set a man against his father, and a daughter against her mother. Your foes will be members of your own household."

▶ Reflection

For Andrew, family life is a struggle. Each day is filled with conflict. His parents don't trust him; they don't accept the way he is and they want him to change and be more like his older brother. But Andrew is different and so he has to endure constant hassles about the clothes he wears, the color of his hair, and the kids he hangs out with. He prays to Jesus to bring peace to his family but it seems to no avail. The paradox of the gospel is still not available to his young mind. Andrew will learn that in the kingdom it is the blind who see, the lame who walk, and the deaf who hear. That's good news for broken families and broken relationships. The day will come when he will break free from his family, leave behind his mother and his father, the expectations of a sinful generation, the values of a passing world, and seek the One he loves more than life. Jesus is the rejected one who calls the rejected of the world to his side.

▶ Prayer

Most loving God, you created me in perfect love, yet I am an imperfect person. I struggle each day for peace, but find division instead. Help me to see your kingdom coming even in my sinful life.

▶ Action

Think of someone in your family with whom you are in conflict. Now imagine Jesus standing with the two of you, bringing you together.

Tuesday of the Fifteenth Week of the Year

Ultimate Justice

MATTHEW 11:20–24

He said to the people of Capernaum, "If the deeds of power done in you had been done in Sodom, it would have remained until this day. But I tell you that on the day of judgment it will be more tolerable for the land of Sodom than for you."

▶ Reflection

When the announcement appeared in the parish bulletin that a gay and lesbian support group was forming in the parish, Archie confronted the pastor. He ranted that it was not right for the church to welcome homosexuals. The pastor's response was gentle, but firm. He pointed out that, according to Jesus, the people of Sodom will get off lighter on the day of judgment than will the people from whom judgment comes. Jesus is confident that those who live under condemnation will show the most mercy. And in the kingdom of God mercy is the key. Jesus came to demonstrate that mercy and forgiveness have the greatest power over sin, and ultimately even over death. But those who persist in judgment claim that righteousness is the deciding factor. Jesus is willing to let those who think they are righteous face the judgment, but warns that they will not fare well. The ultimate justice for the Christian is the love that shows itself in forgiveness.

▶ Prayer

O God, you are the just judge. But you've shown us great mercy in your Son Jesus. Teach us to always walk in the way of your love.

▶ Action

Is there some group or an individual in your life whom you think is definitely condemned? Now think again, with mercy and forgiveness in your heart.

Wednesday of the Fifteenth Week of the Year

Babies Got God

MATTHEW 11:25–27

At that time Jesus said, "I thank you, Father, Lord of heaven and earth, because you have hidden these things from the wise and the intelligent and have revealed them to infants; yes, Father, for such was your gracious will."

▶ Reflection

I sometimes sit on the bus or the subway, or in the mall, or maybe even at church, and watch the babies. And sometimes the babies catch me watching and begin watching back. They gaze at me with such wonder and awe, and I gaze back reflecting, I imagine, the same wonder. Deep within them is the mystery of life and I can almost see it because it hasn't yet been glazed over by even the slightest falsehood or surrender to the passing world. They have not yet learned the guile of deception or the lie of marketing. The babies are totally transparent, totally clear, completely receptive, completely open; no creature is more vulnerable than a baby. As they grow up, they will become more guarded, more opaque, and less assailable. But for now God can be seen in them and can reach out through them to touch our broken hearts and heal us.

▶ Prayer

Dear God, I thank you for the babies. Through them you recreate the world and make new life. Give us the grace we need to become like babies so that we, too, may be open to your love and your light.

▶ Action

At the very next opportunity, engage a baby. Gaze into the baby's eyes and allow the baby to look into yours. See God.

Thursday of the Fifteenth Week of the Year

Yoke of Love

MATTHEW 11: 28–30

"Come to me, all you that are weary and are carrying heavy burdens, and I will give you rest. Take my yoke upon you, and learn from me; for I am gentle and humble in heart, and you will find rest for your souls. For my yoke is easy, and my burden is light."

▶ Reflection

Fred tossed and turned and lay awake because of burdens that weighed heavily on his mind and made his soul restless. Yet, when he looked back, he saw how things worked out in the past and how he worried about many things that really didn't matter. He thought about some of the bad things that had happened in his life and how he suffered, but now here he was, safe and sound. He could see the way that led from the depths of despair to the heights of joy. Maybe disaster and suffering would again be just around the corner. Or maybe he wouldn't live to see tomorrow. Then, in that moment Fred turned to Jesus. "Whether I live or die," he thought, "I belong to Christ." To the degree that Fred continues to live in that faith, so will his soul will find rest.

▶ Prayer

When my soul is troubled, give me rest, O God. When I lie awake at night, remind me of your promise. When I despair over the future, give me faith in your love and in your power to save me. May I always be yoked to you.

▶ Action

What burdens you today? Turn to Jesus and offer that burden to him. Consider his promise to you and live in the light of his love.

Friday of the Fifteenth Week of the Year

Sabbath Blizzard

MATTHEW 12:1–8

Jesus said to those who condemned him and his disciples for breaking the sabbath, "If you had known what this means, 'I desire mercy and not sacrifice,' you would not have condemned the guiltless. For the Son of Man is lord of the sabbath."

▶ Reflection

"Bless me Father, for I have sinned." The woman was troubled. "I missed Mass last Sunday." I inquired why she missed Mass. "Because I was sick, Father." It is a point of particular annoyance when people confess to me that they have missed Mass on Sunday because they were sick in bed. Haven't we taught our members yet that they are lords of the sabbath? An archbishop, a few years ago, got on the radio during a blizzard to announce that he was dispensing his subjects from the obligation to go to Mass. Didn't he know that the law of obligation (Canon 1248) is attenuated in cases of impossibility (paragraph 2)? Why didn't he simply remind them that, under the circumstances of a howling blizzard, they had no obligation to go to Mass on Sunday? We sometimes do more to take away the kingdom of God than we do to announce its presence. We need to remind people that nothing can keep them from entering at any time.

▶ Prayer

O creator of the universe, you have given us charge over the whole world. Teach me to exercise my authority wisely.

▶ Action

Think of a time you were unable to attend Mass due to circumstances beyond your control. How did you feel? How do you feel about this now?

Beloved Servant

MATTHEW 12:14–21

The Pharisees conspired against Jesus. He was aware of this, but continued curing the crowds who followed him. And the prophet Isaiah was fulfilled: "Here is my servant, whom I have chosen, my beloved, with whom my soul is well pleased. I will put my Spirit upon him, and he will proclaim justice to the Gentiles."

▶ Reflection

Those who hold to strict moralism will always conspire against those who hold to the unalloyed love of God. The Pharisees, who were the strict moralists of the gospel stories, didn't like Jesus because he was healing, and therefore, in their eyes at least, letting people out of the strict moral structure of reward and punishment. To the Pharisees, justice meant defeating the enemy, punishing the wrongdoer, and condemning the wicked. But the God revealed in Jesus Christ had his own brand of justice. For God, justice is loving the enemy, finding what was lost, restoring what was corrupted, healing what was broken, freeing what was bound, reconciling what was alienated, raising up what was bowed down, and resurrecting what was dead. The servant who lives in this kind of justice pleases God immensely.

▶ Prayer

Almighty God, your love is beyond my imagining! Thank you for not condemning me for my sins, which is what I deserve. Rather, you raise me up and give me new life. For this I praise and thank you.

▶ Action

Think of someone you know whom you treat according to what he or she does wrong. Today, treat that person according to God's justice.

Monday of the Sixteenth Week of the Year

Parking Lot Angel

MATTHEW 12:38–42

Then some of the scribes and Pharisees said to him, "Teacher, we wish to see a sign from you." But he answered them, "An evil and adulterous generation asks for a sign, but no sign will be given to it except the sign of the prophet Jonah."

▶ Reflection

It was a mistake going to the supermarket on a Saturday afternoon, but an elderly woman from the neighborhood needed a ride so I offered. Now we cruised the parking lot, searching for the space I knew didn't exist. My companion bowed her head and prayed, "Boniface, Boniface, you're my man/give me a parking space fast as you can." I was astonished. I quickly checked through my memory for any references to St. Boniface and parking spaces, but came up empty. I turned into the next aisle and there it was, a holy vacancy. Helping her out of the car I said, "I didn't know St. Boniface did parking spaces." "He doesn't," she replied, taking my hand. "Boniface is the name of my parking lot angel. My sister told me about him years ago and he's never failed me." Every sign given by God is an invitation to believe more deeply in a God who cares.

▶ Prayer

O Lord, I give you thanks for the many signs of your presence you give me in a day. They are like the sign of Jonah; they bring me to believe more deeply in you. May I always recognize your signs.

▶ Action

Look around you right now and see if you can spot the signs of God's presence in your life.

Tuesday of the Sixteenth Week of the Year

Lasting Values

MATTHEW 12:46–50

Someone told Jesus, "Look, your mother and your brothers are standing outside, wanting to speak to you." Jesus replied, "Who is my mother, and who are my brothers?" And pointing to his disciples, he said, "Here are my mother and my brothers! For whoever does the will of my Father in heaven is my brother and sister and mother."

▶ Reflection

Does Jesus toss off his mother in this episode? It sounds that way. Why, if that were *my* mother, she'd be in there in a heartbeat, taking me by the ear and pulling me outside. "You *come* when I call you, do you *hear*?" Yes, Mom. Evidently the mother of God didn't mind Jesus ignoring her for the sake of the kingdom, although Matthew doesn't say what happened next. Perhaps she already knew that kingdom relationships were far more important than worldly ones. Things of the world can only gain the world, but things of heaven gain heaven. Family values are fine, but there are things of far greater value in life: the dignity and respect we show to the least and lowliest of those we encounter today will provide a lasting value for us in heaven.

▶ Prayer

Thank you for my mother, O God. She was the best mother I ever had! But no matter how good she was, you're better. May your love for me always be the model of my love for others.

▶ Action

Decide who the lowliest person will be in your life today and then treat that person like your brother or your sister.

Wednesday of the Sixteenth Week of the Year

Fruit of Their Bodies

MATTHEW 13:1–9

Jesus told them many things in parables. "Listen!" he said. "A sower went out to sow. Some of the seed fell on bad ground and produced nothing. Some of the seeds fell on good soil and brought forth grain, some a hundredfold, some sixty, some thirty."

▶ Reflection

Whenever parents come to me concerned about their ability to be good parents, I tell them about Joachim and Anne. The fruit of their relationship was Mary, the mother of God. Our tradition does not regard them as free from sin, original or otherwise, as it does Mary. So even though they were technically the grandparents of God, we can assume that they were just regular parents with their own particular faults and failures. God sowed the seed of Mary in their bodies, knowing there were thorns and rocks and trampled ground that would prove fruitless, but trusting that the good ground in them would be adequate to produce fruit "a hundredfold." So it is with all of us. Despite our sinfulness, we are called by God to receive the seed of God's grace and bring forth fruit. God trusts that the goodness in us will overcome all our weaknesses.

▶ Prayer

O Mary, my mother, thank God for your parents. They brought you up to be the mother of God. What wonderful gifts they were. Bless my parents, too. They passed on your goodness to me.

▶ Action

Put aside the faults of your parents for a moment and think about the good that you experienced in them.

Thursday of the Sixteenth Week of the Year

Mysterious Presence

MATTHEW 13:10–17

Jesus said to the disciples, "Blessed are your eyes, for they see, and your ears, for they hear. Truly I tell you, many prophets and righteous people longed to see what you see, but did not see it, and to hear what you hear, but did not hear it."

▸ Reflection

A man I know is dying of cancer. As he nears death, he tells me that he is becoming less and less aware of the things that go on around him, and more and more aware of a dark, quiet, mysterious presence within him. He says he often withdraws into this presence; he says it's like a "cocoon of comfort." When he is thus absorbed, he reports that he hears the clatter and chatter of caregiving going on around him but he does not respond, preferring the comfort of his inner world. If, as Jesus says, the kingdom of God is at hand, in our midst, then everything is a parable. We are so caught up in the things of this passing world that we miss the presence of a parallel world within us, where God dwells. It's not that we can't see it or feel it; we simply choose to experience something else.

▸ Prayer

Lord, your kingdom is at hand and those who choose to die to this world are being born into it. Give us the grace we need to let go of the things of this passing world so that we might come to know your presence among us and within us.

▸ Action

Stop what you are doing and sit quietly. Close your eyes. Block out the world, if you can. Know that God is present to you right now.

Friday of the Sixteenth Week of the Year

Berry Bush Dreams

MATTHEW 13:18–23

"The seeds that fell among thorns are those who hear the word, but the cares of the world and the lure of wealth choke it off and it yields nothing."

▶ Reflection

Connie lives in a house where there is a serious problem with thorns. Berry bushes border the property on one side, and they are relentless in trying to grow through the fence and into her yard. Connie's job is to keep them at bay. She spends hours hacking away at them at one end of the fence, only to discover they have grown through on the other end. Some nights she dreams that the thorn bushes are surrounding her and are creeping into her room. It's an endless battle. So it is with the "cares of the world and the lure of wealth." They are a constant presence in our affluent society, relentless as they encroach upon the property of our souls. It is our continual responsibility to keep them at bay through prayer, fasting, practices of self-denial, and works of charity, lest they choke off the word sown in our hearts and leave us fruitless.

▶ Prayer

Dear Lord, you have called us to bear fruit in our lives, yet sometimes I allow the thorns of worldly care and the desire for wealth choke off your word growing in me. Help me deny myself so that I may be united with you completely.

▶ Action

Before you buy something today, stop and ask yourself if you really need it. Let God show you a better way.

Saturday of the Sixteenth Week of the Year

Fruit Ain't Easy

MATTHEW 13:24–30

The servants of the householder came and said to him, "Master, did you not sow good seed in your field? Where, then, did these weeds come from?"

▶ Reflection

Having worked on a farm as a kid growing up in Connecticut, I know what it takes to make good ground. Southern New England is mostly glacial till—that is, a mix of clay, sand, and gravel—and the dirt is full of rocks. Those picturesque stone walls that make such pretty subjects for postcards and vacation photos are the work of generations of kids like me who hauled those rocks out of the fields and piled them up on the edges so that the farmer could scratch the soil and plant his seeds. Weeds, birds, gophers, and bugs all wanted a piece of the action; the battle to produce a yield rages continually. A fruitful life requires the same diligence. When I consider how loud and strong is the call of the world with all its wealth and comfort, and how still and small the voice of the Lord and humble the life to which he calls me, it's a wonder that I produce anything at all.

▶ Prayer

Lord in heaven above, life-giving Spirit within, in me you plant seeds of grace and goodness and beauty. Then you give me all I need to make them grow. Help me always to provide a fruitful harvest.

▶ Action

What seed does God plant in you today to bring forth fruit? Spend the day protecting its growth and then welcome the harvest!

Parables Don't Bite

MATTHEW 13:31–35

Jesus told the crowds all these things in parables to fulfill what the prophet said: "I will speak to them in parables and proclaim what has been hidden from the foundation of the world."

▶ Reflection

"You have to move some things around, you know. It's not going to jump out and bite you on the nose." That was one of my mother's standard aphorisms invoked whenever I stood staring stupidly, mouth agape, in front of the open refrigerator or kitchen cabinet looking for whatever it was I couldn't find. What is true for the kitchen is true also for the kingdom of God. It's not going to jump out and bite you on the nose. You have to search for it, move things around to find out what lies hidden behind life's jar of pickles. The parables of Jesus pique the imagination of seekers, those who are searching for fulfillment and peace. If we are content with things the way they are, we won't be interested in the images Jesus used. They will remain meaningless because they point to things beyond where we are and what we can see. We can believe the kingdom is out there somewhere, but we won't experience it until we act to enter it.

▶ Prayer

Jesus, maker and lover of my soul, you always draw me beyond where I am so that I can make the journey to you. You are my life and my goal. Help me always to be ready to change for you.

▶ Action

Think of what it is you are searching for right now. What do you need to "move" to find it?

Tuesday of the Seventeenth Week of the Year

Loving My Dad

MATTHEW 13:36–43

"Just as the weeds are collected and burned up with fire, so will it be at the end of the age. The Son of Man will send his angels and they will collect out of his kingdom all that causes sin."

▶ Reflection

My Dad died last year. I was not perfect in my love for him any more than he was perfect in his love for me. There were many sinful things that stood in the way of our love: pride, unreasonable expectations, stubbornness, resentment, guilt. Yet, we will see each other again and be together forever in heaven. I look forward to this because I love my Dad and I know he loves me, sinners though we may be. It's good to know that "all that causes sin" will be collected out of the kingdom and burned. That means all the sinfulness within me that has kept me from loving the way I ought, and the way I need, will be removed. And all that has kept others, like my Dad, from loving the way they should and the way they wanted will be removed. God is love, and when we are fully in God, then we will be fully in love with one another.

▶ Prayer

O God, you are love. In you all love exists pure and good and holy. And when I really love the way Jesus taught, I am in you and my love is right and good. Keep me alive in your love. Keep me loving the way I should so that I can feel your kingdom present.

▶ Action

Think of three people you are called to love yet have a hard time loving. What is standing in the way to love? How well does this hold up in God's eyes?

Kingdom for a Car

MATTHEW 13:44–46

"The kingdom of heaven is like a merchant in search of fine pearls; on finding one pearl of great value, he went and sold all that he had and bought it."

▶ Reflection

Lynne would love to be more involved in her daughter's sports, but when she gets home, she's just too tired. Brad wants his relationship with Cindy to work, but weekends are out of the question. Todd would like to go with Jason to the soup kitchen, but he's got other things he has to do. Debbie has to work overtime so that she can meet the payments on her car. It's amazing how much of our time and effort we spend on things that are unimportant and even worthless. We love the soaps, football, travel, movies, restaurants, cars, shopping, clothes…all of which take up large quantities of time and great portions of the energy and resources God gives us to invest in the day. Yet no one ever died saying, "I spent too much time with my kids," or "I did too much for the needy," or "I worked too much on my marriage." Jesus invites us to understand what is important and use the treasure of limited life wisely.

▶ Prayer

My God, you give me so many good things. My time, energy, talent, and all the resources I have all come from you. Teach me to use all these things wisely so that I may be fully alive in your kingdom.

▶ Action

Today, trade in the time and energy you spend on one worthless thing for something that is of truly lasting value.

Thursday of the Seventeenth Week of the Year

Resources Squandered

MATTHEW 13:47–53

"The kingdom of heaven is like a net that caught fish of every kind. Then they put the good into baskets but threw out the bad. So it will be at the end of the age. The angels will come out and separate the evil from the righteous."

▶ Reflection

Every day I am called to goodness that I fail to achieve. Every day love is required of me, yet I fail to fulfill the requirement. God gives me gifts each day that are uselessly spent, and each day I squander my resources on worldly things that do not matter. In the final analysis, there is precious little good in me, I fear. Still, I find comfort knowing that one day the good in me will be saved and all that is bad will be thrown out. I need to work harder clearing out all the bad in me and developing the good, so that when the day comes, there will be enough of me left to provide heaven with a piece of me substantial enough so that my friends will recognize me. Otherwise, almost all of me would get thrown away and that would be too bad.

▶ Prayer

God in heaven, every morning when I rise there are gifts from you placed along the path of my day. My time and talents, even the money I make from my profession, are yours given to me so that I can better live my life. Stir in me the fire of your Spirit so that I may live more fruitfully and more faithfully.

▶ Action

Write down three good things in you that are going largely unused. Now think of ways to use these gifts of goodness.

Friday of the Seventeenth Week of the Year

Mom Can't See

MATTHEW 13:54–58

In his hometown the people took offense at Jesus and said, "Where did he get all this? Isn't he the carpenter's son?" But Jesus said to them, "Prophets are not honored in their own country and in their own house."

▶ Reflection

The mother was really upset with her two young children at church. They were fooling around a little bit, as kids tend to do, but they weren't too bad. The mother, however, was showing signs of exasperation. Finally, she gathered them up and left before communion. She returned by herself to the next Mass and took her place next to another mother with two young children, and these two kids were *really* misbehaving. They weren't terribly bad, but their noise and unruliness were a distraction. After Mass, the first mother came up to the pastor and apologized for the behavior of her children at the earlier Mass. "What did you think of those two next to you at this Mass?" he asked. "Oh," she said, "They didn't bother me. They weren't nearly as bad as my kids." Like many parents, she couldn't see the grace in her own children.

▶ Prayer

When I look at my family and my friends, good Lord, I sometimes can't see the beauty and grace you provide for me in my life. Today, when I encounter them, help me to see past their familiarity.

▶ Action

Think of someone you know or maybe someone in your own family who could be a source of grace for you. Pray to see the grace.

Saturday of the Seventeenth Week of the Year

No Comparison

MATTHEW 14:1–12

When Herod the tetrarch heard reports about Jesus, he said to his servants, "It's John the Baptist! He has been raised from the dead. That's why these powers are at work in him."

▶ Reflection

It was natural that the teachers at the junior high would be reminded of Laura when Sarah showed up in class. Laura was a popular student whom the teachers liked, and Sarah was the image of her older sister. Except Sarah didn't like being compared to Laura. They were two completely different girls and Sarah took offense when the teachers called her Laura by mistake. Jesus was often mistaken for John the Baptist, even after John was executed. But they were two different people. John was a prophet of God's law who would enforce the commandments and the teachings to his death. But Jesus was the prophet of God's mercy who would offer forgiveness to the law-breaker to his death. Nowhere was it written that Jesus ever took offense at being mistaken for John, but make no mistake about it: Jesus and John were two completely different prophets.

▶ Prayer

Loving God, you sent your Son Jesus not to condemn us for our sins, but to save us from our sins. In every moment of my life you offer me grace and mercy. When I fear condemnation, teach me always to trust in your mercy so that my life may bear joyful witness to your love.

▶ Action

Think of how you might be mistaking Jesus for John. In other words, where do you think God is condemning you rather than saving you?

Monday of the Eighteenth Week of the Year

Loaves Given to Us

MATTHEW 14:13–21

Jesus said to his disciples, "We don't need to send the crowd away. You give them something to eat." They replied, "We have nothing here but five loaves and two fish." And he said, "Bring them here to me."

▶ Reflection

In our local parish we run a soup kitchen called "Loaves and Fishes" in honor of this popular miracle story. Through it we feed hundreds of our city's poor and homeless every week. It, and thousands of soup kitchens like it all over the country, are testimonies of what can be done when people respond to the command of Jesus: "*You* feed them." The enormous resources of the federal or state governments do not back these food programs. Rather, the miracle is that they are supported by our contributions and run by volunteers, people like you and me. The answer to the problem of hunger in the world is in our own hands. We already possess everything we need to feed the hungry. In most cases, however, we are using our resources for other things. Loaves and fishes are given to us so that we can take part in the miracle.

▶ Prayer

My Lord, I look around my life and I see all the ways I fall short of what I think I need to do and what I'm supposed to do. Yet you can feed thousands with just a little. Help me always to trust in your grace.

▶ Action

Think of the things you don't have enough of, like savings, time, and patience. Consider what Jesus would do with what you have.

Tuesday of the Eighteenth Week of the Year

Poking at Peter

MATTHEW 14:22–36

Peter tried to get out of the boat and walk to Jesus on the water. But he became frightened and started to sink. He cried out, "Lord, save me!" Jesus caught him and said, "Why did you doubt, O ye of little faith?"

▶ Reflection

Peter was not the undisputed leader of the early church (see 1 Corinthians 1:11–12). Some, perhaps, saw him at best as a bit of a jerk; at worst, someone hungry for power and not to be trusted. Others, of course, acknowledged him as the anointed leader of the apostles and the "keeper of the keys" of the kingdom. Either way, anyone holding a position of authority has to be open to people poking fun at him. This gospel story, I believe, has a little fun with Peter, poking at his vulnerability. If the members of the community to whom the story was addressed knew Peter at all, they would've gotten a good laugh out of Peter's attempt to walk on the water. Part of living in the kingdom is having fun with one another and not taking things like church leadership too seriously. What we need to take seriously is our faith. Peter's faith needed a boost, just like ours.

▶ Prayer

Dear Jesus, you are present in my life in all things, even the things I think are impossible. When I fear, when my faith is weak, show me your power to bring all things to pass.

▶ Action

Close your eyes and think of something you'd like to be able to do in your life but don't feel you can do. See Jesus there calling you.

248

Wednesday of the Eighteenth Week of the Year

The Lord Learns

MATTHEW 15:21–28

Just then a Canaanite woman from that region came out and started shouting,
"Have mercy on me, Lord, Son of David; my daughter is tormented by a
demon." But he did not answer her at all.

▶ Reflection

One thing we always need to remember about Jesus is that he is truly
God and truly human. Nowhere in the gospel stories does the
humanity of Jesus show through more strongly than in his encounter
with the Canaanite woman. One can say he was testing her on
purpose when at first, he did not answer, but this would be
inconsistent with his responses in other stories. No, I believe Jesus is
learning something here. Just as God "changed his mind" on a few
things in the Old Testament (see Exodus 32:14, Jonah 3:10), so now
the Lord of the New Testament "repents" of the standard cultural
attitude about foreigners and people of other races and religions he
learned growing up. Even though the Canaanites are historical
enemies of the Jews, Jesus sees in the woman a cause to celebrate
God's goodness and grace. She is like he, simply another human
being. And so he heals her daughter.

▶ Prayer

O Lord Jesus, how sensitive and open you were to the woman who
sought your help, even though everything you learned to that point
would have closed your mind to her. With your grace, help me to be
open and accepting to all people who come to me for help.

▶ Action

Think of the racial and ethnic stereotypes you learned growing up.
Now consider how they've been changed by your faith in God.

Thursday of the Eighteenth Week of the Year

Peter Drops the Ball

MATTHEW 16:13-23

Jesus told his disciples that he must undergo great suffering and be killed, and on the third day be raised. Peter took him aside and began to rebuke him, saying, "God forbid it, Lord! This must never happen to you." But he turned and said to Peter, "Get behind me, Satan! You are setting your mind not on divine things but on human things."

▶ Reflection

It's significant that the first discernment Peter makes as the keeper of the keys of the kingdom is worldly, that is, judging by human standards and not by God's. That's why it's not enough just to believe that Jesus is the Christ, the Son of God. Even the devil believes that! In order to rightly judge the things of the world, a person must know the teachings of Jesus and have some experience practicing those teachings. The church already has plenty of members and leaders who accept the divinity of Jesus yet judge the things of life according to worldly values. The suffering and death of Jesus had to become a lived experience for Peter in order for him to understand the ways of the kingdom and exercise right judgment. This must also be so for followers of Jesus today.

▶ Prayer

Dear God, I am constantly tempted to pursue the things of this world, for they are always before me. But you call me to pursue the lasting things of heaven because you love me. Keep me always in your grace.

▶ Action

Write down three human things upon which you have set your mind. How would turning your attention to divine things be different?

Friday of the Eighteenth Week of the Year

Profit Motive

MATTHEW 16:24–28

Jesus told his disciples, "If any of you wants to become my follower, you must deny yourself, take up your cross, and follow me. What profit would you show if you gained the whole world but lost your own soul?"

▶ Reflection

As each of Terry's three daughters graduated from college, she would write to them with advice about a career. She always included today's gospel passage because it, or a variation of it, appears six times in the Bible, one of the very few sayings of Jesus that appears in all four gospels. Terry realizes that this teaching must have had a huge impact on those first-century communities that spawned the gospels. A millennium later, in 1212, Clare Offreduccio of Assisi, Italy, offered her life in service of this same ideal. She began the Order of Poor Ladies, dedicated to complete personal and communal poverty. They were the Second Order of St. Francis, or Poor Clares, as they would come to be called. Together they embodied the joy of living the lives they found through giving up the lives they had. Terry wants what is best for her kids and she believes Jesus knows the way.

▶ Prayer

God of goodness, what cross awaits me to carry this day? Will I lay down my life to carry it and follow you? I hope so. Please, dear Lord, give me the grace I need to lose the world and gain my soul.

▶ Action

Write down a list of the last five worldly things you gained. Next to it list the spiritual things you may have lost in the process.

Saturday of the Eighteenth Week of the Year

Driving Home Empty

MATTHEW 17:14–20

Jesus said to his disciples, "I tell you truly, if you have faith the size of a mustard seed, you will say to a mountain, 'Move from here to there,' and it will move; and nothing will be impossible for you."

▶ Reflection

Mrs. Benson loves to tell the story about the night she, her husband, and another couple were driving their old car back from a prayer meeting in the city. Traveling across a long lonely stretch of road, they ran out of gas. Mr. Benson confirmed the predicament with his flashlight, announcing that the glass bowl of the old-fashioned fuel pump was dry. That's when Mrs. Benson and the other woman began to pray in the back seat. "Oh, we prayed up a storm," she says. "We called upon the Father, Jesus, the Holy Ghost, and everybody, praisin' God and shoutin' glory! just askin' to give us the gas we need to get us back home." This is the part where Mrs. Benson likes to pause to make sure everybody is listening. "Then I felt the Spirit come upon me and I said to my husband, 'Start up the car, Emile. We're goin' home.'" Then Mr. Benson tells his part: "I started it and we drove home. When we got home, the tank was still empty."

▶ Prayer

O God of miracles, I know you can do anything. It's just hard sometimes believing you'll do it for me. When I am in need and things look impossible, come to my aid. Give me the faith to believe.

▶ Action

Think of a mountain you need to move in your life. Ask God to move it and then begin to live like that mountain is moving.

Monday of the Nineteenth Week of the Year

Fish Story

MATTHEW 17:22–27

Jesus asked Peter, "Do the children of kings pay taxes?" Peter said, "Of course not." Jesus said, "Then the children are free. But so that we don't give offense, cast a line into the sea and take a fish. In its mouth you will find a coin to pay our taxes."

▶ Reflection

What a great trick! Unfortunately, the story concludes without any indication as to whether or not Peter ever caught the fish or extracted a coin from its mouth. The playful tone of Jesus' dialogue with Peter, however, indicates that the fish story may have had a more colloquial meaning. What goes unnoticed is the conclusion of Jesus: "Then the children are free." I know a guy who became a priest because he was very ill as a teen and promised God that if he got well he would become a priest. The trouble was God never called him to be a priest and the man ended up leaving the priesthood after many unhappy and unfruitful years. If only he had known that, as a child of God, the healing he received was free. He didn't have to pay for it.

▶ Prayer

Heavenly Father, each day you fill my life with so many good things. You create a world just for me and sustain me each day with your love. You have saved me from death and forgiven all my sins. All these things are your gift to me, given in love. May I always believe in your generous grace and be thankful for all you do for me.

▶ Action

Make up a bill of things that you "owe" God. Now in red crayon write PAID IN FULL over the bill.

Tuesday of the Nineteenth Week of the Year

Turning the Tables

MATTHEW 18:1–5, 10–14

The disciples asked Jesus, "Who is the greatest in the kingdom?" He put a child among them and said, "Unless you change and become like children, you will never enter the kingdom of heaven. If a shepherd has a hundred sheep and one of them goes astray, doesn't he leave the ninety-nine and go in search of the one that went astray?"

▶ Reflection

The good Lord was never at a loss to show his disciples how to figure out the kingdom. In their worldly estimations, they figured the one of greatest importance in the kingdom would probably be someone they could recognize as great in the world. Perhaps it was a religious leader or someone who had achieved a high level of spiritual development. Jesus, as always, turns the tables on their thinking because the kingdom is just that: a turn of the tables. If the last are to be first and all that, then the most important in the kingdom will be the lowliest in the world. That's why the shepherd in the parable is interested in the poor lost sheep. Although a worldly shepherd would not risk the herd searching for a loser, God would risk everything to find the lost.

▶ Prayer

I was lost, Lord, and you found me because you loved me and valued me more than even your own life. Turn me around and show me who I am to value in turn.

▶ Action

Who is the greatest person in your world? Who is the least? Imagine the kingdom comes and the value of these two people gets reversed.

Wednesday of the Nineteenth Week of the Year

Carla's Offense

MATTHEW 18:15–20

If someone offends you, go and discuss the matter between the two of you. If the other listens, you have gained a friend. If not, bring others into the discussion. If that doesn't work, bring the matter before the entire community.

▶ Reflection

When Jessie had gathered all her friends on the patio of the senior citizen's home during lunch, she told them what Carla had done to her. "I can't believe she was so mean to me," she cried, her voice trembling. Megan consoled her. "You should talk about this with Carla," she told Jessie. They all agreed that Jessie and she could work this out together. Jessie's approach to the conflict was common: if we've got a problem with somebody, we tend to tell everybody else first, and then finally bring it to the individual. But Jesus taught the way of the kingdom, which is paradoxically opposite of the way we usually do things. Jesus recognized the sacred dimension of the individual first, the power of the relationship second, and the authority of the community after that. Jesus said that he didn't come to condemn; rather, he came to save. When we save relationships through reconciliation, we participate in the life of Christ among us.

▶ Prayer

Lord Jesus, you came among us to reconcile us to God and to one another. May we always act in the spirit of your love.

▶ Action

Think of a relationship in your life that needs saving. Now consider what you could do to save it.

Thursday of the Nineteenth Week of the Year

Eternal Forgiveness

MATTHEW 18:21—19:1

Then Peter asked Jesus, "If someone offends me, how often should I forgive? Seven times?" Jesus said to him, "Try seventy-seven times! You have been forgiven all your debt, so you should have mercy on your fellow debtors."

▶ Reflection

"Do you know that you're forgiven?" I asked the child who had just confessed his sin. "Yes," he said solemnly, "but not if I do it again!" This is what we call a teachable moment. The child may have learned that particular rule of forgiveness under the care of his well-meaning parents, but an upgrade will be necessary if the child is to grow up with a truly Christian understanding of forgiveness. When Jesus died on the cross "once for all" (see Hebrews 10:10), the eternal reality of forgiveness became available to all people for all time. It is like the parable of the banquet in Matthew 22:1–14: all are invited to participate. Like participating in love, we do it through both giving and receiving. God neither holds back forgiveness nor parcels it out; it's an eternal and infinite gift. Rather, to the degree we participate in the gift, to that degree we experience it. Therefore, forgiveness must be both given and received. You can't have one without the other.

▶ Prayer

O God, through the passion of your Son Jesus, my sins have been forgiven. Help me every day to extend this forgiveness to others.

▶ Action

Make a list of some of the ways you've been forgiven. Next to it write a list of some of the ways you need to forgive.

Friday of the Nineteenth Week of the Year

One Flesh

MATTHEW 19:3–12

Some Pharisees tried to test him by asking, "Is it lawful for a man to divorce his wife for any cause?" He answered, "In the beginning God made them one flesh. Therefore what God has joined together, no one should separate."

▶ Reflection

The woman sat before me, wringing her hands and sobbing. Her daughter had just gotten a divorce and now the woman was certain that the daughter was going to hell. The question of divorce is one that so very much plagues the Catholic church. While the church's prohibition of divorce is based on the teaching of Jesus found only in this passage and its parallel in Mark 10:2–9, it must be understood that Jesus was answering the Pharisees who were trying to "test" him. In other words, his enemies were trying to get him into trouble. Throughout the gospel stories, the typical response of Jesus in this situation was to turn the tables on his questioners and give them something even more difficult to ponder. Here he may simply have been challenging the double standard of a male-dominated religion.

▶ Prayer

From the beginning, O God our creator, you made us for each other. In the sacrament of marriage you make two people one flesh to live their lives in a sacred union. Bless your married children and keep them on the way that leads to fulfillment.

▶ Action

Think of a divorced friend of yours, or consider your own divorce. Think of three blessings that have come from God because of this divorce.

Owners of the Kingdom

MATTHEW 19:13–15

Jesus said, "Let the little children come to me, and do not prevent them. It is to such as these that the kingdom of heaven belongs."

▶ Reflection

"He wants me to 'get in touch with my inner child.'" Fred was coming off his third visit to a psychotherapist and he was a little frustrated. "Heck," he said, "I didn't even know I had an inner child." Evidently Fred did. When he was a little kid, Fred was emotionally traumatized by his aggressively punitive father. Sensing danger, his little psyche built protective structures in his personality to prevent his father from getting through and wounding him inside. This isolated his world of feelings from the outside world and his inner child was created. These structures remained into adulthood and prevented important people like his wife and kids from getting through to him, too. So he needed a little help. Jesus wanted absolutely nothing to stand between him and the children who came into his life: no violence, no threats, no disrespect of any kind. Children were to be esteemed as the owners of God's kingdom.

▶ Prayer

Dear God, you give us children to care for and raise to the light. They begin life filled with the values of your kingdom but we quickly change them to become like us, full of the world. May we change and become more like them.

▶ Action

When you encounter children in your life today, treat them as you would treat the ones who own the kingdom of heaven.

Monday of the Twentieth Week of the Year

Grieving My Possessions

MATTHEW 19:16–22

A rich young man asked him, "What must I do?" Jesus said to him, "If you wish to be perfect, give all you have to the poor; then come and follow me." When the man heard this, he went away grieving, for he had many possessions.

▶ Reflection

In defense of the rich man, the story offers no indication that he didn't do what Jesus asked of him. It simply says that he was sad because he had many possessions. I understand the feeling. Last year I moved across the country and could only take what would fit in the trunk and back seat of my little car. So I had to leave a lot behind. It grieved me, as it grieved the rich young man in the story. It should. I am attached to all my possessions. They are all symbols of many friendships, since most of what I have was given to me by the people I've served over the years. Yet there came the call to leave them all behind. It grieved me to do it, but I'm glad I did. I feel better. The experience gave me more freedom to live my call. My hope is that the rich young man had the same experience.

▶ Prayer

You call us to travel light, O God, yet you give us so many things to possess. Why is it necessary for us to deny ourselves? Could it be that you are teaching us to love what is beyond us? I hope so. I hope I can give up everything in this world to possess you.

▶ Action

Make a list of all the things of this world that you love. Now answer this question for each: do you possess it or does it possess you?

Tuesday of the Twentieth Week of the Year

Your Money or Your Life

MATTHEW 19:23–30

Jesus said to his disciples, "It's hard for a rich person to enter the kingdom of heaven. It is easier for a camel to go through the eye of a needle than for someone who is rich to enter the kingdom of God."

▶ Reflection

"What's the problem?" my wealthy friend asked. "Does Jesus have something against rich people?" We were sitting in his million dollar house having lunch on his million dollar porch looking out at his million dollar view. "No, no," I said. "Jesus loves rich people, too. It's just that rich people are understandably happy in their wealth and don't want anything to change. They have everything they need. Jesus taught that in the kingdom, the first shall be last and the last shall be first. So, when the kingdom comes, you and I will be having our lunch in a soup kitchen while the poor folks will be dining on this porch. Is that how you want it?" My friend pondered this for a while. Like the rich young man in yesterday's gospel, he has many possessions. But whether or not he'll adjust his life to take advantage of the coming kingdom remains to be seen.

▶ Prayer

You send me to feed the hungry and care for the poor and those in need, dear God. You give me everything I need to accomplish my mission, yet I squander your wealth on my own desires. I make myself rich in the things of this world. Help me to change, Lord.

▶ Action

Look at your bank statement. Do you simply need more money to live the way you want? Or is God needed more than money?

Wednesday of the Twentieth Week of the Year

Such a Deal

MATTHEW 20:1–16

Jesus told a parable about an owner who paid the workers working one hour the same as those who worked all day. "I am doing no wrong," the manager said. "We agreed on the daily wage. I simply chose to give the last the same as I gave the first."

▶ Reflection

"So, the rich miss out on the kingdom?" my wealthy friend asked as we finished our lunch. "Not at all," I replied. Then I told him how in Luke 6:20–26 it can be said that Jesus sets the terms of the working contract. "Blessed are you who are poor," he says, "for yours is the kingdom of God." Okay, that's a pretty good deal, at least for the poor. Then he goes on to say, "But woe to you who are rich, for you have received your consolation." In other words, everybody gets to be rich; the poor of the world will get it in the kingdom and the rich get it here. The big advantage the rich have in this world is that they get to choose which it will be for them. They can stay rich and get their reward here, or they can use their wealth in such a way that they are poor in this world but rich in the kingdom. It sounds to me like a pretty good deal all around. My wealthy friend doesn't think so. He thinks the rich earn their wealth so they should get to keep it.

▶ Prayer

Merciful Lord, you give us all a chance to be rich. May we so live our lives that when your kingdom comes, we will be among the first.

▶ Action

Find someone who needs a helping hand. See to it that the person gets your help without knowing from where it came.

Thursday of the Twentieth Week of the Year

Going Elsewhere

MATTHEW 22:1–14

"The kingdom of heaven may be compared to a king who gave a wedding banquet. But there was a guest who was not properly dressed. So the king said to the attendants, 'Bind him hand and foot, and throw him into the outer darkness, where there will be weeping and gnashing of teeth.' For many are called, but few are chosen."

▶ Reflection

So, what is "proper dress" for the wedding feast? What is this "wedding garment" we must somehow find and put on to avoid ending up bound hand and foot in teeth-gnashing darkness? It would seem to be the baptismal garment that signifies a new birth by water and the Holy Spirit. At the same time, it is the garment of good deeds mentioned in Revelation 19:8. In order to remain at the feast, one must be born again and live a life of good works. But we may be putting our eschatological cart before the horse here. We need to concentrate a little more on our response to the invitation, which we sometimes take for granted. Money, business, and career are often put before the kingdom. And how do we treat the poor beggars who come to us with the invitation?

▶ Prayer

You saved me from sin and death, O Lord. You gave me a new life and called me to be a witness of your love. Give me opportunities for good works today, that I may be an instrument of your grace.

▶ Action

Wear a white garment today as a sign of your intention to do good works. Every time you notice the white, do something good for someone.

Friday of the Twentieth Week of the Year

His Mother Too?

MATTHEW 22:34–40

One of the Pharisees asked him, "Which commandment of the law is the greatest?" He said to him, "You shall love the Lord your God with all your heart, and with all your soul, and with all your mind."

▶ Reflection

Marilyn's mother was on the phone and very upset. "The new priest at church said that Jesus was Jewish!" she cried in amazement. " Not only that, he said the Blessed Mother was, too!" Marilyn was astonished that her mother had never learned that, but thankful for the new priest in her mother's parish. Jesus was indeed Jewish and taught the law in a perfectly orthodox manner, acceptable to both the Pharisees and the Sadducees. But in the passages bracketing this one, versus 23–33 and versus 41–45, he stymies both groups with conundrums involving a point of law or pronouncement of the prophets. The factions of first-century Judaism were consistently cast in adversarial relationships with Jesus. But as the story evolves, it becomes apparent that Jesus is not in conflict with Judaism, but with religion in general and religious leaders in particular. Therefore, the teaching of Jesus can be applied to any time and any religion, including Christianity.

▶ Prayer

Jesus, you taught your own people how to see injustice and hypocrisy in religion and to speak against it. May we see our religion clearly and be ready to speak the truth boldly to our own religious leaders.

▶ Action

Think of three things about your religion to which Jesus might take exception. Imagine what he would say.

No Help

MATTHEW 23:1–12

Jesus said to his disciples "Do not do as the Pharisees do. They tie up heavy burdens, hard to carry, and lay them on the shoulders of others; but they themselves are unwilling to lift a finger to help with the load."

▶ Reflection

Yvonne lay dying in a nursing home. She was in great distress until the priest arrived. "Please, Father," she gasped, "Hear my confession." The priest listened while she told her story. As a young mother with five children, she became frightened of having another baby. After much worry and anguish, she and her husband decided to use birth control. Wracked with guilt, she took her burden to a priest, but he refused to help her. So all her life she carried that load, convinced she had sinned mortally and could not be absolved. Now the priest at her side had a chance to lift the load from her shoulders. "You are forgiven," he said to her. They recited the Act of Contrition together, and he laid hands on her and gave her absolution. Later, the priest said to me, "Why is it that the great burdens of Catholic women are marriage, birth control, and abortion, things we priests never have to worry about?" I had no answer for him.

▶ Prayer

Lord Jesus, you are the Lamb of God who takes away the sins of the world. May the leaders of your church always live by your love.

▶ Action

Think for a moment what it would be like if married women ran the church. Write down some of the things that would change.

Monday of the Twenty-first Week of the Year

Hiding the Keys

MATTHEW 23:13–22

"Woe to you scribes and Pharisees, you hypocrites!" Jesus cried. "You lock up the gates of the kingdom of heaven to those who are trying to enter. You don't enter yourselves, so you won't allow anybody else to enter either."

▶ Reflection

"How come we were weren't taught to read the Bible when we were kids growing up like the Protestants were?" It's a common enough question among older Catholics. The answer is simple. For the better part of Christian history, the general population of the world was illiterate. Usually only the clergy could read and write, so only the clergy read the Bible and taught its contents to the people. In the last few centuries, literacy has become fairly commonplace, but the clergy has been slow to let go of their power over the contents of the Bible. Victor Hugo wrote: "To learn to read is to light a fire; every syllable that is spelled out is a spark." That "spark" is the key to the kingdom of heaven and those who have traditionally held the keys have been loath to give them up. Martin Luther, a Catholic priest, was one of the first to encourage people to read the Bible, and that began the Protestant Reformation. Maybe that has something to do with why the Protestants traditionally have been better versed in the Bible.

▶ Prayer

Jesus, you are the word of God made flesh. May we learn your word and keep it always in our hearts.

▶ Action

Pick up your Bible and look through it. If there is anything about the Bible you don't understand, ask someone who knows.

Tuesday of the Twenty-first Week of the Year

Gnats and Camels

MATTHEW 23:23–26

"Woe to you, scribes and Pharisees, hypocrites! You tithe mint, dill, and herbs but have neglected the weightier matters of the law: justice and mercy and faith. It is these you ought to have practiced without neglecting the others. You strain out a gnat but swallow a camel!"

▶ Reflection

Lynnelle's eyes filled with tears as she poured out her story to me. Coming home late had not been her intention when she went with her girlfriends to the church fair. But they were having so much fun and the time had somehow slipped away. By the time she realized how late it was, it was too late. She rushed straight home, but was five minutes past her curfew. Her mother was livid and grounded her for a week, which included the first big dance of the school year. Now Lynnelle was seeking my intercession. Lynnelle was a very dependable girl; this was her very first infraction and I think it caught her mother off guard, which may account for her harsh reaction. She was straining out the gnat and swallowing the camel. In this case I thought mercy was called for and I felt it would be a good idea to have a little talk with Lynnelle's mom on Sunday.

▶ Prayer

O God, you are gentle and merciful. You see all sides of a situation and always give your children the benefit of the doubt. I am your servant and I want to do right. May I always be merciful as you are.

▶ Action

Today is a good day to be merciful; let somebody off the hook, whether it's the one in front of you in the market or behind you on the freeway.

Wednesday of the Twenty-first Week of the Year

Lotto Hypocrisy

MATTHEW 23:27–32

"Woe to you, scribes and Pharisees, hypocrites! For you are like whitewashed tombs, which on the outside look beautiful, but inside are full of dead men's bones. So on the outside you look righteous to others, but inside you are full of hypocrisy and lawlessness."

▶ Reflection

What would you do if you won the lottery? Most folks say they would give a substantial amount to their favorite charity and to their church. Does that mean they are good and faithful stewards of their money? Not necessarily. Talk is cheap. It's quite possible that the same people dispose of the thousands and thousands of dollars they earn each year in ways that hardly reflect the values of a good and faithful steward. We tend to take care of ourselves first and worry about the poor later. What would you do if Jesus were to show up at your front door? Again, most of us think we would invite him in and show him great hospitality. In reality, Jesus shows up at our doors every day in the person of the poor and needy of the world. We ignore him; we turn him away; we even make laws prohibiting his presence. We are sometimes like whitewashed tombs.

▶ Prayer

God ever faithful and true, make me faithful and true to you. In my heart is the desire to be a good steward, but I'm fearful of losing out to worldly pleasure. Please help me change my heart.

▶ Action

Take a good account of your life and determine where you look good on the outside but are not so hot on the inside. Begin to change.

Thursday of the Twenty-first Week of the Year

God the Thief

MATTHEW 24:42–51

Jesus said, "Keep awake because you do not know when your Lord is coming. If the owner of the house knew when the thief was coming, he wouldn't let him break into the house. In the same way you must be ready, for the Son of Man is coming at an unexpected hour."

▶ Reflection

Freeman's laugh echoed down the steel and concrete halls of the prison where he was serving time for petty theft. He told his story with glee, recognizing the irony of it. "So the judge says to me, 'Freeman, stop breaking the law.' So I says, 'But judge, I'm a criminal! It's what I do!'" One of Jesus' closest friends was a known thief (see John 12:6). Could it be that Jesus learned something about thievery from Judas and formed it into a parable about God? Jesus warns his followers that time forecloses on life like a thief in the night. Day by day the opportunities of grace come and go, and the chances we have to respond to God's call are limited. Think of all the time, talent, and money God gives us to put into the service of the kingdom, and consider what we do with it all. If an accounting were made right now, how would we fare? Perhaps it is time to wake from our sleep.

▶ Prayer

O God, I know this world of time has a beginning and an end. Teach me always to be ready for the coming of your kingdom.

▶ Action

Make a list of all the things God has given to you today. Ask yourself, "How have I put these things in service of the kingdom?"

Friday of the Twenty-first Week of the Year

Opportunities

MATTHEW 25:1–13

The kingdom of heaven will be like ten bridesmaids who took their lamps and went to a wedding. Five of them were foolish and brought no fuel. When it was time, their lamps went out and they missed the wedding. Stay alert, therefore, for you know neither the day nor the hour.

▶ Reflection

Giving up smoking isn't the easiest thing in the world. I tried it several times and failed. Then a friend of mine suggested we try to do it together, citing Matthew 18:19, "If two of you agree on earth about anything you ask, it will be done for you." We prayed for each other earnestly every day, encouraging each other in our triumphs and confessing to each other our failures. That was seventeen years ago and neither one of us has had a cigarette since. I believe that somehow the time was right; the opportunity was there and we took it. We could have easily let it pass and we would probably still be smoking today. Life offers many such windows of opportunity when the bridegroom arrives. "Keep awake therefore, for you know neither the day nor the hour."

▶ Prayer

Sweet Jesus, you are always present in my life, protecting me and guiding me. Whenever I am in trouble you come to my rescue. May I see in every opportunity to grow your hand outstretched to save me.

▶ Action

Write down on a piece of paper the opportunity God is giving you today. Carry the paper around in your pocket all day.

Kitchen Stewardship

MATTHEW 25:14–30

The master said to the good steward, 'Well done, good and faithful servant; you have been trustworthy in a few things, I will put you in charge of many things; enter into your master's joy.'

▶ Reflection

When Phil got the promotion he'd been hoping for and a raise to go along with it, he called Lisa with the news right away. "Now we can get the kitchen remodeled like you've been wanting," he told her. But Lisa hedged. "I don't know, Phil," she said. "God has blessed us with so much. We really need to think more seriously about what we do with our money...or I should say, the money God gives us to manage. I think God is putting us in a position to help people. How about if we pledge that raise to our diocesan mission in Haiti? I think we could manage a few more years with the kitchen we've got. We could put food in a poor family's kitchen instead of new cabinets in ours." Phil was incredulous. This was a new side of Lisa. She'd always been a Catholic but now for the first time she was studying the Bible and it was making a difference in her life.

▶ Prayer

O God, you entrust me with time, money, and talent. You teach me in the gospel of Jesus to use these resources with your kingdom in mind. Yet passing things are so inviting and I feel like I'm supposed to be getting more. Help me always to make my choices for you.

▶ Action

Decide today to stop spending so much money on yourself and start spending it on people who really need your help.

Monday of the Twenty-second Week of the Year

Truth and Trust

LUKE 4:16–30

Jesus said, "The truth is, there were many widows in Israel during the famine, yet Elijah was sent only to a widow in Sidon, just as there were many lepers in Israel when Elisha healed Naaman the Syrian." When they heard this, all in the synagogue were filled with rage.

▶ Reflection

This passage could be called, "Jesus yanks their chain." Essentially he was pointing out that in the biblical history of Israel there were instances when God seemed to ignore the plight of the "chosen people" and rescued Israel's bitter enemies instead. Several years ago a schoolgirl I know incurred the wrath of her teacher when she pointed out that, contrary to what the teacher had just taught, America had lost two wars in its history. "And which two?" the teacher asked irately. "Vietnam and the Civil War." My little friend had moved north from Alabama. Now, there are Americans who don't like to hear such truth, but truth is one of those divine attributes that constantly challenges us to trust in God, not in what or whom we think God ought to favor.

▶ Prayer

Loving God, you love everybody! You even love the people that I don't like. When my attitudes and prejudices get the better of me, remind me that your love is universal and undivided, that you don't love anybody less for who they are or what they do.

▶ Action

Make a list of all the people in the world that you think are probably God's enemies. Spend some time believing that God loves them, too.

Tuesday of the Twenty-second Week of the Year

Demons Obey

LUKE 4:31–37

The demon cried out, "Let us alone! I know you are the Holy One of God." Jesus rebuked him, saying, "Be silent, and come out of him!" And the demon came out of him without having done him any harm.

▶ Reflection

Did you ever notice that sometimes the bad people are better at being good than the so-called good people are? It's like the demons. They seemed to do well by Jesus. They recognized Jesus for the person he was and they obeyed him, two areas in which his mortal companions consistently failed. There are other stories in the Bible that show at least a civil relationship between the divine and the demonic. In the first chapter of the Book of Job, Satan pays God a social visit and they have a little conversation about Job, God bragging and Satan disrespecting. The point is that there seems to be, at least in the inspired minds of some biblical authors, a certain affinity between good and evil, God and the devil, which may affirm the suspicions of a lot of us. The good news is that Jesus, the final and complete revelation of God, takes total authority over evil and commands it not to abuse humans.

▶ Prayer

O God, you are good above all things, but evil scares me sometimes. I see it at work in the world and at work within me. Deliver me from evil and keep me free from my sins.

▶ Action

Consider the evil you sense is at work in you. Compose a prayer to Jesus asking him to protect you and keep you free.

Wednesday of the Twenty-second Week of the Year

Addressing Pain

LUKE 4:38–44

Simon's mother-in-law had a fever. Jesus addressed himself to the fever and it left her. Then they brought him all who were sick with various diseases. He laid his hands on them and cured them. And demons came out from them.

▶ Reflection

Over drinks after a movie, Mike was telling the guys how difficult it was for him at work because of the way his boss managed things. His friends joked with him a little, pointing out that he had a very good job that paid well and his boss had a good reputation among his colleagues. "That's the trouble," Mike complained. "Nobody will pay attention to what's hurting me. I need somebody to care." His friends were taken aback because they never knew Mike to be so vulnerable. They had to consider Mike's pain just as Jesus turned his attention to what was bothering Simon's mother-in-law and the others who were afflicted in various ways. Although there may be deeper causes to one's ills, sometimes it's necessary simply to address the pain.

▶ Prayer

Pain is not attractive to me, dear God. I avoid it at all costs. But you humbled yourself to be born of a woman, accepting all the suffering that goes along with being human. In this there is great love. Teach me how to love others as you love me.

▶ Action

Listen to people today. When you say, "How are you?" to somebody, be prepared to hear the answer.

Slot Machine Blessing

LUKE 5:1–11

Simon Peter and his partners James and John were astonished at the catch of fish they had made. Jesus said to Simon, "Do not be afraid; from now on you will be catching people." And when they brought their boats to shore, they left everything and followed him.

▶ Reflection

"Boy, am I lucky!" Julia screeched as she scooped up the coins raining down into her cup from the ringing machine. Halfway through her roll of quarters she'd hit a minor jackpot and the slot machine was paying her a hundred dollars. "You're not lucky," replied her friend Dotty helping her with the coins, "you're blessed. Remember where you got the money in the first place." Sr. Rosemary from the church had given Julia the roll of quarters to play the slots. "Win some money for the school," Sister had told her. Peter didn't chalk up the extraordinary catch of fish to luck. He knew where it came from. In the same way, invoking luck misses the point about God's blessings. Luck is only a fifty-fifty deal at best. God's blessings are a sure thing all the time.

▶ Prayer

Gracious God, whose love is from beginning to end, you order all things for my benefit. You call me to walk in the ways of your love so that I may experience the fullness of life. Remind me today that your blessings await me at every turn.

▶ Action

At the end of this day, write down all the good things that God did for you. Include any missed opportunities. Give God thanks.

Friday of the Twenty-second Week of the Year

Ten Commandments?

LUKE 5:33–39

Jesus told them this parable: "No one tears a piece from a new garment and sews it on an old garment; otherwise the new garment will be ruined and the piece from the new will not match the old. And no one puts new wine into old wineskins; otherwise the new wine will burst the skins and will be spilled, and the skins will be destroyed. But new wine must be put into new wineskins."

▶ Reflection

Sometimes, the way our religion is presented, we can get the distinct impression that our faith is in the law of Moses with Jesus thrown in for good measure. We say we believe in Jesus; that he is the Son of God and all. But if you want to go to heaven, you've got to obey the Ten Commandments. If you break the rules, you're toast. Jesus broke the rules. "I came that they might have life, and have it to the fullest," Jesus said (John 10:10). For him that meant, among other things, eating, drinking, and going to parties while other religious leaders fasted and prayed. Isn't that one of the reasons why Jesus got into so much trouble? And if following the Ten Commandments is the way to salvation, what was the point of Jesus' suffering and dying?

▶ Prayer

O loving God, you guide me in the way of holiness so that I might know the fullness of your life within me. Keep me ever mindful of what is good and right and pure and helpful to my salvation.

▶ Action

There's no law against love. Practice love today with someone who needs it. Let love flow from your heart.

The Hoover Rule

LUKE 6:1–5

Some of the Pharisees found fault with Jesus and his disciples for picking grain to eat on the Sabbath. Jesus answered, "David and his men ate the forbidden bread when they were hungry. The Son of Man is lord of the sabbath."

▶ Reflection

One of the fundamental moral principles I learned from my mother was always expressed as a question: "If Herbert Hoover jumped off the Brooklyn Bridge, would that mean that it was okay for you to jump off too?" So if Jesus is looking to justify breaking a serious religious law by pointing out that David did the same, it's not going to fly with my mother. Evidently the author of Mark's gospel didn't think so either. So Mark included an aphorism in his version of the story (Mark 2:23–28): "The sabbath was made for humankind, not humankind for the sabbath." In other words, divine law, even the Ten Commandments, is there for the benefit of people. It can never be used as an absolute to block people from satisfying their essential needs. The law of God is meant to give people charge of their lives.

▶ Prayer

You give me your law to guide me, O Lord. Yet you provide me with mind and heart and conscience so that I might be free to find a new way, a way that gives you glory and praise. Give me the grace to treasure this freedom always.

▶ Action

Think of all the rules you follow in your life. Which ones benefit you and which ones do you follow simply because they exist as rules?

Monday of the Twenty-third Week of the Year

Pushing It

LUKE 6:6–11

On another sabbath Jesus entered the synagogue. The scribes and the Pharisees watched him to see whether he would cure on the sabbath, so that they might find an accusation against him. They were filled with fury and talked about what they might do to Jesus.

▶ Reflection

I wonder if Jesus did his grocery shopping on Saturdays, too. He did seem to pick the worst days. He could have avoided a lot of trouble if he would have just performed his healings on Wednesdays or any days of the week other than the sabbath. Doing almost anything on the sabbath was against one of the most important of the Ten Commandments. By healing on the sabbath, Jesus was defying what had long been accepted religiously as God's unchanging law. So, was God changing? Or was Jesus challenging people to change their understanding about God and God's law? When religion evolves, as it must in order to incorporate the ever-evolving human understanding of God, people get upset. It's unnerving to think that God is changing. The reality is that we are changing, moving towards God, and every step along the way gives us a different view of God.

▶ Prayer

You are the God who always was, is now, and ever shall be, my creator. Yet every day I discover something new about you. Show me again who you are today so I may rejoice in your revelation.

▶ Action

Remember what you believed about God twenty years ago; ten years ago; five years ago; and now. How has your vision of God changed?

Tuesday of the Twenty-third Week of the Year

Faith Healing

LUKE 6:12–19

They had come to hear him and to be healed of their diseases; and those who were troubled with unclean spirits were cured. And all in the crowd were trying to touch him, for power came out from him and healed all of them.

▶ Reflection

Mr. Chang next door goes to the movies every Tuesday. He says he goes to laugh and be entertained, but if the movie isn't funny, he leaves halfway through. The gospel says that people came to hear Jesus and to be healed of their diseases. I wonder what would have happened if they came for other reasons. In virtually every healing story, Jesus tells the one healed that it was his or her faith that had got the job done. Healing is like forgiveness; indeed the two work together (see Luke 5:18–26). It cannot be that God parcels out healing any more than God parcels out forgiveness. As St. Paul says, "Jesus Christ was not 'Yes and No' but always 'Yes'" (2 Cor 1:19). But we connect to God's forgiveness and healing through faith. If I do not believe God will forgive, I will not seek forgiveness. If I don't believe God will heal, I will not seek healing. But if in faith I come to Christ to be healed, I will experience healing.

▶ Prayer

My Lord, I turn to you in time of need and I know you will come to my aid, for you are always faithful to your promise.

▶ Action

Think of areas in your life where you do not believe God is healing you. Ask God to help you find the healing you're looking for.

Wednesday of the Twenty-third Week of the Year
Call Him Evil

LUKE 6:20–26

"Blessed are you when people hate you, and when they exclude you, revile you, and defame you on account of the Son of Man. Rejoice in that day and leap for joy, for surely your reward is great in heaven."

▶ Reflection

Scott was deeply hurt by what the other boys had said about him in the locker room. He was embarrassed by their horseplay and vulgar language and felt uneasy and vulnerable when he had to shower with them after gym class. He was different; he knew he thought different thoughts and felt different feelings than they did. But that didn't give them the right to say the things they said about him. He felt alienated and rejected by them, much the way he felt the day he overheard somebody at church say that all homosexuals were going to hell. He found comfort in the words he'd read in the little Bible his grandmother gave him: "Blessed are you when they hate you and exclude you and call you evil." This was good news for him and gave him hope that maybe there was a way for him to go on. So far he had few friends at school and no friends at church. But he did have a friend in Jesus.

▶ Prayer

O God, sometimes I reject people who are different from me. But in your goodness and love, you accept them and love them. Help me to love them, too, so that I might share their blessings in the kingdom.

▶ Action

Remember a time when you felt rejected. Think of someone you reject. Ask God to show his acceptance of you and those you reject.

Thursday of the Twenty-third Week of the Year

Wealth in Poverty

LUKE 6:27–38

"Love your enemies, do good to those who hate you, bless those who curse you, pray for those who abuse you. If anyone strikes you on the cheek, offer the other also; and from anyone who takes away your coat do not withhold even your shirt. Give to everyone who begs from you; and if anyone takes away your goods, do not ask for them again. Do to others as you would have them do to you."

▶ Reflection

Loving your enemies sounds fine until the shooting starts. Then, if you want to protect what you value in this world, you shoot back. Turning the other cheek will result in your enemy winning the victory and ultimately you will lose everything: your land, your home, your family, your freedom, your way of life. The bad guys will succeed and all that is good, all you stand for, will fail. So what good is this gospel of peace? Simply this: we live for the sake of a greater reality, which is the kingdom of God. The suffering, death, and resurrection of Jesus demonstrated the power of his gospel. "Follow me," he said—and leave the world behind. This is pretty serious business. We're fortunate now that our freedom is not at stake. But what if it were?

▶ Prayer

My Lord and master, you suffered, died, and rose so that I might have new life. But what is this new life if I don't live it? I'm afraid sometimes. Show me your presence and give me the courage I need.

▶ Action

Today you will find yourself in a conflict with someone or something. When all else fails, try surrendering and see what happens.

Friday of the Twenty-third Week of the Year

Now I See

LUKE 6:39–42

"How can you say to your neighbor, 'Friend, let me take out the speck in your eye,' when you yourself do not see the log in your own eye? You hypocrite, first take the log out of your own eye, and then you will see clearly to take the speck out of your neighbor's eye."

▶ Reflection

A perfect example of what the grace of God's kingdom can do is St. Paul. He reminds his readers in 1 Timothy 1:13 that he was once "a blasphemer, a persecutor, and a man of violence." But then he encountered Jesus, risen from the dead (see Acts 9:1–9), and everything changed. What he thought he could see turned out to be darkness, and what was the real light he found he couldn't see. Human science teaches a similar paradox: we are often blind to the truth about ourselves, but we can readily see the same truth in others. My encounter with another is like looking in a mirror, only I don't know the mirror is there. The task of life is to discover the truth about ourselves, as did St. Paul. When we do that, Jesus said we would truly be free (see John 8:32). Then we can see well enough to help others with their discoveries.

▶ Prayer

O Lord, open my eyes to the truth about myself. Give me the courage to accept my faults and failures as you do, and to love myself as you love me. Then send me to others so that I may share your love.

▶ Action

Do you know somebody who "pushes your buttons"? Sit down and write out all the things about that person you don't like. Guess what?

Saturday of the Twenty-third Week of the Year

Good Treasures

LUKE 6:43–49

Jesus said to his disciples, "The good person produces good out of the good treasure of the heart, and the evil person produces evil out of evil treasure of the heart. It is out of the abundance of the heart that a person produces."

▶ **Reflection**

"I don't want to be like that," Molly cried to Fr. Jim. "I want to be a good person." She had just confessed the fights she was having with her parents at home and was perplexed by all the evil she experienced coming out of her. Fr. Jim had this to say. "Sometimes when people annoy me, I think, 'What jerks!' But if I keep that up, it won't be long before I'm being mean to them, because I've been storing up evil in my heart against them. What I need to do is store up good things in my heart. So I forgive the people who annoy me right away and try to remember the things I like about them. Molly, what you need to do is store up good things in your heart for your parents. Whenever they do something that annoys you, bless them. Think of your favorite thing about them. Be sure to pray for them every day. Your gracious thoughts will produce gracious deeds; generating the goodness you love will displace the evil you hate."

▶ **Prayer**

I look in my heart, dear Lord, and I don't always find a treasure of goodness there. Help me store up goodness that I may produce good.

▶ **Action**

Think of the person you dislike most in your life. Ask God to bless that person. Write down three good things about that person.

Words of Comfort

LUKE 7:1–10

When Jesus drew near to the house, the centurion sent friends to say to him, "Lord, do not trouble yourself, for I am not worthy to have you come under my roof. But only speak the word, and let my servant be healed."

▶ Reflection

"It's the most important part of the Mass, as far as I'm concerned." You might think that Sharon was talking about Holy Communion. But she and her husband don't receive communion, although they attend Mass regularly. They are waiting for her annulment to come through. Sharon was talking about the part of the Mass when everybody recites the words of the centurion in today's gospel: "Lord, I am not worthy to receive you, but only say the word and I shall be healed." She knows that those words were put in the Mass centuries ago because many people didn't go to communion out of a sense of unworthiness. She also knows that Holy Communion isn't a matter of worthiness; it's a gift from God to be received and be thankful for. Still, while she waits for the day when she and her husband can receive together, the words comfort her.

▶ Prayer

Lord, I am not worthy to receive your many gifts, but time and time again you give them to me out of your infinite love for me. Your love is beyond my imagining. Thank you, Lord, for your love.

▶ Action

Compose a prayer of thanksgiving to God for all the things God has done for you that you didn't deserve.

Tuesday of the Twenty-fourth Week of the Year

Faith in Sorrow

LUKE 7:11–17

A widow's only son died. The Lord had compassion for the mother and said to her, "Do not weep." Then he touched the dead man and said, "Young man, I say to you, rise!" The dead man sat up and Jesus gave him to his mother.

▶ Reflection

If Jesus were the moderator in one of our parish bereavement groups, we wouldn't want him to say, "Do not weep." Instead we'd want the Lord to encourage people to express their emotions and assure them that weeping is a natural and healthy thing to do when a loved one dies. But the gospel story predates our modern scientific understanding of the psychology of grief; it was simply meant to proclaim the victory of Christ over death. It's like when Jesus says, "Do not be afraid" (Luke 12:7, 12:32). It doesn't mean life won't scare us from time to time or that we shouldn't feel fear. It means that the Lord is always with us. So while it's natural and appropriate to weep at the death of a loved one, we are called to understand that death is not the end of life and we will see our loved ones again.

▶ Prayer

Eternal God, all life comes from you. You created me as an expression of your own self and gave me eternal life. As I was born into this world, so I will die leaving it. But I will always live in you and be an expression of your love. Keep me always in this faith.

▶ Action

Write down the names of all your loved ones who have died. Think about what it will be like to see them again.

Wednesday of the Twenty-fourth Week of the Year

Authoritarian Blindness

LUKE 7:31–35

Jesus said, "John the Baptist came eating no bread and drinking no wine, and you say, 'He's crazy.' I come eating and drinking, and you say, 'Look, a glutton and a drunkard, a friend of tax collectors and sinners!' But wisdom will reveal herself in the end."

▶ Reflection

John the Baptist seems to have been some kind of religious fundamentalist who lived in strict adherence to the Jewish law, scrupulously avoiding food or drink that might have been considered unkosher. His insistence on rigorous obedience to the rules got him into trouble with the authorities, and eventually he was put to death. Jesus, on the other hand, played it fast and loose with the religious law, frequently showed up at parties and banquets, and hung around with those who were considered to be sinners and excluded from the community of the righteous. His compassionate application of grace got him, like John, into trouble with the authorities and he also was put to death. The trouble with religious authoritarians is that sometimes they're so caught up in their authority that not even God can get through to them.

▶ Prayer

My precious God, you sent John to announce my need for repentance and then sent Jesus to save me from my sins. May I always be thankful to you and responsive to your word alive in me.

▶ Action

Write down the names of the religious authorities in your life: the pope, your bishop, and your pastor. Pray for them.

Great Sin, Great Love

LUKE 7:36–50

A woman came to Jesus while he was at dinner and knelt at his feet, weeping, and began to bathe his feet with her tears and to dry them with her hair. She covered his feet with kisses and soothed them with ointment. His host, a Pharisee, disapproved because she was a sinner. So Jesus said, "Her sins, which were many, have been forgiven. That is why she shows such great love."

▶ Reflection

Isn't it great that *she* welcomed the body of Christ, washed it and soothed it and delighted it? Sure, she had many sins; of that both Jesus and the Pharisee were in agreement. But while the Pharisee saw condemnation, Jesus saw forgiveness. Think of all the people we forbid to touch the body of Christ today. I wonder how many of them would love greatly if given half a chance? In the early church, many priests and bishops didn't want to reinstate lapsed Christians who wanted back in, and there was great conflict between them and those who recognized the potential of a forgiven sinner to love greatly. Pray that this new millennium sets the tone for a new spirit of welcome to sinners who want to draw near to Christ.

▶ Prayer

Open the doors of our church wide, Lord, to welcome sinners to attend to the body of Christ with love. I have known your love in my own sinfulness, and I am joyful because of it. Praise you, Jesus!

▶ Action

Welcome a sinner into your life today. There are plenty of them around. Begin to forgive someone who needs your forgiveness.

Friday of the Twenty-fourth Week of the Year

Women Called

LUKE 8:1–3

Jesus and the twelve went on proclaiming the good news of the kingdom of God. There were women with them who had been cured of evil spirits and infirmities: Mary Magdalene, Joanna, Susanna, and many others, who provided for them.

▶ Reflection

Debate over the ordination of women has given rise to questions about the gender of Jesus' followers. The gospels report that Jesus chose twelve men as apostles ("apostle" is a Greek term meaning "one who is sent"). The name "apostle" was also applied to Matthias, chosen by lot (Acts 1:26), and to Paul who claimed the title for himself (See Romans 1:1). Paul also bestows the title of apostle on others such as the companions of Titus in 2 Corinthians 8:23 and a woman named Junia (or Julia) in Romans 16:7. In today's gospel, Luke identifies three more women along with "many others" in conjunction with the apostolic mission of "preaching and proclaiming the good news of the kingdom of God." Clearly both men and women are called to be witnesses of the gospel.

▶ Prayer

My loving Jesus, you gathered people around you, men, women, and children, to share your life and be lifted up by your teaching. Your Spirit came upon all who believed in you and witnessed your resurrection. Teach me to live free of prejudice and fear.

▶ Action

Think of women you know who are powerful witnesses to Jesus Christ. Consider that God has sent them into your life to proclaim the gospel.

Saturday of the Twenty-fourth Week of the Year

Got Parables?

LUKE 8:4–15

Jesus said to his disciples, "To you it has been given to know the secrets of the kingdom of God; but to others I speak in parables, so that looking they may not perceive, and listening they may not understand."

▶ Reflection

As they left the conference room and headed out for lunch, Ryan turned to Seth and said, "I don't understand any of this. What are they talking about?" They had just been to a staff development program. Ryan, fresh out of college and newly recruited into entry level management, was still of the old school, an autocrat in the making. "It's about shared responsibility," replied Seth. "We're supposed to be learning how to empower our subordinates to work independently." Ryan shook his head. "I don't get any of that stuff. The way I look at it, we tell people what to do and they do it. Why make it so complicated?" Seth laughed. He knew Ryan wasn't going to change. Jesus knew that people looking for a better life would hear his words and seek meaning from them. Others, who felt no need to change, would just hear stories about farmers and seeds.

▶ Prayer

O Lord, in my heart I feel a great need to change, but there's so much of me that doesn't want to change. Transform me. Make me good ground that receives your word and produces an abundant harvest.

▶ Action

Make time today to sit and ponder something about the gospel that you don't understand. Ask God to open your heart to its meaning.

Monday of the Twenty-fifth Week of the Year

Lose Less, Get More

LUKE 8:16–18

"Nothing is hidden that will not be revealed, nothing is secret that will not come to light. So pay attention to how you listen; to those who have, more will be given; and from those who have not, even what they seem to have will be taken away."

▶ **Reflection**

It's difficult to imagine how a system of justice based on giving to the poor would result in those who have getting more, and those with little losing what they have. But Jesus is talking here not about the things of the world, but about the things of the kingdom. One of the "secrets" of the kingdom is that the last will be first and the first will be last. One of the "hidden" mysteries of the kingdom is that you can gain the whole world but lose your own soul in the process. So if I don't pay attention when Jesus says that in the kingdom, one gains by losing the things of the world, I'll settle for going to church on Sunday and trying to gain the things in the world. In the end I'll lose it all. But if I pay attention and put the Lord's words into practice, I will lose much in the world but there's much to be gained in the kingdom.

▶ **Prayer**

Gracious God, your Son Jesus announced an eternal kingdom of joy where the last are first. Help me to always surrender the things of this passing world to enjoy the coming of your kingdom.

▶ **Action**

Think of an area in your life where you gain from giving. Plan now to give more so you can gain more.

Tuesday of the Twenty-fifth Week of the Year

New Parents, New Life

LUKE 8:19–21

His mother and his brothers came, but they couldn't get near him. He was told, "Your mother and your brothers are outside, wanting to see you." But he said to them, "My mother and my brothers are those who hear the word of God and do it."

▶ Reflection

Connie's life was a mess, at least in her mind. She had grown up in a totally dysfunctional household filled with alcoholism, abuse, and neglect. Though in her forties now, Connie was still bound tightly to her family, glued to these painful people by unmet expectations, unfulfilled hopes, and a large, gaping emptiness within her where her childhood was supposed to be. She identified this gnawing attraction to her parents and her siblings as love, for it was all she knew of it. But whenever she encountered them, the pain simply grew worse. Jesus was calling her to trade them in for a new family, a fellowship shaped by the word of God, a life spent in the practice of Christian love. "Leave your parents and siblings," he was saying, "and come follow me" (see Luke 14:26).

▶ Prayer

O God, you gave me good parents and a good family. Still, you call me beyond them to a heavenly family that will raise me to fulfillment. Bless me in my efforts to move beyond my beginnings, and bless all those anchored to the unmet needs of broken families.

▶ Action

Write down the names of all the members of your family of origin. Thank each from your heart and move on to God.

Wednesday of the Twenty-fifth Week of the Year

Buried Power

LUKE 9:1–6

Jesus sent the twelve out to proclaim the kingdom of God and to heal. He said, "Take nothing for your journey, no staff, nor bag, nor bread, nor money—not even a change of clothes. Whatever house you enter, stay there, and leave from there."

▶ Reflection

"I wonder how much of the healing power that Jesus gave to the apostles has been lost," a priest friend of mine mused over lunch. We had been discussing the "motives of credibility" God gives to the faithful through the action of miracles (see the *Catechism*, #156). In other words, what happened to the power to heal miraculously? My friend was speculating that because Jesus sent his disciples with instructions not to take anything with them for the journey and to live off the generosity of others, the subsequent accumulation of wealth and comfort by the leaders of the church has resulted in the loss of miraculous powers. "Do you think God took the power away from us?" I asked. "No," he said. "I think we've just invested it poorly. We've taken what was meant for the kingdom and committed it to the world. We buried it."

▶ Prayer

My loving God, the wealth and comfort of the world is so attractive to me, yet I know fulfillment is only in you. Help me to leave behind this passing world for the sake of your coming kingdom.

▶ Action

Leave your watch home today and try to exist off the generosity of others who will tell you what time it is.

Thursday of the Twenty-fifth Week of the Year

Herod's Soul

LUKE 9:7–9

Herod heard about the events and was perplexed, because some said that John had been raised from the dead, or that Elijah or one of the ancient prophets had appeared. Herod said, "John I beheaded; but who is this I'm hearing about?" And he tried to see him.

▶ Reflection

The concept of resurrection from the dead wasn't new to the people of Jesus' time. It was part of the prophetic treasury of the Scripture (Ezekiel 37:12–13). The idea of a return to life after death was solidly placed in the Book of Wisdom (3:1–9) and resurrection from the dead in 2 Maccabees 12:43–44. That people were speculating about the possibility of Jesus being the resurrection of John the Baptist was simply an expression of contemporary religious belief. Herod, a man of power with little taste for religion, seems to indicate his own disbelief that such a thing was possible, especially after one's head was separated from one's body. Herod's interest in Jesus seems to come more from an inward resonance. There is something Jesus is saying and doing that stirs Herod's soul.

▶ Prayer

My Lord, the first time I ever read your words and heard them proclaimed in the power of the Holy Spirit, they stirred my soul. You drew me to yourself with your mercy and your love. Keep me always close to you and never let me stray.

▶ Action

Write down your favorite passage from the words of Jesus in the gospel. Tape it to your mirror and read it aloud every morning.

Friday of the Twenty-fifth Week of the Year

Jesus or John?

LUKE 9:18–22

Jesus asked the disciples, "Who do the crowds say that I am?" They answered, "John the Baptist; but others, Elijah; and still others, that one of the ancient prophets has arisen." He said to them, "But who do you say that I am?" Peter answered, "The Messiah of God." Then he said, "The Son of Man must undergo great suffering, and be killed."

▶ Reflection

John the Baptist was very popular among the people. After all, he was first on the scene and he seemed sincere in his words. He preached reform and a return to righteousness. Because he lived in the wilderness and subsisted on what he could find, the people knew he realized no gain from his preaching. Besides, John made more sense. He was a preacher of the law. Jesus was teaching about loving your enemies, turning the other cheek, and giving your money away to the poor. So when folks heard about the holy man who was making an impression (they didn't have the benefit of newspapers or TV) they assumed it was John the Baptist. Even the identity of "Messiah" or "Christ" didn't fit. Jesus preferred "Son of Man," and regular person, a human being like everybody else who would suffer and die.

▶ Prayer

My Lord, you come to me so humble, in flesh and blood, born of a woman. You share my humanity so that I might have a share in your divinity. So I suffer sometimes just like you. But I rise with you, too!

▶ Action

Something will go wrong today; it always does. In your suffering, discover the presence of Jesus suffering with you. Endure it in love.

Saturday of the Twenty-fifth Week of the Year

Blindness to Addiction

LUKE 9:43–45

Jesus said to his disciples, "Let these words sink into your ears: the Son of Man is going to be betrayed into human hands." But they did not understand this saying; its meaning was concealed from them, so that they could not see it. And they were afraid to ask him about it.

▶ Reflection

"I don't have to smoke," Kelly told Devon while she lit one up on the way home from school. "I smoke because I choose to. I can quit anytime I want." If you've ever been addicted to nicotine, you know that Kelly is in pure denial. We tend to be blind to our addictions. Admitting there's a problem is the first step of any Twelve Step program designed to address addictions. We can be addicted to many things: nicotine, alcohol, caffeine, drugs of any kind, gambling, sex, chocolate, food, power, money. The disciples were addicted to loyalty. They had followed Jesus everywhere and had stuck by him through thick and thin. So his talk of betrayal fell on deaf ears. The truth is that they all betrayed him then, just like we all betray him now. In order to live in right relationship with God who is truth, I must know the truth about myself; that I am a sinner in every way and that Jesus is the one who saves me from my sins.

▶ Prayer

My dear Jesus, you deliver me from the evil of my life and restore me to union with God in love. Thank you for your forgiveness.

▶ Action

What is one of your addictions? Write it down on a piece of paper. What do you think Jesus might be saying about it that you can't hear?

Monday of the Twenty-sixth Week of the Year

Up the Lowly!

LUKE 9:46–50

An argument arose among them as to which one of them was the greatest. But Jesus took a little child and said to them, "Whoever welcomes this child in my name welcomes me, and whoever welcomes me welcomes the one who sent me; for the least among all of you is the greatest."

▶ Reflection

The gospel writers never tell us whether these discussions among the disciples about who was the greatest (there were several of them) involved supporting one another for the honor, or were exercises in self-promotion. Either way, they missed the point. Worldly greatness has no place in the Kingdom of God. The prophet Zechariah understood this and pointed to the rubble heap that was Jerusalem destroyed by her enemies, and proclaimed a vision of joyful children filling her streets once again (see Zechariah 8:1–8). This is what it means when we say God is a God of justice. God restores what was lost, reconciles what was alienated, fixes what was broken. As Mary proclaimed in Luke 1:52, God "has cast down the mighty from their thrones and lifted up the lowly."

▶ Prayer

You have fixed my life, Lord. You found me when I was lost. You saved me when I was condemned and welcomed me when I was forsaken. Open my heart wide to receive your grace and your love.

▶ Action

Take out an old photograph, or a long unused piece of jewelry, or a necktie you haven't worn in a long time. Recall the love that's in it.

Tuesday of the Twenty-sixth Week of the Year

Bringing Down Fire

LUKE 9:51–56

When the Samaritans would not receive him, the disciples said, "Lord, do you want us to command fire to come down from heaven and consume them?" Jesus turned and rebuked them.

▶ Reflection

You wonder how the apostles would come with Jesus as far as they did and still be looking to bring down lethal vengeance on the foreigners because of a social snub. But deeply ingrained cultural prejudices are not quick to die. Even after repeated social reforms and church teaching, many Catholic Americans still harbor unacceptable prejudices and justify all kinds of vengeful activities. I still find myself being passive aggressive on the freeways, punishing those who in my opinion have violated one of my personal rules of the road. What the United States. has done to Iraq over the last decade is unconscionable, but evidently justified by many who would call themselves "good Catholics." We still want to bring down fire, and Jesus still rebukes us for it.

▶ Prayer

My Jesus, in your gospel story, it says you didn't come to do your own will, but to do the will of the one who sent you. What was your will, dear Jesus? Were you tempted in the same way I am to bring wrath upon sinners? Thank you for doing God's will: shedding your blood for me and for all so that sins might be forgiven.

▶ Action

Using a red marker, circle the people in today's newspaper whom you would condemn. Now ask: what would Jesus do?

296

Wednesday of the Twenty-sixth Week of the Year

Family as Obstacle

LUKE 9:57–62

As they were going along the road, someone said to him, "I will follow you, Lord; but let me first say farewell to those at my home." Jesus said to him, "No one who puts a hand to the plow and looks back is fit for the kingdom of God."

▶ Reflection

Family gets consistently bad play in the gospels. We like to think that the love of family is among the noblest of values, and it is. But whenever he was given an opportunity to comment on family, even his own, Jesus preferred to cast it as an obstacle to entering the kingdom of God. Perhaps it is that no matter how good the experience of family can be, a better experience awaits in the kingdom. And if I subject my entrance into the kingdom to my love of family, I'm doing myself and God a disservice. The church presents us with the images of a heavenly Father and a blessed Mother for a reason. For some, this is a welcomed alternative. For others, perhaps like the man in today's gospel, it's a struggle believing there is something better than what we've got.

▶ Prayer

O God, my creator, you gave me a human family that responded to your call of love and provided for me a good, wholesome upbringing. I love my family and I thank you for that gift. But Jesus calls me to an even greater family. Help me to leave behind mine and join yours.

▶ Action

On a scale of one to ten, rate your family, the household you grew up with. Now rate God, the Blessed Mother, and Jesus. Who wins?

Thursday of the Twenty-sixth Week of the Year

Welcoming Strangers

LUKE 10:1–12

Jesus said to his disciples, "Whenever you enter a town and they do not welcome you, go out into its streets and wipe off the dust of that town from your feet. On the judgment day it will be more tolerable for Sodom than for that town."

▶ Reflection

The divine retribution inflicted on Sodom and Gomorrah in Genesis 19 is an enduring biblical image of the ultimate punishment the wrath of God has to offer in response to wickedness. Subsequently, the instruments of that destruction, fire and brimstone, became emblematic of a style of preaching that focused on the eternal consequences of mortal sin. Yet Jesus taught his disciples that a simple failure to welcome a stranger merits a far worse penalty. It seems hard to imagine until we examine the story of Sodom and Gomorrah and find that the wicked act that put them over the top was indeed gross inhospitality (see Genesis 19:1–13). Once again Jesus reminds us how critically important it is to welcome the strangers life places before us.

▶ Prayer

God of all goodness, throughout history you have called people forth from the comfort of their own surroundings and sent them as strangers to be your witnesses. May I always welcome these strangers, even when they come to me dirty, hungry, and needy.

▶ Action

Look at all the strange faces you see today. Welcome each in your heart and say a graceful prayer for each one.

Friday of the Twenty-sixth Week of the Year

Forgiveness Power

LUKE 10:13–16

"Woe to you! If the deeds of power done in you had been done in Tyre and Sidon, they would have repented long ago. But at the judgment it will be more tolerable for Tyre and Sidon than for you."

▶ Reflection

"The trouble with kids today is that their parents don't give them 'the strap' any more," griped Sam. He went on to recount how, when he was a kid growing up, misbehavior was met with swift, corporal punishment. Sam had in turn inflicted the same punitive parenting on his kids. While it was true that his kids were very well-behaved, they were also very subdued. It seemed that out of fear of misbehaving, they didn't behave at all. Though a Catholic all his life, Sam had not yet realized the transforming power of mercy and forgiveness. In today's gospel, Chorazin and Bethsaida had experienced such grace. The Lord had worked his saving power there and it was now time for them to change their ways. Some day someone is going to show Sam great mercy and forgiveness. When that day comes, he's going to have to make some changes.

▶ Prayer

O God, I never knew your kindness and mercy until I experienced it in flesh and blood. Your servants, whom you sent into my life to demonstrate the good news of my forgiveness, did your will and I came to know you love. Help me to love others the way you love me.

▶ Action

Think of the most profound act of kindness and mercy ever performed for you. Know that God was speaking to you through that act.

Saturday of the Twenty-sixth Week of the Year

Playing With God

LUKE 10:17–24

Jesus rejoiced in the Holy Spirit and said, "I thank you, Father, Lord of heaven and earth, because you have hidden these things from the wise and the intelligent and have revealed them to infants; yes, Father, for such was your gracious will."

▶ Reflection

Mrs. Todd loved to sit in church and play with the little children. She was never able to have any of her own, and now that she was old, she wasn't going to pass up any opportunities to enjoy them. She would always make it a point to sit behind a family with children so that she could play with them during Mass. Sometimes the people around her would get annoyed because the children squealed with delight at the funny faces she would make. She ignored the criticism. "Age has its privileges," she would say. "Besides, the children have so much more to teach me than the boring sermons I get in church. I think they're sent to me to help me understand more about God. They play so wonderfully. It's like playing with God. I can't get *any* of the grownups to play with me at church. The children are wiser. They know how to live in God's world."

▶ Prayer

You came among us as a little child born of a woman, dear Jesus. You revealed God in human form and continue to visit me in the little children. Help me to see your Spirit in their shining faces.

▶ Action

The next time you get a chance, allow a little child to explain things to you. Ask questions and listen carefully to the answers.

Monday of the Twenty-seventh Week of the Year

Beyond Next Door

LUKE 10:25–37

A lawyer wanting to test Jesus asked, "Who is my neighbor?" Jesus told the story of a priest, a Levite, and a Samaritan who saw an injured man, but only the Samaritan stopped to help. Asked which of the three was neighbor to the man, the lawyer said, "The one who showed him mercy." Jesus said to him, "Go and do likewise."

▶ Reflection

"I don't like Mrs. Talbot," the boy confessed. Fr. Haney looked down at the child and asked, "And how is that a sin?" The child looked up at him. "Well," he sighed, "you told us that we're supposed to love our neighbor. Mrs. Talbot is our neighbor next door and she's mean and I don't like her. So I figure that's a sin, right?" Fr. Haney smiled at the big brown eyes looking up at him. This would be a challenge. How do you explain to a kid that our neighbors pop up everywhere in our lives? In the story of the Good Samaritan, Jesus taught that we are neighbor to whomever we encounter in poverty. As the Samaritan met the needs of the injured person, so we are called to do the same, regardless of the inconvenience this imposes. The child waited for Fr. Haney's answer.

▶ Prayer

All people are your children, dear Lord, and my sisters and brothers. There are times when I am in conflict with others in ways great and small. Whenever I need extra love for them, give me your grace.

▶ Action

Think of your least favorite person and resolve today to do something good for that person, even if it's only saying a little prayer.

The Better Part

LUKE 10:38–42

Jesus said to Martha, "Martha, Martha, you are worried and distracted by many things; but there is need of only one thing. Your sister Mary has chosen the better part, which will not be taken away from her."

▶ Reflection

Alicia lived alone in a tiny apartment in the big city. She was forty-two, no children, never married. Unlike her sisters who all had families and important careers, she was content to write her stories for magazines and work four days a week in the little dress shop down the street. She volunteered at the soup kitchen whenever she could and participated as much as possible in parish life. She went to the movies on Tuesdays, and led a small book discussion group on Thursdays. Her parents and most of her married friends tolerated her curious lifestyle. Still, they harbored a hope that one day she would marry, or at least get a "real" job. When she gave up a lucrative book offer to spend two years caring for a dying friend, the dam broke and she endured much criticism from her friends and family. They could not understand that for her this was the better part.

▶ Prayer

God in the heavens, you make people with your purpose in mind. You set them in the world to do your will and reveal your presence to others in unique and beautiful ways. Help me always to see the differences in others as your creative self-expressions.

▶ Action

Think of the strangest person you know. Consider that God created that person to be different for a reason.

Wednesday of the Twenty-seventh Week of the Year

Commanding God

LUKE 11:1–4

Jesus said to the disciples, "When you pray, say: Father, hallowed be your name. Your kingdom come. Your will be done, on earth as in heaven. Give us each day our daily bread. Forgive us our sins, as we forgive everyone indebted to us. Do not bring us to the time of trial."

▶ **Reflection**

Pam asked: "Why do you say it that way?" I responded: "Say what what way?" She said, "Say the 'Our Father' the way you just did with the big 'will.' You said 'thy *will* be done' as if 'will' was a verb." "I dunno," I said, "that's the way I learned it." I recalled (how could I forget!) the catechism classes where Sr. Frumentius, waving her ruler like an orchestra conductor, would lead the class in reciting the Lord's Prayer. She would sweep her arms up into the air and our voices would rise with her, "thy *will* be done" as if commanding God to do something. Pam had a point: "will" is not a verb. Religion just gets so darn authoritative, sometimes, that it spills over into the way we say our prayers. Jesus was insistent that he hadn't come to do his own will (see John 6:38). He instructed his disciples to pray for the same wisdom.

▶ **Prayer**

O God my Father, how holy is your name. Manifest your kingdom here and now. I pray that your will be done rather than mine. Provide what I need today and keep me safe.

▶ **Action**

Write out the Lord's Prayer in a completely different way using completely different words to say the same thing.

Thursday of the Twenty-seventh Week of the Year

Good Mother

LUKE 11:5–13

Jesus said to the disciples, "If your child asked for a fish, would you give him a snake? Or if he asked for an egg, would you give him a scorpion? If you, in your sinfulness, know how to give good things to your children, how much more will God give good things to you?"

▶ Reflection

Denise is a good mother. She is always looking out for her kids, making sure they eat well, get their rest and exercise, attend to their studies, and always have clean clothes to wear. She is closely attentive to the details of their medical histories and is careful that they get regular checkups from the doctor and the dentist. She doesn't neglect the soccer mom stuff, either. She drives them everywhere and always tries to be there for the games and the plays and the concerts. And every Sunday and holyday, she gathers them together and brings them to church. Sometimes, though, especially when there's a quiet moment, like at church, she'll worry about her life and her finances and her family and her future. But she needn't worry. She just needs to know that God is a better mother to her than she is to her kids.

▶ Prayer

O God my salvation, your love for me is more than I'll ever know in this life. Every breath I take and every moment I live is a gift from you to be celebrated. You have rescued me from sin and death and have given me your Spirit. For this I give you thanks.

▶ Action

Write down all the ways that you are a good parent or that your parents were good to you. Consider now how your heavenly parent treats you.

Friday of the Twenty-seventh Week of the Year

Go Away, Giraffe!

LUKE 11:15–26

"When the unclean spirit has gone out of a person, it wanders looking for rest. Finding none, it returns and discovers things swept and put in order. Then, with seven other worse spirits, it moves in; and the last state of that person is worse than the first."

▶ Reflection

Close your eyes and try not to think of a giraffe. Doesn't work, does it? You really can't concentrate on not thinking about something. That's the trouble with the negative "thou shalt not" moral imperatives. St. Paul wrote in the Letter to the Romans that the law cannot save; it can only condemn (see Romans 7:7–25). So often people try to banish evil from their lives and are unsuccessful. Then they lose heart and give up on the whole business of trying to lead virtuous lives. A virtuous life is not a matter of banishing evil. Rather, it is the process of filling your life with good so that there's no room for evil. So now, instead of trying not to think of a giraffe, picture in your mind an elephant! See? Concentrate on the elephant and the giraffe goes away!

▶ Prayer

Thank you, Lord, for showing me how to live a good life! When evil comes my way, so often I fear it and try to hold it at bay. Next time I'm tempted to turn to the darkness, may I instead embrace the light so that my life will always be a witness to your goodness.

▶ Action

Today, as soon as you notice you've said or done or thought evil, say a prayer of praise and thanksgiving to God. It drives the devil nuts!

Saturday of the Twenty-seventh Week of the Year

Our Lady Blessed

LUKE 11:27–28

A woman in the crowd raised her voice and said to Jesus, "Blessed is the womb that bore you and the breasts that nursed you!" But he said, "Blessed rather are those who hear the word of God and obey it!"

▶ Reflection

It is obvious that Jesus didn't have to deal with groups of ardent Catholics devoted to Our Lady. Otherwise, he would have thought twice about passing up an opportunity to acknowledge another blessing for the Blessed Mother. But he did acknowledge Mary. She was certainly among those who heard the word of God and obeyed it. God said that she would "conceive and bear a son" who would be called "Son of the Most High" (Luke 1:31–32). Even though she had no husband, she accepted God's word. "I am the servant of the Lord," she said. "Let it be done to me" (Luke 1:38). At our baptism, the word of God proclaimed that we had eternal life and forgiveness of our sins. Even though we journey towards death and discover ourselves as sinners at every turn, we have the ongoing opportunity to be blessed through out hearing that word and believing it.

▶ Prayer

O Mary, my mother, pray for me. You heard the word of God and you obeyed it, bringing forth from your womb the savior of the world. In my need, intercede for me. May your response to God, born of a faithful heart, be a model and example for me.

▶ Action

Think of someone in your life whom you believe hears the word of God and obeys it. How blessed is that person?

Monday of the Twenty-eighth Week of the Year

Out-of-Towner

LUKE 11:29–32

Jesus said, "An evil generation asks for a sign, but no sign will be given to it except the sign of Jonah. For just as Jonah became a sign to the people of Nineveh, so the Son of Man will be to this generation."

▶ Reflection

Bob had been working with his executive staff for months, trying to get them to adjust their management styles to reflect the new organizational system that came down from the home office. Unsuccessful, he called in an "expert" in the field to conduct a conference. It worked. His staff eagerly participated in the exercises and worked up a new organizational plan. Later, Bob asked his expert, "How come you could get them to do that and I couldn't?" The expert laughed. "Well," she said, "the only difference between you and me is that I'm from out of town!" When Jonah preached to the Ninevites, they listened because he was a foreigner with no vested interest in their repentance. Jesus, too, was certainly from "out of town," God come down to save us. We listen to Jesus because we know that he's from God.

▶ Prayer

O loving God, you come to me, born of a woman, to share my humanity. You call me to repentance, to believe in your ways rather than in my own ways. May your will be done in my life.

▶ Action

How would you have done things differently in your life today if there were no God? How does God make a difference?

Tuesday of the Twenty-eighth Week of the Year

St. Paddy's Fish

LUKE 11:37-41

A Pharisee was amazed that Jesus did not wash before dinner. Jesus said to him, "You Pharisees clean the outside of the cup and of the dish, but inside you are full of greed and wickedness. You fools! Did not the one who made the outside make the inside also?"

▶ Reflection

Every few years there's a great controversy in many dioceses over whether or not Catholics should be allowed to eat corned beef on St. Patrick's Day when it falls on a lenten Friday. I was amused when a guy came up to me after Mass once and asked, "So, can I be dispensed from eating fish on Friday?" I said, "Sure, you can eat broccoli instead." The question served as an example of the reason why the church abrogated the general rule about not eating meat on Fridays in the first place. The action had ceased to be devotional and had become so superficial that it had lost its meaning. In some minds at least, eating fish on Fridays became the rule, further blurring the significance of the abstinence. So it was dropped. Jesus did not tolerate superficial religious observance in today's gospel, so the church isn't going to tolerate it either.

▶ Prayer

I practice a religion out of reverence for you, O divine master. But sometimes religions can get a little silly. May I always be guided by the Spirit you have given me.

▶ Action

Think of a religious custom we perform all the time. For instance, blessing a sneezer! See if you can find out why we do that.

Wednesday of the Twenty-eighth Week of the Year

Tombs

LUKE 11:42–46

"Woe to you Pharisees! You love to have the seat of honor in the synagogues and be greeted with respect in the marketplaces. You are like unmarked graves, and people walk over them without realizing it. Woe also to you lawyers! You load people with burdens hard to bear, and you yourselves do not lift a finger to ease them."

▶ Reflection

There's a wonderful rhetorical trap in St. Paul's Letter to the Romans, in chapters 1 and 2. In chapter 1 he draws his readers into the snare of condemning the Greeks for their intellectual, religious, and social sinfulness, then he nails them in their self-righteousness for doing "the very same things." Romans 2 needs to be required reading for everyone who condemns others based on Romans 1. It works every time! It comes down to a simple teaching of Jesus in Luke 6:37: "If you don't want to be judged, then don't judge. If you want to avoid condemnation, don't condemn." Period. We who are devout sometimes fall victim to our own outward appearance. We seem to have our moral ducks in a row and therefore feel justified judging others. Jesus would call us "hidden tombs," a Jewish insult.

▶ Prayer

O Lord, I am guilty of judging others. Because I am careful about my behavior, I condemn other who are less careful or who don't conform to my values. Help me to be merciful as you are merciful.

▶ Action

What social group have you learned to condemn? Spend some time today undoing the damage you've inflicted on your own soul.

Holding the Keys

LUKE 11:47–54

Jesus cried out, "Woe to you scribes! You take away the key of knowledge; you do not enter yourselves, and you hinder those who are trying to enter." Then they began to be very hostile toward him.

▶ Reflection

The tribunal of the archdiocese was holding up Terri's annulment, so she sought help from her parish priest. She explained to him that she really needed the annulment soon so that she could get her marriage blessed and keep her job. She worked for a Catholic school in the next town and the principal was threatening to fire her unless she was married in the church. The priest told her to be patient. She told him she had been waiting almost two years, but he said there was nothing he could do. In desperation, she went to a priest in a neighboring parish. He called the tribunal and they said one of the judges was delaying all the cases because somebody in Rome was upset about the number of annulments in the United States and there was nothing they could do about it. Our Holy Father Pope John Paul II declared a Jubilee Year so that on the dawn of a new millennium the doors of the church would be opened for all. Some holders of the keys, however, haven't gotten the message yet.

▶ Prayer

You have given me authority in this world, O Lord, so that I might be a servant to others. Remind me each day that my authority is for the purpose of helping people enter into your kingdom.

▶ Action

List all the various ways you have authority in this world. Today, find new ways of helping others with your influence.

Friday of the Twenty-eighth Week of the Year

Watching Birds

LUKE 12:1–7

Jesus said to his disciples, "Are not five sparrows sold for two pennies? Yet not one of them is forgotten in God's sight. Even the hairs of your head are all numbered. Do not be afraid, therefore; you are worth more than a whole flock of sparrows."

▶ Reflection

Where Marek used to live in Poland there were few birds; he lived in a large city. But after moving to the United States he discovered many birds in the suburb where he'd bought a house for him and his wife. He would go out every day with his binoculars and look for the birds in the trees along the street and in the lot behind his house, naming as many as he could and trying to find new ones to add to his list. He told his wife one day, "Sometimes I think that God feels among us the same way I feel among the birds; that God watches us with delight and love, calling us each by name and looking carefully for the ones he hasn't seen in a while. Jesus says that God even knows all the hairs on our heads!" His wife laughed and playfully caressed his handsome bald head. She said, "That would be hard to do in your case, honey!"

▶ Prayer

How many times, O Lord, have you said to me, "Do not be afraid?" Yet every day I find myself being afraid of something. You are always with me, protecting me and showing me the way. May I never be afraid with you at my side.

▶ Action

Write down three things that you know will frighten you today. When those things come up, remember that God counts your hairs.

Breaking the Washer

LUKE 12:8–12

"And I tell you," Jesus said, "everyone who acknowledges me before others, I will also acknowledge before the angels of God. Words spoken against the Son of Man will be forgiven; but whoever blasphemes against the Holy Spirit will not be forgiven."

▶ Reflection

Brian loved his new washing machine. The purchase maxed out his credit card, but it was worth it. The first thing he did after the installer left was to load all the dirty rugs from the porch into it and measure in three cups of detergent to handle the load. Imagine his horror when the machine clanged and banged and whirred and whizzed and ground to a halt. The repair guy told him point blank: "You're never supposed to wash rugs and you're never supposed to use three cups of detergent. Didn't you read the instructions?" Brian had glanced at them but had ignored them. Now he would pay the price. Jesus promised that the Holy Spirit would provide instructions for living our lives. We disregard the Spirit's guidance at our own risk. If the Spirit warns us of danger and we proceed anyway, we will pay the price. God can only do so much. We are free to listen or ignore.

▶ Prayer

Holy Spirit, giver of life, you come to me with God's love and care, providing me with counsel and protection. May I always listen to your voice within, showing me the way to fulfillment.

▶ Action

Think of a time when the Holy Spirit pointed one way and you went the other. What were the consequences?

Monday of the Twenty-ninth Week of the Year

Collectible Cupidity

LUKE 12:13–21

Someone said to Jesus, "Tell my brother to give me my share of the inheritance."
But he said to him, "Take care! Be on your guard against greed of any kind;
your life does not consist in the abundance of your possessions."

▶ Reflection

Beanie Babies are brilliant. They represent a most successful marketing
strategy: start the consumer off young and make the product small
and cute. We never think to call it greed if a kid does it. And who gets
greedy over a cute little fuzzy Sally the Salamander? Even more
importantly, make the product a collectible so that the child's greed—
oops, we don't call it greed do we—so that the child's, er, avid
infatuation with the product is amplified every time a new model is
introduced. That way, when the avaricious little tyke grows up, he or
she will be just like the rest of us and keep the whole retail
establishment going. Grownups need to hear the word of the Lord:
avoid greed in all its forms. We need to give up buying all the things
we buy just for the sake of having them. Children learn from our
example and all too often we provide a lousy example for our kids.

▶ Prayer

My Lord, each day as I move through my life I see things that I want
and I often give myself permission to buy what I want for no good
reason. Help me live a better life.

▶ Action

Take stock of your possessions. What things do you have because you
need them and what things do you have because you want them?

Tuesday of the Twenty-ninth Week of the Year

Missed Opportunity

LUKE 12:35–38

Jesus said to his disciples, "Be like slaves waiting for their master's return from a wedding. If the master comes home near dawn and finds them alert and ready, he will put on an apron and serve them supper. How blessed will those slaves be!"

▶ Reflection

Diane had been trying for two months to get a date with Pablo, but the guy never knew it. She was the prettiest, most popular girl in the class but Pablo figured that he didn't have what it took to attract a girl like her. He couldn't see her flirtations; he thought that she was just teasing him, and so the opportunity passed him by. God's grace, which comes in many different ways every day, can pass us by too if we're not ready and waiting for it. Jesus paints the absurd picture of a master coming home at an ungodly hour all full of wine and merry from a wedding party. Finding the house staff waiting up for him, he assumes the unlikely role of a waiter and playfully serves them supper. In the same unexpected way God's universal grace is received by those who are alert and waiting for it in joyful hope.

▶ Prayer

Each day you come to me with blessings and grace beyond my imagining. You love me so much, but I am still learning to love myself. Teach me to always look for your gifts and to be alert for your surprises. May I be ready and waiting when you come.

▶ Action

What are three blessings you need to be looking for today? Write them down and carry them with you all day.

Wednesday of the Twenty-ninth Week of the Year

Responsibility Lesson

LUKE 12:39–48

The Lord said to his disciples, "Who is the faithful and prudent manager whom the master puts in charge of his servants, to give them their allowance of food at the proper time? Blessed is that manager whom the master finds at work when he returns."

▶ Reflection

The class was in a quandary. They had spent the last fifteen minutes discussing how a good God could allow horrible tragedies to befall the human race. Mrs. Burton, the religious education teacher, patiently moderated the debate. The speculations ranged from ardent atheism to feckless fundamentalism. One of the students appealed, "How can there be a God who lets those little children in Africa starve to death?" Mrs. Burton challenged the question: "Why are they starving? Who's in charge of feeding them?" For the rest of the class, Mrs. Burton's fifth grade religious education students were going to learn about God's plan for the human race; how God provides enough for everybody and how it is the responsibility of those who have charge over these things to be sure that those who are in need have what they need when they need it.

▶ Prayer

O God, giver of every gift, you desire people to experience your love. You send the rich to help the poor so that both may rejoice in charity, the giver and the receiver. Show me what I must do today.

▶ Action

Look in your parish bulletin for the opportunities you'll have this week to share what you have with the poor. Exercise your options.

Thursday of the Twenty-ninth Week of the Year

Consuming Fire

LUKE 12:49–53

Jesus said to his disciples, "I came to bring a fire upon the earth, and how I wish it were already kindled! I have come to experience a baptism, and how anxious I am till it is completed!"

▶ Reflection

The disciples must've wondered about Jesus sometimes. First he says one thing, and then he says another. First he reprimands them for wanting to call down fire upon the Samaritans (see Luke 9:51–56); then he wants "to bring a fire upon the earth." He had been baptized back in Luke 3:21; then he talks about being baptized again. What's going on? John the Baptist provides the answer in Luke 3:16. He says, "I baptize you with water. He will baptize you with the holy Spirit and fire." Fire is a good image of that which consumes the material and transforms it into the ethereal, something spiritual that rises. Jesus will be consumed by suffering and death and ascend like smoke into the heavens. When he is glorified, he will send "a fire upon the earth" so that all who would make the same choices he made may be likewise consumed.

▶ Prayer

O Jesus, savior of all, you willingly gave up your life, all that you loved in the world, so that all people might be set free from the slavery of sin and the bondage of death. I want to stay free. Remind me always that the choices I make determine where I am going.

▶ Action

If you were to be called from this world today, what thing would you miss the most? Ask the Spirit to cleanse you of that possession.

Friday of the Twenty-ninth Week of the Year

Case Closed

LUKE 12:54–59

Jesus said to his disciples, "When you are accused, make an effort to settle the case, or you may be dragged before the judge and the judge may throw you in prison where you will not get out until you have paid the last penny."

▶ Reflection

Henry had a wake-up-call heart attack. It didn't kill him, but it caused him to take a good look at his life and change a few things, including the way he looked at sin, God, and judgment day. "I used to try to equivocate about my sins," he said. "Ever since I learned there were conditions necessary for committing mortal sin, I tried to use those conditions to argue my culpability. Somehow I thought that if I was less guilty, I was in a better position with God. Then I realized that Christ died for *all* my sins, that I am a forgiven man! So why beat around the bush? Now I confess everything, even the little stuff. My priest says I'm being too scrupulous, but I just enjoy celebrating God's mercy and forgiveness. God's love inspires me to live a better life. God's pardon of all my offenses frees me from anxiety and heals my guilt so now I can do more for God. My case is closed."

▶ Prayer

Lord Jesus Christ, you won the victory over sin and death for me so that I am free to serve you completely. Keep me always mindful of your love in my life so that I am not overcome by fear and guilt.

▶ Action

Is there sin in your life that causes you to worry? Spend the day remembering that your sins are forgiven. Go to confession soon.

Saturday of the Twenty-ninth Week of the Year

Victims of Foolishness

LUKE 13:1–9

They told Jesus about the Galileans whom Pilate had executed. He asked them, "Do you think that because these Galileans suffered in this way they were worse sinners than all other Galileans? Or were those eighteen who were killed when the tower of Siloam fell on them worse offenders than all the others living in Jerusalem? No, but unless you repent, you will all perish just as they did."

▶ Reflection

In the time of Jesus it was the general understanding that if ill fortune came upon a person, it was probably because he deserved it. Here and elsewhere in the gospel stories, Jesus insists that this is not the case. God does not will bad things to happen to people. That is why God reveals a way of life that leads to goodness, not evil. It's like my mother telling me to look both ways before I cross the street. If I fail to heed my mother's good direction and get run over by a bus, is that my mother punishing me for not obeying her? Neither does God want us to be hurt, but persistence in evil will eventually lead to an evil end. While we may sometimes be the victims of the wrongdoing of others, we don't want to be the victims of our own foolishness.

▶ Prayer

Lord, you are like a mother to me, guiding me and showing me what is right and good for my own welfare. Yet sometimes I turn away from you to follow another path. Lead me safely back to you.

▶ Action

Remember the times you have asked, "Why is this happening to me?" or "What did I do to deserve this?" Think of a better question to ask.

Monday of the Thirtieth Week of the Year

Halloween Sneak

LUKE 13:10–17

The synagogue leader was indignant because Jesus had cured on the sabbath. But the Lord said to him, "You hypocrite! You let out your animals on the sabbath. Shouldn't this woman, a daughter of Abraham, be set free from bondage on the sabbath day, too?"

▶ Reflection

Mid-October is the time of year when the altar server robes start disappearing from the sacristy. They will reappear shortly at my front door worn by various ghosts, angels, ninja warriors, ghouls, and goblins extorting treats by threatening tricks. I want to say that this would never have happened in the old days, but I seem to recall liberating a cassock or two from the altar boy closet prior to Halloween in my mischievous youth. Of course, all borrowed items would be returned the next day, none the worse for the wear with the exception of a few shaving cream stains. I think Fr. Picher, God rest his kindly old soul, was aware of the shenanigans but never said anything because he knew compassion was the better part of the rules every time.

▶ Prayer

O God, you are so wonderful. You gave the law so that people might live in peace and grow in prosperity. People broke your law, but you sent Jesus to rescue them from the consequences of their sinfulness. May I always be free to follow your guidance to what is good.

▶ Action

Think of a time when God saved you in some way from the consequences of a foolish act. Offer God a prayer of thanksgiving.

Tuesday of the Thirtieth Week of the Year

Overdoing It

LUKE 13:18–21

"The kingdom of God is like a mustard seed that a man planted. It grows and becomes a tree, and the birds make nests in it. It is like a little bit of yeast that a woman puts in a mountain of dough. All of it rises and is baked into bread for an entire village."

▶ Reflection

Kathy needed to back off her kids. She harped on them constantly about this and that, unrelenting in her criticism and unceasing in her supervision of them. It was clear, even to her Mom who came to visit that day, that she was beginning to really alienate her children. That would mean trouble later on. "Honey," her Mom said gently over coffee, "I know I'm only the grandmother, but I think the kids do really well. You're too critical of them." Kathy protested, "But I'm so afraid they won't get it right." Her Mom understood. "Maybe that's the problem: you're afraid. What I've learned about being a mother is that you have to trust the goodness of your kids. God made them good and you're putting good things into them. Somewhere you have to just sit back and watch the goodness grow. You know, there were even times I had my doubts about you, but look how well you turned out!"

▶ Prayer

You are the great planter of seed, O my God. You sow goodness into the field of who I am, the person you made me to be. I pray that you bring forth an abundant harvest from this barren little field.

▶ Action

Plant seeds in people's lives today. Tell people how good they are or how bright their futures look. Water the seeds daily with prayer.

Wednesday of the Thirtieth Week of the Year

Know God

LUKE 13:22–30

"Strive to enter through the narrow door; for many, I tell you, will try to enter and will not be able. When once the owner of the house has got up and shut the door, and you begin to stand outside and to knock at the door, saying, 'Lord, open to us,' then in reply he will say to you, 'I do not know you.'"

▶ Reflection

"You don't know me," a fan begins her letter from halfway across the country, "but I know you." Well, she doesn't really "know" me. She's seen my picture and read my stuff, but we're not friends or anything like that. She simply knows a little something about me from what I write. Jesus uses the same comparison in his teaching. People know a lot about Jesus, but do they really "know" Jesus? Do they have a relationship with the Lord? Unless we really come to know Christ, we remain blind to his presence in our lives and miss our opportunities. For instance, do we really believe that God can make everything in our lives work together for good? (see Romans 8:28). Often we fall victim to our fears and doubts because we place limits on God's love and God's power to bring about goodness in our lives.

▶ Prayer

My Lord, you dwell within me; your flesh and blood are joined with mine in a sacred union. Yet, while you know me, I have not known you all that well. Turn my heart more to your presence in me.

▶ Action

Talk to your Creator in your heart today. Ask Jesus about the "narrow door." Listen to the Spirit answering you from within. Know God.

Thursday of the Thirtieth Week of the Year

A City Unwilling

LUKE 13:31–35

As they neared Jerusalem, Jesus cried out, "Jerusalem, Jerusalem, the city that kills the prophets and stones those who are sent to it! How often have I desired to gather your children together as a hen gathers her brood under her wings, and you were not willing!"

▶ Reflection

In biblical stories, "the city" always seems to play the bad guy, from Babylon, the first city built on the plains of Shinar (see Genesis 11:1–9), to the great Babylon of Revelation 18:1–22, the city of final destruction on judgment day. The city is the enduring biblical image of people coming together for the purpose of gaining wealth and security. And while that's not bad in itself, desire for it turns hearts, corrupts intentions, and, finally, perverts the purpose of creation. Only in the city, set apart from the self-sufficient farm, does the dynamic of supply and demand power a market economy in which the value of a commodity is determined by how much a buyer is willing to pay for it. There it is possible for the rich to get richer at the expense of the poor who get poorer. Such a system soon becomes unwilling to hear the voice of compassion and hostile to the warnings of judgment.

▶ Prayer

O my God, I am so sorry for the times I do not hear your voice gathering me to your love, for the times when I love money more. Help me to be more compassionate to the poor and faithful to your call.

▶ Action

Somewhere in your life, love of money gets in the way of compassion for the poor. See if you can find at least one point of conflict today.

Friday of the Thirtieth Week of the Year

Grape Juice Compassion

LUKE 14:1–6

Jesus asked the lawyers and Pharisees, "Is it lawful to heal on the sabbath?" But they were silent. So he asked them, "If your son falls into a well on the sabbath, wouldn't you pull him out?"

▶ Reflection

I used to celebrate Mass with a group of inmates in a local prison. Most of them were in jail because of problems with drugs and alcohol and so they were all in some kind of recovery program. I wanted them to be able to drink from the cup at communion time, but I knew that the form of alcohol in the Precious Blood of the Lord could adversely affect their recovery. So I substituted grape juice for the wine and told them so. I knew I wasn't supposed to do that, but it was very important to the men to drink from the cup. One day my good bishop came to celebrate with us. After communion we sat with our little congregation and I could hear him quietly smacking his lips, signaling to me, I suppose, his awareness of my unlawful grape juice. But he never said a word to me. Although the law states that wine is necessary for a valid celebration of the Eucharist, the bishop cared more for these poor souls than for the rules.

▶ Prayer

O God, when law keeps me from reaching out to another in compassion, give me the courage to be bold and fearless, trusting in your grace and mercy. Teach me to live according to your Spirit.

▶ Action

Think of how the rules could sometimes stand in the way of justice and compassionate action. Resolve to always do the right thing.

Saturday of the Thirtieth Week of the Year

Gone Nuts?

LUKE 14:1, 7-11

"When you are invited to a banquet, do not sit at a place of honor. Rather, sit at the lowest place. All who exalt themselves will be humbled, but those who humble themselves will be exalted."

▶ Reflection

They must've thought Jesus had gone nuts. From the start, the point of the Jewish religion was that they would work their way to the front of the line. When it began with Abraham, he had no family and no land. He and his descendants would strive all their lives to gain what was at the beginning only a hope. When Moses led them out of Egypt, they had nothing except what they could carry running as they escaped from slavery. They would have to struggle against other strong tribes to possess the land they were promised, and even then couldn't hold on to it without a fight. Eventually, only the strongest won the places of dignity and respect in the society. The weak became the poor and the lowly, excluded from honor. The coming kingdom that Jesus proclaimed would exalt those on the bottom rungs of society and recruited followers who would serve as examples of this new hope for the poor. In that way *all* people would come to know God's love.

▶ Prayer

When there is poverty in my life, you fill me with riches, O Lord. You lift me up in my lowliness and show me the greatness of your love. May I always be a sign of hope for others who are needy.

▶ Action

Lift up a friend today. Give something secretly to a person in need. Encourage someone who needs to hear good news.

Monday of the Thirty-first Week of the Year

Love or Money

LUKE 14:12–14

"When you give a luncheon or a dinner, invite the poor, the crippled, the lame, and the blind. You will be blessed because they cannot repay you. Your payment will come at the resurrection."

▶ Reflection

What if Bill Gates offered you ten million dollars to throw a dinner party at your house for the local street people, the bag ladies and the shopping cart guys, the people from the soup kitchen, AIDS and cancer patients from the hospital downtown, the "special" folks from the local group homes, and people from that "high crime" neighborhood on the other side of town? Would you do it for ten million? So would I. But what if the payment was deferred? What if you wouldn't get paid until, say, you rose from the dead on the last day? Would you still do it? Well, that's what Jesus is offering. He gives us an opportunity to be paid far more than ten million dollars to offer our lives in service to the broken people of our world. Do we take our Lord Jesus at his word? Are we willing to take him up on his offer?

▶ Prayer

God my creator, all the world is yours and you give it all to me. You fill my life with the wealth of family, friends, community, and enough resources to clothe, feed and shelter me. You only ask that I share what I have. In return you give me eternity. Such a deal.

▶ Action

Start small. Invite a lowly acquaintance to lunch. Have a humble family in the neighborhood over for dinner. Rack up a reward.

Tuesday of the Thirty-first Week of the Year

Drug Dealers Invited

LUKE 14:15–24

"A man gave a great dinner and invited many. But they all made excuses and didn't come. So he opened his doors to the poor, the blind, and the lame. Then he went out into the highways and byways and compelled people to come. But none of those who were originally invited tasted his dinner."

▶ Reflection

"They ought to extend the death penalty to include drug dealers, too!" shouted the outraged woman shaking her copy of the parish bulletin in the pastor's face. The bishops had just announced their call for an end to the death penalty in the United States and the pastor had printed excerpts in the bulletin and, from the pulpit, called for support from his parishioners. Now he was taking the abuse he expected. The poor woman's daughter had been the victim of a drug dealer and her heart was broken. Still, a change of heart was necessary for her to be healed. It's hard to imagine that all people, even the drug dealers, are invited into God's kingdom. Sure, many won't respond, just like many Catholics who go to church every Sunday will refuse to come, too. The big questions are: will you come? Will I?

▶ Prayer

Your mercy and compassion extend to everyone, my God, because you made them all yourself and you love them like a mother loves her children. Help me to try and understand your universal love.

▶ Action

Read today's newspaper and make a list of all the people you would condemn if you were God. Now consider how you would save them.

Wednesday of the Thirty-first Week of the Year

Give Up

LUKE 14:25–33

Jesus said, "If you wanted to build a tower, you would first count the cost to see if you had enough to finish the job. Otherwise you would fail and people would say, 'He began to build what he could not finish.' In the same way, you can't be my disciple if you do not give up all your possessions."

▶ Reflection

When the refugees from the fighting in Kosovo began arriving in this country, Don began an effort in his parish to find homes for them. There were many large houses in the community where folks lived comfortably in retirement, or at least with the kids gone, had room to spare. Don thought that surely these people would open their homes at least temporarily for the Kosovar refugees. Some did, but many begged off, saying they didn't have the room. "You know," he said later, "I would've felt better about it if they just said that they had room but were unwilling to share it with strangers. At least that would've been honest." Jesus may be saying the same thing in today's gospel. If you're not willing to give it up for the sake of others, don't bother even trying to be a disciple.

▶ Prayer

O God, it's scary to think about giving up the things I possess. Yet you call me to be your disciple and be a witness to your kingdom. Help me to let go of my possessions so I can better serve you.

▶ Action

Give up a part of your home that you usually claim for yourself. Give it to your spouse or to one of the kids, or to someone in your parish or neighborhood who might need the space.

Thursday of the Thirty-first Week of the Year

Bad Shepherd?

LUKE 15:1–10

The Pharisees were grumbling and saying, "He welcomes sinners!" So Jesus told them a parable: "Which one of you, having a hundred sheep and losing one of them, does not leave the ninety-nine in the wilderness and go after the one that is lost? And when you find it, you rejoice. In the same way there is more joy in heaven over one sinner who repents than over ninety-nine righteous who need not repent."

▶ Reflection

You have to wonder what kind of shepherd would leave ninety-nine perfectly good sheep alone in the wilderness in order to track down one dumb sheep that managed to get itself lost. Yet that is the image Jesus presents. God goes to extraordinary lengths to rescue the lost. The grace of salvation is directed towards those who need to be saved. If anyone is going to level a judgment on another, it must be the judgment of love. Therefore, Jesus says, "love your enemies, do good to those who hate you, bless those who curse you, pray for those who mistreat you" (Luke 6:27–28). The paradox of the gospel is so evident here. In order to engender repentance in another, that repentance must first be engendered in ourselves.

▶ Prayer

Your incredible love turned my heart to you, O Lord. You rescued me from the foolishness of my own pursuits. Now, Lord, soften my heart so that I may have compassion for other who are lost.

▶ Action

For what sin are you most sorry? What is it like for you to be totally and completely forgiven of that sin? Carry that joy around all day.

Friday of the Thirty-first Week of the Year

God's Beauty Queen

LUKE 16:1–8

Jesus told a story about a steward who was commended by his master for being shrewd with his wealth; for the children of this age are more clever in dealing with their own than are the children of light.

▶ Reflection

Rose was very pretty. She was always the prom queen in school and the object of a great deal of attention wherever she went. In college she won a beauty contest, which got her into the finals of the Miss America pageant in her state where she finished third runner-up. Later on she went to work modeling for an agency that produced catalogues for a national clothing chain. Through it all she never missed her weekly trip to the children's hospital to visit the kids in the critical care unit. There her beauty worked magic on the kids. She was like a fairy princess to them; they seemed transported by her loveliness. "It's what God gave me," she'd say. "So I use it for his purposes." Like the steward in the gospel story, she took initiative with her worldly treasure and used it wisely in this world to gain an advantage in the world to come.

▶ Prayer

Almighty God, you put me in charge of the wealth of my life. Then you show me all the good that could be done with what I hold in my possession. You send me the hungry to feed, the lowly to lift up, and people to love. May I always be a wise steward.

▶ Action

Take a look at the wealth you possess and decide how you can best use it to gain an advantage in the kingdom of God.

Saturday of the Thirty-first Week of the Year

Panhandler Opportunity

LUKE 16:9–15

"Whoever is faithful in a very little is faithful also in much; and whoever is dishonest in a very little is dishonest also in much. No slave can serve two masters. You cannot serve God and money."

▶ Reflection

The panhandler was standing at his usual place on the corner, shaking his paper cup and asking for spare change as Lydia and Charlene walked by. Lydia stopped, reached in her purse, took out two quarters and dropped them into the man's cup. He smiled and said, "Thank you, ma'am, and God bless you." Lydia replied, "You're welcome. And God bless you, too," and the two continued on their way. They walked along in silence for a while, and then Charlene said, "Why do you give your money to those people?" Lydia knew the question was coming and had a ready answer. "Well," she said, "the Lord gave it to me so I'm just passing it along. I reckon I'd rather love that poor man than those two quarters. And besides, no one ever went broke giving their spare change away." Lydia was being faithful in a little thing. There is a good chance that she'll have the opportunity to be faithful in much more. That is the way things are with God and money.

▶ Prayer

O God, thank you for the money you give me. I sometimes think it's not enough, but that's only because I spend too much of it on worldly things. Help me always to use my money for what it was intended.

▶ Action

Sit down today and determine just how much of your income you give to real charities. Ask yourself: is this how much I trust God?

Monday of the Thirty-second Week of the Year

Where's the Scandal?

LUKE 17:1–6

Jesus said to his disciples, "Offenses are bound to come, but woe to anyone by whom they come! It would be better for you if a millstone were hung around your neck and you were thrown into the sea than for you to give offense to one of these little ones."

▶ **Reflection**

The Greek word Luke uses for "offense" is *skandalon*, from which derives the English word "scandal." A certain amount of tension always exists between social scandal—that which arises from behavior generally considered to be inappropriate—and gospel scandal—that which comes from behavior which is contrary to the gospel. A friend of mine was hired by a certain archdiocese to work in an urban social outreach capacity. In the course of his employment, he began to make the rounds of bars in the evening, getting to know the folks. His boss, the director of the ministry, thought that was inappropriate. "It causes scandal," he said. In Jesus' day, the keepers of the social conscience claimed the Lord caused scandal, too. "Look, a glutton and a drunkard, a friend of tax collectors and sinners!" they'd say (Luke 7:34). So where do you draw the line?

▶ **Prayer**

O Lord, only with the guidance of your Holy Spirit can I understand what is truly God's will for me. And only with your grace can I do the things you call me to do. Guide me and bless me always.

▶ **Action**

Think about what the Lord might be calling you to do that you avoid doing out of fear that you would give offense to others.

Tuesday of the Thirty-second Week of the Year

Hero? Not!

LUKE 17:7–10

"Does the master of the house reward his servants for following orders? In the same way, when you have fulfilled all that you were commanded to do, say, 'We are unworthy servants; we have only done what we were supposed to do!'"

▶ Reflection

Cassian was embarrassed by all the fuss people were making over him. A friend had taken gravely ill and Cassian had come to his rescue. Since the friend had no family, Cassian took a leave of absence from work and spent many months nursing his friend back to health. Because of what he did, they called him a hero and a saint. "I didn't do anything anybody else wouldn't do in the same circumstance," he told an acquaintance. "Isn't that just what we're supposed to do?" Cassian understands that life is more than money and career and comfort. He sees himself as a servant to the poor and the lowly. A devout Christian, Cassian is certain he will not go without his reward. In the meantime, he lives his life according to what he sees is its purpose.

▶ Prayer

My God, you created me in love so that I might experience life and come to know you and serve you and live in your love. Keep me focused on doing your will and accomplishing my purpose. May I always follow you wherever you lead me.

▶ Action

Think of three things you do each day that you know are part of God's purpose for you in your life. Give thanks to God for the opportunity.

Wednesday of the Thirty-second Week of the Year

Fear of Priests

LUKE 17:11–19

Ten lepers cried out, "Lord, have mercy on us!" Jesus said, "Go and show yourselves to the priests." And as they went, they were made clean. One of them returned praising God. Jesus said, "Where are the other nine?"

▸ Reflection

You have to wonder about the poor guy who returned to thank Jesus. The story says he was a Samaritan, which means that not only would the Jewish religion have been alien to him, it would also have been hostile toward him. The ten, ethnically, religiously, and perhaps even racially diverse, had no doubt been thrown together by their common catastrophe. Imagine the man's horror when Jesus sent the group off to show themselves to the priests, presumably in Jerusalem. Imagine his prayer along the way: "Oh please, please don't make me go to the priests." And of course God hears his prayer and heals him along the way. You can bet he raced back to thank Jesus. The others, happily looking forward to being declared cured by the priests (as was required by the religious law of Leviticus 14:1–33), continued on their way.

▸ Prayer

Dear Jesus, when I come to you in prayer, you always respond because of your infinite love. You give me all I need, yet my response is sometimes inadequately human. Thank you for your merciful love.

▸ Action

Recall a blessing God gave you for which you made an inadequate response. Take the time now to thank God from your heart.

Kingdom Inside

LUKE 17:20–25

Once they asked Jesus when the kingdom of God was coming, and he answered, "The kingdom of God doesn't come with things that can be observed. You can't say, 'It is here!' or 'There it is!' The kingdom of God is within you."

▶ Reflection

"So the doctor says I have to see a gastroenterologist," my mother informed me over the phone. "What's that?" I had to admit that I wasn't quite sure, but I looked it up. A quick check of the dictionary showed me everything I needed to know. It's a doctor who looks at your "insides." The root word in gastroenterologist is "enter" which means exactly what you think it means. It's from the Greek "entos" which means, "within." It's the same word Luke uses in the original language of his gospel to identify the location of the kingdom of God. It's "inside" you, Jesus says. What an amazing revelation! Inside you is the kingdom of God in its completeness and in its entirety. And it is the same kingdom that is in all of us. We need not look for signs of the kingdom's coming. It's already present to us and is a reality within us. God's kingdom, as Jesus describes in his teaching, is an inner happening going on right now.

▶ Prayer

You are at peace in your kingdom, O God, and that kingdom is within me. Help me to know your peaceful and secure presence in my life.

▶ Action

Look up one of the many gospel teachings about the kingdom, like Matthew 13:44–47 or 18:23–34. Imagine all that going on within you.

Friday of the Thirty-second Week of the Year

Godly Buzzards

LUKE 17:26–37

"On the day when the Son of Man is revealed, those who attempt to secure their life will lose it, but those who surrender their life will preserve it. Where the carcass is, there the vultures will gather."

▶ Reflection

"When the kingdom comes," crackled the voice from the car radio as I drove through the night, "the Lord will show us where it is. All we have to do is watch for the eagles to gather, for he saith unto them wheresoever the body is, thither will the eagles be gathered together, Luke 17:37, praise God!" I chuckled to myself. He got the first part right. The Lord will definitely show us where the kingdom is coming and lead us to its fulfillment. But the sign won't be supernatural; we won't have to look for any bizarre assembly of eagles. The image is metaphorical. It means simply that finding the kingdom will be as natural for us as it is for vultures to spot road kill, the source of their daily nutrition. You always know where the road kill is; you see the vultures gather. If God so loves the buzzards and cares for them and guides them to where they need to go, how much more will God love you and care for you and guide you to where you need to go?

▶ Prayer

I sometimes get anxious, O Lord, about where I am to go and what I am to do in order to be good and right. But you always guide me. Help me to really believe in your abiding love.

▶ Action

Keep track of all the things that make you afraid today. When day is done, review how God worked to protect you from what you fear.

Saturday of the Thirty-second Week of the Year

Bugging the Judge

LUKE 18:1–8

A widow kept coming to a judge and saying, "Grant me justice!" After a while the judge said to himself, "I respect neither God nor people, but I will grant her justice or she will wear me out!"

▶ Reflection

Jesus tells the amusing story of a callous magistrate who doesn't give a hoot about anyone, including God or the people he allegedly serves. Into this man's life comes a woman who makes it clear to him that she is going to hound him day and night until he does what he's sworn to do, which is to satisfy the demands of justice for her. His response comes neither out of a sense of duty nor responsibility, but rather the fear that she will wear him out with her demands! Jesus is simply saying that if a judge with no dedication whatsoever to justice, God, or humanity would respond favorably to the woman out of his own self-interest, then how much more will God, who is dedicated to us out of an infinite love and whom the prophet Jeremiah called, "our Justice" (23:6), do justice for the poor? Another question: if in God's justice the last are first and the first are last, where will God's exercise of justice leave me?

▶ Prayer

O God of justice, you "cast down the mighty from their thrones and lift up the lowly" (Luke 1:52). You are the champion of the poor and the needy. May I always be an instrument of your justice.

▶ Action

Today you will experience a person who is in need. Resolve now to do what is necessary to provide justice for that person.

Monday of the Thirty-third Week of the Year

Jesus First

LUKE 18:35–43

The blind man shouted out to Jesus, "Son of David, have mercy on me!" Jesus stopped and asked him, "What do you want me to do for you?" He said, "Lord, let me see again." Jesus said to him, "Receive your sight; your faith has saved you."

▶ Reflection

Their relationship was faltering and their marriage was in trouble. Tonya wanted to see a counselor, but Herve would have none of it. He said he didn't believe in such things and besides, Tonya just had to understand that he needed to spend a lot of time at work to make his business successful. The relationship would just have to wait. Tonya knew that the relationship couldn't wait. She was like the blind man in the gospel story who only wanted one thing. The blind man wanted to see and Tonya wanted to save their marriage. With virtually nothing in his life to distract him, the blind man could focus on what he needed to get what he wanted. In the same way, Tonya was focused on what she wanted, but Herve had a divided heart. He wanted to be married to Tonya but he also wanted his business to succeed. Jesus tells the story in Matthew 22:5 of such a man who missed out on the kingdom because of his business. It happens.

▶ Prayer

O God, I want your kingdom. I desire the riches of your grace. May no worldly thing ever stand between me and your love.

▶ Action

What do you want most in your life? Compose a prayer to God and recite the prayer every day until you receive what you ask for.

Tuesday of the Thirty-third Week of the Year

Jesus for Dinner

LUKE 19:1–10

They began to grumble when Jesus went to Zacchaeus' for dinner. They said, "He's gone to the house of a sinner." But Jesus said, "Today salvation has come to this house, for I came to seek out and save the lost."

▶ Reflection

The day Jesus showed up at Zacchaeus' house, the diminutive tax collector was about as "lost" from God as one could get. He had literally sold his soul to the devil, abandoning the covenant with God and working a deal with the pagan Romans. The emperor in Rome hired his revenue collectors locally because they knew where the money was, and Zacchaeus (his Hebrew name means "pure") knew how to work the locals. He grew rich quickly and rose to become the chief tax collector of Jericho, despised by his fellow Jews. But Jesus began to change all that. There's nothing to suggest that Zacchaeus quit his job, but he changed the way he did business. His repentance had begun; what had been lost was found. As Jesus said in the story, this is why he came. Today Jesus is coming to your house for dinner. What changes will you make?

▶ Prayer

My Lord, I sit at your table and you feed me with your flesh and blood presence in my life. You are with me now, seeking to save what is lost to my sinfulness. Help me to repent and amend my life.

▶ Action

Write down three things you should be doing differently in recognition of the presence of Jesus in your life.

Wednesday of the Thirty-third Week of the Year

Going To Get It

LUKE 19:11–28

"A nobleman went away to be crowned king and then return. But the citizens of his country hated him and sent a delegation after him, saying, 'We do not want this man to rule over us.' So when he returned as king, he had his enemies put to death."

▶ Reflection

Luke throws a little political intrigue into the popular parable of the talents found in Matthew 25:14–30. He adds the story of the nobleman who goes away to be crowned king. Some scholars think Luke may have had local history in mind and was drawing a parallel between the story of how Archelaus, the son of Herod the Great, went to Rome to be made king of Judea after his father's death in 4 BC, and how Jesus "went away" and would return as king to defeat his enemies. Many in the first-century Christian community thought that the return of Jesus would happen in their lifetime, and that he would establish the kingdom in Jerusalem. But the apostle Paul, a friend of Luke's, developed the theology of a "delay" in Christ's return, which, evidently, worked its way into Luke's gospel. It is possible that Luke felt it would be some comfort to his persecuted Christian readers that, when Jesus returned, the persecutors were going to "get it."

▶ Prayer

Lord Jesus, I don't want my earthly enemies hurt. But I hope you put to death my spiritual enemies: greed, envy, pride, and all the others.

▶ Action

Make a list of the enemies you would like to see Jesus put to death when he returns. Then wait in joyful hope for his coming.

Thursday of the Thirty-third Week of the Year

Victory of Surrender

LUKE 19:41–44

Jesus wept for Jerusalem saying, "If only you could see the path to peace available to you this day! But it is hidden from your eyes. The time will come upon you when your enemies will besiege you, and surround you, and hem you in on every side."

▶ Reflection

The "path to peace" would have saved Jerusalem from destruction by the Romans in 70 AD, but the ancient Judeans were bent on fighting for their independence from Rome. Forty years earlier, the preaching of Jesus about the kingdom led many Judeans, including some of his own followers, to conclude that it would be Jesus who would lead the revolt against the Romans and re-establish the ancient realm of King David. But the road to peace for Jesus was not victory in a worldly fight. "My kingdom is not here," he said in John 18:36. Rather, to establish his kingdom, he would surrender to the forces of darkness and the evil of this world. I see in my life how often I am visited with an opportunity to surrender, to give up my will for the sake of peace. But just as often I fail to recognize it and peace escapes my grasp.

▶ Prayer

O loving Jesus, the sinfulness of the world overwhelmed your human life and crucified you. Yet you died as a friend of sinners, and you rose again to set me free and give me a new life. Establish your kingdom in me, Lord. Give me a share in your victory of surrender.

▶ Action

In the next battle of wills you encounter, surrender. Give in, entrust yourself to God, and see what happens.

Friday of the Thirty-third Week of the Year

Prayer and Thievery

LUKE 19:45–48

Then he entered the temple and began to drive out those who were selling things there. He said, "It is written, 'My house shall be a house of prayer,' but you have made it a den of thieves!"

▸ Reflection

A strong tradition of ancient Jewish spirituality, as it was understood and practiced in the time of Jesus, was that of purity. The Mosaic Law seemed to disfavor "mixing" things. You couldn't, for example, harness an ox and an ass together to plow your field, or plant your vineyard with two different kinds of seed, or wear clothing made of fabric woven from two different kinds of thread—a poly-cotton blend would have been a no-no (see Deuteronomy 22:9–11). Some contemporary kosher regulations, such as the prohibition of mixing dairy and meat, in a way reflect that ancient concern. Formed in these traditions, Jesus stormed into the temple that day, outraged at the mixing of commerce and worship. Prayer and thievery had no truck in the Lord's mind, but the keepers of the religion, who loved the money, were offended. When the leaders of a religion make their living from the religion, it's hard to mix things up.

▸ Prayer

Oh Lord, I thank you for the gift of my religion and the people you have chosen to lead me in faith. Bless them and strengthen them in their weaknesses. Keep them faithful to your call.

▸ Action

Think about how often anxiety about money occupies your attention and enters your prayers. Look up and read Matthew 6:24–34.

Saturday of the Thirty-third Week of the Year

Religious Repartee

LUKE 20:27–40

The Sadducees asked Jesus, "If a man marries a woman and dies, and then his brother marries her and dies, and the next brother, and so on; and seven brothers in turn marry her and the all die, then she dies, whose wife will she be in the resurrection? All seven married her."

▶ Reflection

The Sadducees couldn't care less about the answer to their question. They were ridiculing the whole idea of resurrection and life after death. The Pharisees, on the other hand, held that there was indeed a resurrection, a theology already a century old by the time of Jesus (see Wisdom 2:23—3:10). Neither did the Sadducees believe in angels (see Acts 23:6–10). So, reading the full text of the passage, Jesus incorporates angels into his reply, an unmistakable gibe tossed back at them. Or, as a liturgist I know once said while in a dispute with a priest over a fine point of liturgical procedure, "You can do things your way, but I will do things God's way." Jesus evidently favored the theological position of the Pharisees. But he seemed to enjoy a little religious repartee with people of other persuasions. A mark of real faith, perhaps, is that one is not put off by those who disagree.

▶ Prayer

O God, my love, you are not diminished by differences in faith and your glory is not made less by the disagreement of believers. May I always be steadfast in my religion and not fear the rejection of others.

▶ Action

Recall an argument about religion you may have had with a friend or relative. Evaluate your part. Resolve next time to enjoy it.

Monday of the Thirty-fourth Week of the Year

God's Annuity

LUKE 21:1–4

Jesus saw rich people putting their gifts into the temple treasury. Then he saw a poor widow put in two cents. He said, "I tell you, this poor widow put in more than all of them. The others contributed out of their abundance, but she out of her poverty put in all she had."

▶ Reflection

So, do you think God will take care of the widow because she tossed in everything she had? If your answer is "yes," you're half right. God will indeed take care of the widow, but not because she made such a great offering. No, God takes care of everybody; God's love and faithful providence are not conditioned by anything people do or don't do to deserve them. But the widow's offering will sure put her in a position to notice God's care for her. When God makes the divine move, she'll know for certain it was God coming to her rescue and not her annuity check coming in the mail. People with money, however, even if they make great offerings, tend not to notice God's care because they are rarely in a position to be consciously aware of their complete reliance on God. The rich are secure in their wealth. Their income is regular and they expect it to show up. But you have to empty the cup once in a while so that God can fill it.

▶ Prayer

O God, you give me the whole world, but I want the sun and the moon and the stars. May I be blessed in giving rather than receiving.

▶ Action

Make a space for God to bless you in your life today. Pour out a cup of time, money, or attention so that God may fill it up again.

Tuesday of the Thirty-fourth Week of the Year

Church or God?

LUKE 21:5–11

They were speaking about how beautiful the temple was with its many precious stones and memorial offerings. Jesus said, "These things that you see? The day will come when not one stone will be left upon another; it will all be torn down."

▶ Reflection

"Ralph was very upset when they closed St. Isadore's," Sylvia told her neighbor Fran over coffee. "He's saying he's had it with the church and he won't go to Mass any more." St. Isadore's was a rundown parish in a neighborhood of abandoned factories. It had been a "throwaway" where the bishop had sent priests who were "problems" in other parishes. After years of poor pastoring, the people had lost interest and migrated to other parishes nearby. Ralph had been a stalwart supporter, and when it finally closed he was outraged. "But it's just a building," Sylvia pleaded. Ralph, however, was adamant. Sylvia confided in Fran, "I sometimes think it's that old church he loves. I don't think he cares that much about religion." Sylvia could say that about many devout churchgoers. We sometimes love our religion more than we love God. But for God, it is the love that lasts. God is in it till the end of time, no matter what happens to the church.

▶ Prayer

My Lord Jesus, your Spirit fills the church and makes it alive. Fill me with the same Spirit and make me a living member of your body.

▶ Action

Go inside your church today, if you get a chance, and observe how nice it is inside. How would you feel if it were all torn down?

Wednesday of the Thirty-fourth Week of the Year

Enduring Betrayals

LUKE 21:12–19

You will be persecuted, betrayed by your own. But I will give you words and a wisdom that cannot be opposed. You will be hated because of my name. But not a hair of your head will be harmed. By your endurance you will gain your souls.

▶ Reflection

Suddenly, without warning, Andrea screamed in protest against Pat. She ranted and raved at full volume while Pat stood dumbfounded. In twenty years of happy marriage, there had never been such an outburst between them. Pat knew that Andrea was under a tremendous amount of stress with her work, her recent surgery, and the tragic death of her father. And Pat knew that he could be annoying sometimes and was indeed doing so when Andrea blew up at him. But he felt betrayed nonetheless, and Andrea was fuming. Later, he took his wife in his arms and held her tenderly while she wept. "I love you, Andy," he said. "I love you too," she sobbed. At times married couples have to endure patiently the betrayals and persecutions that come their way. And to those who do, God gives words and a wisdom to sustain them through difficult times.

▶ Prayer

You taught me in your gospel, gentle master, that I would fare no better than you did in this world; that if the teacher suffered, so would the student. Help me to endure and to always trust in you.

▶ Action

Think of the worst betrayal you ever endured. Write down the words and wisdom God gives you now for that time in your life.

Thursday of the Thirty-fourth Week of the Year

Salvation Is Near

LUKE 21:20–28

*"There will be signs in the sun, the moon, and the stars, and on the earth
distress among nations. People will faint from fear of what is coming upon the
world. Then they will see the Son of Man coming in glory. Now when these
things begin to take place, stand up and raise your heads, because your
redemption is drawing near."*

▶ Reflection

There is a great image in Isaiah 2:19 which is repeated in Revelation
6:15–16. In it "the Lord arises" to judge the earth. The response of
many is to hide in the caves out of fear and cry out to the rocks, "Fall
on us!" Others, in confidence, go out to meet the Lord. The
distinction between the two groups can hardly be one of sin and
virtue, since "*all* have sinned" (Romans 3:23). Rather, what would
drive people to hide in the caves would be fear of retribution and
condemnation, while faith and hope in God's mercy and kindness
would buoy those going out to meet the Lord, sinners though they be.
This confidence is one of the hallmarks of God's people, from Daniel
in the lions' den to those who would raise their heads to the Son of
Man coming on the clouds. So we wait in joyful hope for the coming
of our savior.

▶ Prayer

Dear God, I am a sinner and I am guilty in my sins. But you are
merciful and kind and have forgiven me completely. Jesus Christ paid
the price and now I am free. Thank you, thank you, O my God.

▶ Action

Our savior Jesus Christ may come for you in glory today. Put a pebble
in your pocket as a reminder of your expectant hope.

Friday of the Thirty-fourth Week of the Year

Good Wins

LUKE 21:29–33

He told them a parable: "Look at the fig tree. When you see it sprout leaves, you know that summer is near. So also, when you see these things taking place, you know that the kingdom of God is near. This generation will not pass away until all things have taken place."

▶ Reflection

"The beast" is an enduring image of all that goes wrong in the world. Taken from the apocalyptic books of Daniel, chapter 7, and Revelation, chapter 13, it personifies evil and all forms of human depravity. But as Jesus points out in the parable of the fig tree, the presence of evil assures the greater presence of good. Or, as St. Paul says, "where sin increased, grace overflowed all the more" (Romans 5:20b). It is the very nature of good to be in the presence of evil and vice versa. (For an unusual image of that, read Job 1:6–12.) Often we're given to think that when evil is upon us and we are experiencing our sinfulness, God is far from us. But the opposite is true. Jesus teaches that when evil surrounds us, "know that the reign of God is near." It is God's will to rescue those caught in the trap of sin. Out of infinite love for you, God is motivated to save you. And God wins the victory over evil.

▶ Prayer

The light of your love finds me in darkness, O God, and leads me to safety. You cleanse me from all my sins and restore me to life. May I always be thankful for you and ready to serve your will.

▶ Action

Where do you struggle the most with sin and evil in your life? Remember all day today that God is closest to you there.

Saxophone Salvation

LUKE 21:34–36

"Be on guard so that your hearts are not weighed down by worrying about the things of this life, and the day of salvation catch you off-guard. For it will come upon everyone. Be alert at all times, praying that you may have the courage to stand before the Son of Man."

▶ Reflection

I grew up learning how to worry. I had the sense that it was natural to entertain a certain amount of anxiety about things in general, like what people would think if I got into an accident wearing dirty underwear. Coming to Christ as a grownup, I realize that worry does great harm to the human soul. Fear is an attitude contrary to how I need to be toward God if I am to enjoy being a child of God. I had to learn confidence and joyful hope in God. I have come to understand that the kingdom of God is like playing the saxophone. When you first start to play, it is very difficult and the sound you make is absolutely horrible. But practice, practice, practice, and in time you get pretty good at it. In the same way, trusting in God's all-conquering goodness is difficult at first; we're so used to worrying and feel awkward being confident. But practice every day and soon you'll become an expert!

▶ Prayer

O Lord, I thank you that you are always with me, creating for me a way of goodness and showing me the path that leads to fulfillment. May I be ready for you when you appear as my salvation.

▶ Action

At the end of the day, make a list of the things you worried about. Tomorrow, practice trusting God to take care of those things.

Special
Feasts

January 1: Mary, Mother of God

Angels Told Them

LUKE 2:16–21

The shepherds went with haste and found Mary and Joseph, and the child lying in the manger. When they saw this, they made known what had been told them about this child; and all who heard it were amazed at what the shepherds told them. But Mary treasured all these words and pondered them in her heart.

▶ Reflection

Sometimes when Jonathan bursts through the door with his wild stories of what goes on in school, Theresa, Jonathan's mom, doesn't quite know what to make of it all. Jonathan can be quite imaginative and he loves the thrill of telling his stories, although sometimes his perceptions of the events of his day are far different from what others, like his teacher, have to offer. Still, Theresa treasures these things. It's more important to her to build trust in her son than always to get the facts of his day straight. Theresa is not unlike Mary who received a fantastic story from the shepherds about angels and the glory of the Lord. Mary knew that shepherds, the dregs of first-century Palestinian society, were not to be trusted. Still, she withheld her judgment and pondered their story. What could it mean?

▶ Prayer

Mother Mary, join me in my prayer. All kinds of stories came your way about angels, spirits, and the promise of God. You trusted God at his word. Pray that I, too, trust God the way you did.

▶ Action

Recall the most fantastic thing that ever happened to you. How would you best describe it to another? Do you think you would be believed?

Leaving Family Behind

LUKE 1:57–66, 80

Now Elizabeth gave birth to a son, and her family wanted to name him Zechariah after his father. But his mother said, "No, he is to be called John." They said to her, "None of your relatives has this name." Zechariah told them, "His name is John." And they were all amazed.

▶ Reflection

There was a young man in a parish where I served who wanted to make movies. His parents wanted him to become a professional, like a doctor or a lawyer. They fought. In the end, he moved to Hollywood and became a successful moviemaker. His parents were very disappointed that their agenda was not met, and the relationship between them and their son was broken. Yet he followed his heart and fulfilled his dream. When Elizabeth and Zechariah broke family tradition and named their son John, they probably disappointed a few of their relatives, but when God calls, it's often in a direction that would not be found on the pathways of cultural and family expectations. Later on Jesus would teach that if you want to follow him, you have to leave your family behind (see Luke 14:26).

▶ Prayer

Each day the world draws us one way, O God, and you draw us in another. When our desires are in conflict with the expectations of the world, give us the courage to follow you with all our hearts.

▶ Action

Give a call to your parents, either on the phone or in spirit, and thank them for helping you become who you are.

June 29: Peter and Paul, apostles

Gas and Brakes

MATTHEW 16:13-19

Jesus said to them, "Who do you say that I am?" Simon Peter answered, "You are the Messiah, the Son of the living God." Jesus answered him, "I will give to you the keys of the kingdom; whatever you bind on earth will be bound in heaven, and whatever you loose on earth will be loosed in heaven."

▶ Reflection

Katherine and Paul were put together as a management team to head up a new work group for the company. They were matched up based on their profiles on file with the human resource department. They were very different, but their skills and personalities could be complementary if they could learn to work together in harmony. There was no more unlikely pairing in the New Testament than Peter and Paul. It does seem like they were always at loggerheads, Peter staunchly defending the conservative tradition, Paul pressing for his freedom to think and act "outside the box." And that's what makes church. If the church were a car, Paul would be the gas, always pressing forward, and Peter would be the brakes, slowing things down and keeping it on the road. You can't have one without the other.

▶ Prayer

O God, you called Peter to lead the church, and you called Paul to teach the leader. Bless their successors today. Make them faithful to Jesus who is our savior. Help them to get along.

▶ Action

Think of someone in your life who sometimes gets on your nerves. Ask God to show you how you can harmonize with that person.

August 6: The Transfiguration

Universe Transfigured

LUKE 9:28–36

Jesus took Peter, John and James up on the mountain to pray. There he was transfigured; the appearance of his face changed and his clothes became dazzling white. They saw Moses and Elijah talking to him. A voice from the clouds said, "This is my beloved Son; listen to him!" In the end, they saw that is was only Jesus.

▶ Reflection

Since this is a story about God, you would certainly expect that God would be glowing somewhere, and that there would be sightings of the late but great holy heroes of history. And of course, what God sighting would be complete without a voice from heaven? Still, the real miracle in this episode is the simple recognition that it was "only Jesus." In so many of the stories of the gospels, the real question— "Who is this?"—holds the plot's tension. Our world is full of "only's": it's only a baby crying, it's only a beggar, it's only water, it's only bread, it's only you, it's only me. But if we look with eyes of faith, everyday things are transfigured to become the living, flashing presence of God; the ordinary becomes extraordinary, the mundane, holy. God transfigures the universe.

▶ Prayer

At my best, I see you in the things you create, O my God. Your glory shines through them. But so often my sight is dimmed because I am a sinful person. Heal my blindness and help me to see your presence.

▶ Action

Look intently upon the things you are given to see today. Try to perceive the presence of God in the ordinary things of your day.

August 15: The Assumption of Mary

A Woman's Body

LUKE 1:39–56

Elizabeth was filled with the Holy Spirit and cried out, "Blessed are you among women, and blessed is the fruit of your womb!"

▶ Reflection

Even if Luke had known he was composing part of what would eventually become one of the most recited prayers in Christian history, he could not have come up with a better image for the savior of all humanity than "the fruit of thy womb." Our Christ, like every single human being on the planet, came forth from the sacred body of a woman. In the case of Jesus, the body was Mary's. From as early as the second century, Christians have believed that Mary was so blessed among women that, at the end of her life, her body was preserved from the corruption of death and she was assumed body and soul into heaven. She is our model of human person and of faith; she is the prototype of all Christians. The same gift of salvation given to her is offered to all, and all who embrace her faith are preserved from death. Therefore Mary is our mother, too, and the mother of all the church.

▶ Prayer

O God, you always were, are now, and ever shall be. But in time you sent your only begotten Son to be born of Mary and enter fully into our human world. Jesus was the fruit of Mary's womb, and you gave eternal life to her who bore him. May we who also receive Jesus in our bodies be like her in faith.

▶ Action

Spend a quiet moment with your eyes closed, remembering what it was like in your mother's womb.

November 1: All Saints

Saved by Divorce

MATTHEW 5:1–12

Blessed are you when people revile you and persecute you and utter all kinds of evil against you. Rejoice and be glad, for your reward is great in heaven.

▶ Reflection

Sandra divorced her husband because he was beating her up, not every day, but often enough so that she was afraid of him every day. Besides, a woman doesn't have to get beaten up every day to know that she's in danger and she has to do something about it. So she got a restraining order, put his stuff out on the sidewalk, and changed the locks on the doors. Then she got a divorce. What surprised her was that her own family disapproved of what she did. "You're a Catholic," her mother told her. "You're not supposed to get a divorce. I put up with your father's abuse for years and I never got a divorce. You shouldn't either." Sandra's mother was wrong. The Catholic church supports women who divorce abusive husbands. Church law says that if a husband "causes serious danger of spirit or body" to wife or children, or if living together becomes "too hard," a woman has just cause to leave her husband (see canon #1153).

▶ Prayer

O my God, you make love my call and my hope. I ask for the goodness of love in my life and the willingness to love in return. May my efforts to love be fruitful. May I be fulfilled in love.

▶ Action

Do you know a woman who's being abused? Talk to her. Tell her she needs to protect herself.

November 2: All Souls Day

Abortion Forgiven

JOHN 6:37–40

"Everyone who comes to me is God's gift to me, and I will not reject anyone who comes to me. It is not God's will that I should ever lose those who are given to me."

▶ Reflection

When Arlene stopped in to see her neighbor Janna, she never expected to tell her about the abortion. But since her dream a week ago, the one about the little baby alone and crying, Arlene had been haunted by her secret, which she had kept hidden from everyone for twelve years. "You should confess it to a priest and get absolution," Janna advised. "I couldn't," replied Arlene. She hadn't been to church in… well, since the abortion and she was afraid. She figured she could never be forgiven for her sin. The priest would probably yell at her and throw her out of the church. "Oh, no, Arlene!" Janna took Arlene's hand and her big brown eyes filled with tears of compassion. "Jesus never rejects anyone," she said. "You go talk to Fr. Clark. You'll see." Arlene went to the church and celebrated the sacrament of reconciliation with her priest. Absolved of her sin and healed of her guilt, she began again to walk with Christ.

▶ Prayer

Dear Jesus, is it true you will accept anyone who comes to you? You make me so peaceful in your love. I know you will always be there for me and you will never reject me. Thank you, Lord.

▶ Action

Call up a friend who may be feeling low or insecure and remind your friend that your love is constant and always there, no matter what.

December 8: The Immaculate Conception

Conception Misconception

LUKE 1:26–38

The angel Gabriel was sent by God to a virgin named Mary. And the angel came to her and said, "Hail Mary, full of grace! The Lord is with you. Blessed are you among women!"

▶ **Reflection**

"No, no," said Catherine shaking her head. "The Immaculate Conception isn't the conception of Jesus; it's the conception of Mary." Catherine was conducting the second RCIA inquiry session and dealing with a common…misconception. "Today's gospel can be confusing because it's the story of the virgin conception of Jesus and, of course, Christmas is in three weeks. But today we celebrate the conception of Mary! While her parents conceived her in the normal way, she was kept free from original sin from the very first moment of her life in the womb of her mother. It was God's gift to her, seeing that she would become the mother of Jesus. That's why the angel said she was full of grace. Baptism cleanses us of original sin, too, so we can be full of grace just like Mary. Then, in the sacrament of the Eucharist, we receive Jesus in our bodies and bring his presence to the whole world. Mary is a model for us all."

▶ **Prayer**

Holy Mary, Mother of God, pray for us. Your parents conceived you in love and your mother brought you forth in hope. May we rejoice together with you in the salvation won for us by your Son, Jesus.

▶ **Action**

Find out the date of your baptism and circle it on your calendar. Plan a little celebration of your salvation that day.